"Twenty years after the hit teen drama *The O.C.* first aired, its creators are taking us all for a romp down memory lane with an oral history of the series, featuring interviews with its stars, writers, directors, and more. It's a fascinating peek behind the making of a megahit, and a delightful bit of nostalgia for those of us who remember life before streaming TV."

— *Town & Country*

"Will most likely satisfy any *O.C.*-heads (Newpsies?) craving a glimpse into the backstage drama, network chaos, on-set romance, and, of course, the show's iconic music. . . . The riveting book features enthralling and often hilarious interviews with the entire principal cast, memorable guest stars, directors, producers, and even some big-name musicians whose work was featured on the show. The oral history is both a story about a once-in-a-lifetime hit . . . and the highly competitive landscape of network television in the early 2000s."

—Daily Beast

"A splendid retrospective. . . . A must-read for viewers of the show's original run, but it works, too, for those meeting the Cohens and their fellow Orange County residents for the first time via streaming services."

—Associated Press

"Fans of the series will devour. . . . The only thing missing from this definitive dive is Ryan's trademark brooding."

— *Paste*

"Sepinwall talked to basically every important actor, creative person, and executive associated with the series. He also knows his *O.C.*, having written about it extensively when it was on the air. . . . I was blown away by how many new tidbits Alan uncovers."

—Vulture

"The ultimate tell-all book."

—*Cosmopolitan*

"[A] juicy look behind the scenes of the television series *The O.C.* . . . The insider perspectives are refreshingly candid and offer new insights into what went into making the much-loved show. *The O.C.* fans won't want to miss this."

—*Publishers Weekly*

"A revealing oral history of the unlikely teen drama. . . . Skillfully captures the show's surprising sizzle without letting anyone off the hook for its many shortcomings."

—*Kirkus Reviews*

"The perfect companion for any TV fan feeling a little nostalgic."

—TVLine

"An oral history of the seminal teen drama (which, if we're all being honest, has stood the test of time because it's so much more than a teen drama). . . . Happy early Chrismukkah."

—InsideHook

"Packed with juicy, behind-the-scenes scoop about making the show, from the casting process to the way the stars behaved."

—Yahoo! Entertainment

"A comprehensive oral history of the addictive soap, featuring interviews with its creators, cast, and crew, revealing how a modern TV classic (barely) got made."

—*Rolling Stone*

"Breezy, entertaining."

—Salon.com

WELCOME TO **THE O.C.**

WELCOME TO

MARINER BOOKS
New York   Boston

THE O.C.

The Oral History

ALAN SEPINWALL

in conversation with **JOSH SCHWARTZ**
and **STEPHANIE SAVAGE**

HarperCollins books may be purchased for educational, business,
or sales promotional use. For information, please email the
Special Markets Department at SPsales@harpercollins.com.

The Mariner flag design is a registered trademark
of HarperCollins Publishers LLC.

A hardcover edition of this book was published in 2023 by Mariner Books.

FIRST MARINER BOOKS PAPERBACK EDITION PUBLISHED 2025.

Designed by Renata DiBiase

Library of Congress Cataloging-in-Publication Data has been applied for.

ISBN 978-0-06-334280-4

25 26 27 28 29 LBC 5 4 3 2 1

For Stacy

Contents

The Party

ON SEPTEMBER 9, 2003, the Fox network threw a party at a Manhattan Beach bar where radio contest winners could watch the latest episode of *The O.C.* with the stars of TV's hottest new drama. The cast and members of the creative team piled into the backs of cars to make their way over from their nearby production facility, and writers' assistant Lauren Gussis found herself in the same vehicle with series star Adam Brody, who played the already beloved, adorkable Seth Cohen.

"We're driving, we're chatting," recalls Gussis. "The show had just aired a few times, and everybody continued to be super humble and kind."

No one in the car was prepared for the scene about to unfold before them.

"We get to the place," says Gussis, "and the door to the car opens, and Adam Brody steps out to a sea of screaming teenage girls. And I watched his face change. Like, this is the moment that this guy realizes he's famous. He didn't know until that moment that he had become a teen icon. I watched it. I saw it happen. This is maybe one of the greatest moments of my career, and it has nothing to do with me. To watch that realization dawn on someone's face, it was amazing. How many times in your life do you get to see that moment for anybody? That's the Beatlemania moment."

That night at the bar—where Brody, Ben McKenzie, Mischa Barton, Rachel Bilson, and the rest of *The O.C.* cast were overwhelmed with the love and adoration of their rapidly growing fan base—was not the start of *The O.C.* experience for anyone who attended. But it was the moment that transformed the way all of them thought about the reach and power of the show on which they were all working so hard—the moment they recognized they were part of something that could be described as a phenomenon, without hyperbole. It was the beginning of a wild, turbulent ride with gorgeous highs and shocking lows—on-screen and off—that would not soon be forgotten by the people making the show, nor by those who watched it.

The O.C. was, depending on who you asked, a teen soap opera that was smart and funny enough to be enjoyed by adults, or a self-aware comedy punctuated by occasional melodrama. Its creator, Josh Schwartz, and his producing partner, Stephanie Savage, viewed it as a Trojan horse that they would use to hide all the nuanced character work they cared about inside a sexy package the Fox network would be willing to air. It put a mainstream spotlight on indie rock music and comic book culture. It put seemingly nonsense words like "Chrismukkah," "Newpsies," and "yogalates" into the vernacular. In characters like brooding outsider Ryan Atwood, lonely and self-destructive Marissa Cooper, wisecracking nerd Seth Cohen, and reformed mean girl Summer Roberts, it helped create new archetypes, or brought unexpected spins to familiar ones.

And, oh yeah, at its best, it was pretty goddamn great.

The story of *The O.C.* is typically summarized this way: a terrific, wildly popular first season, followed by a rapid decline in both quality and ratings, until the show all but faded from the discourse. But the truth—as told by the people who made the show, who starred in it, and even by those who watched it obsessively—is more complicated than that. Well, yes, the third season of the show is largely indefensible. But even that—including the shocking character death at the end of that year, which in turn accelerated the demise of the show itself—isn't necessarily for the reasons you might think.

This book is a conversation with Schwartz, Savage, the entire regular cast, key members of the creative team, studio and network executives, and more. It's also a time capsule of a particular crossroads in the history of television, music, comic books, the Internet, celebrity culture, and more. And it's a case study of how desperation can lead to creative inspiration, as well as how, when showrunners plan, network television laughs.

So put on that white tank top and crank up Phantom Planet's "California," because here comes our oral history.

Welcome to the O.C., bitch!

CHAPTER 1

The Origin Story

SOME TELEVISION SHOWS come from ideas that germinate from a deeply autobiographical place. Some are thrown together in a rush. What this chapter about the tumultuous development phase of *The O.C.* presupposes is . . . maybe some shows are both?

Welcome to the Orange County

In the beginning, there was McG. Well, no. In the beginning, there was a kid named Joseph McGinty Nichol growing up in Orange County, California. He was not a fan.

McG (executive producer): It was a place devoid of any meaningful artistry, filled with planned communities, generalized divorce malaise, and a lovely, dreamy, laid-back Beach Boys vibe. Certainly not a breeding ground of anything creative that the world would be interested in sharing.

Melinda Clarke would eventually become the queen of the fictionalized Orange County. She was the only *O.C.* cast member to have grown up in the real version, about thirty minutes south of Newport Beach in Dana Point.

Melinda Clarke (Julie Cooper-Nichol): I did a lot of theater, and I had to seek it out outside of Orange County, because my mother used to call it "a cultural wasteland." I didn't actually experience Newport

Beach the way it was perceived or portrayed in the show until I was in high school. My friends and I would go, "There's a party in Newport," and that's where you would see the kids driving the Porsches and the Lamborghinis. I drove my parents' '64 Volvo.

Colin Hanks, who would make a memorable Season One guest appearance, studied for a year at Chapman University in the city of Orange.

Colin Hanks (Grady Bridges): It felt like there were definitely haves and have-nots in Orange County. That's very much baked into the DNA of that region.

McG: I was a scrawny, red-haired kid that never saw a day in high school without braces. I was a virgin, and I went to high school with those very same Adonises that were on the national water polo team and were beautiful and were like the *Big Wednesday** poster come to life.

That scrawny kid grew up to become a prolific music video director, working not only with Orange County–bred acts like Sugar Ray, but other popular nineties artists like Smash Mouth and Barenaked Ladies. Eventually, he parlayed that into a chance to direct the 2000 film *Charlie's Angels*, starring Cameron Diaz, Drew Barrymore, and Lucy Liu. It was there that he met future *O.C.* executive producer Stephanie Savage. Savage had always loved pop culture—for a while, she wrote for a 'zine called *Mickey Rourke*—and went to Los Angeles to do research for her PhD dissertation on film history and theory.

Stephanie Savage (executive producer): I needed to get a job, and then I ended up working for Drew Barrymore and Nancy Juvonen's company, Flower Films. I worked on *Never Been Kissed* and *Donnie Darko*, then *Charlie's Angels*. That's how I met McG.

* A 1978 movie about surfers, starring Jan-Michael Vincent, William Katt, and Gary Busey.

McG and Savage hit it off and set up their own production company, Wonderland Sound and Vision. In time, they had a TV development deal with Warner Bros., and produced a *Miami Vice*–esque cop drama called *Fastlane*. It only lasted a season on Fox, but now McG and Savage were in the television business, and that business wanted more from them.

Stephanie Savage: The WB* had really wanted *Fastlane* but couldn't afford it, so we said we would bring them something else down the road. Jordan Levin was the head of The WB at the time, and he said that he really wanted something personal from McG, that was not what we would think of at the time as a McG show—exploding cars and girls in bikinis and people shooting guns. So what could that be?

McG: I was the guy from Orange County. It was a moment for Orange County, and it was a moment for me too because of what was happening theatrically. And I had a stupid name that cut through. There was the Orange County scene and I had helped bring the Orange County bands with the videos for Sublime. And I was buddies with Gwen Stefani, and Zack de la Rocha with Rage Against the Machine. There was a synthesis of energies that went into it.

Part of that moment? A hit movie comedy simply titled *Orange County*, starring Colin Hanks.

Colin Hanks: I hate the phrase, but it is true: there was just something in the zeitgeist at that point. Orange County was in the conversation enough at that point that it was ripe to be either lampooned or popular enough to have something set in that world that people would be able to identify, you know, and understand.

---

* Once upon a time, when the traditional broadcast networks ruled television, there were The WB and UPN, each of them fighting it out for the prestigious title of America's fifth-place broadcaster. Just before the final *O.C.* season debuted, the two decided that the only way to win this particular game was to join forces, and they merged into The CW.

Stephanie Savage: I thought about the idea of Newport Beach, because that's where McG was from, and that would hopefully help us fulfill that obligation of making it seem personal to him.

Meanwhile, a young writer named Josh Schwartz was struggling to get his first project made. A precocious film nerd from Providence, Rhode Island, he had sold his first screenplay, titled *Providence* and inspired by his relationship with his high school girlfriend, while he was still an undergrad at USC.

Josh Schwartz (creator/executive producer): There was a bidding war. I was in my fraternity house, it was very weird. Jules Asner from E! television came to my fraternity to do the "college kid sells homework" story.

Providence never escaped years of development hell. Schwartz began trying television, selling a few pilot scripts that didn't go to series, but that would later prove useful for material on *The O.C.* One was *Wall to Wall Records*, set in the music industry and featuring a young Bradley Cooper. The other was an ABC drama called *Brookfield*.

Josh Schwartz: It was a boarding school–set drama. And I did not know at the time that I was going to be writing about high schoolers for the next twenty years. It was about a blue-collar kid who goes to a preppy boarding school where he does not fit in. So there were definitely some bones there for what would later become *The O.C.*

Peter Roth (president, Warner Bros. Television): We had so much in development with Josh at the time,* and he was such an important part of our strategy. I loved his talent. I thought, *My God, this guy is*

---

* In the same development season as *The O.C.*, Schwartz was working on an NBC sitcom about a moving company. "I thought that was going to go and that was going to be my *Scrubs*," recalls Schwartz. "That was the dream. And then there was this other show, like, 'Oh yeah, maybe it'll work.'"

going to speak to an audience that is underserved and he can do so in a way that is compelling and smart and fun and funny.

Josh Schwartz: The consensus was that both of those projects were missing the eight-hundred-pound gorilla—the person who was attached to projects who can push it through no matter what.

Schwartz needed an eight-hundred-pound gorilla. The eight-hundred-pound gorilla's producing partner needed a writer. And all the producing partner had when she met with the writer in the summer of 2002 was a location.

Stephanie Savage: I started pitching that story area to people, including Josh. It could have been anything. It could have been a soap about sexy real estate agents.* It could have been a cop show. Josh is going to bring up extreme sports, because *XXX* was a big movie at the time.

Josh Schwartz: Stephanie was like, "This would be a very McG thing: extreme sports cops." I asked, "Does that mean that they jump out of the plane, land on a skateboard, and arrest people?"

Stephanie Savage: And I said, "Yes, Josh, that's exactly what it means." That was the beginning of a beautiful friendship.

"Extreme sports cops" soon turned back to the search for something more personal. Though Schwartz grew up a continent away from Orange County, he felt he understood the area well.

Josh Schwartz: I went to USC, and that is a direct pipeline for kids from Newport Beach to go to college. As a Jewish kid from the East

---

* "Sexy real estate agents" was a common suggestion from McG, especially when it came time to develop potential *O.C.* spinoffs. "We can laugh about it now," says Schwartz, "because it presaged all these shows like *Selling Sunset*."

Coast, I felt very much like a stranger in a strange land at USC. I definitely felt my Judaism in ways that I had not in Providence. I didn't even know water polo was a sport before I had arrived there.

Stephanie Savage: I brought Josh to the set of the *Charlie's Angels* sequel, where he pitched McG in a trailer with Demi Moore entering at some point during the pitch.

McG: Josh and I bonded over realizing we have that same sort of Seth point-of-entry experience to this world. And there were some giggles there.

Soon, they had an idea, and a title—neither quite what we would come to know.

Josh Schwartz: It was called *Newport Beach*. The show was initially about a girl named Lucy Muñoz, who was the daughter of this rich family's gardener. They were worried about her in the public school that she was at, and her family lived in the guest quarters of this rich family called the Atwoods. She was kind of the Ryan. Ryan was kind of the Marissa. There was a Seth and Summer.

Stephanie Savage: The Needlemans are the next-door neighbors.

Josh Schwartz: That's the Cohens.

Schwartz begins reading from the initial pitch document:

Josh Schwartz: "This is a show about finding your place in the world. A show about people struggling for a sense of identity. We will wrestle with issues of where do we fit in? But in Newport Beach, with its blue skies and oceans bluer still, its new money and gated communities and McMansions, the amount of wealth and disparity between rich and poor intensifies everything. The characters in this town and the town itself give off a false sense of identity—seemingly beautiful and tranquil and suburban. But underneath is a world of shifting loyalties and identities, of kids living secret lives hidden from their parents, and of parents living secret lives hidden from their children. It is a place where everyone feels like an outsider, where no one feels quite at home."

He pauses to note that what he's read so far is largely what the show would become, then resumes with the big divergence:

Josh Schwartz: "It is also a love story anchored by two people. One, Lucy Muñoz, an outsider who wants in. The other, Ryan Atwood, someone born into the world who wants out, both driven by the sense that a life different from theirs must be better. And it's finally a coming-of-age story for these two characters, about those choices and experiences that drive us out of youth to adulthood as they try to find the courage to make decisions that will set them different from their parents, different from their friends. It is a story with themes universal to any community in the country, with characters and style unique to Newport Beach."

Sounds great, right? Not to the studio.

Stephanie Savage: I think it got kiboshed in that first meeting. They said, "You need to retool this one element," which was pretty significant.

Warner Bros., it turned out, already had two other teen dramas in development that season that were *Romeo and Juliet*–esque star-crossed love stories between white and Latin characters: *Skin*, about the white daughter of a pornography magnate and the Latin son of a prosecutor,* and *No Place Like Home*, about the white daughter of an incarcerated criminal and

---

* If you were watching the 2003 World Series on Fox, you may have this fact permanently etched into your memory, since every game was peppered with *Skin* commercials that featured Ron Silver, playing the pornographer, screaming, "His FATHER is THE DISTRICT ATTORNEY!"

the Latin son of a successful landscaper, from *Party of Five* creators Chris Keyser and Amy Lippman. And the studio felt that three shows with that theme in the same year was somehow one too many.*

> **Stephanie Savage:** There was no conversation—no version of, "Can't we all develop in this area?"

At a crossroads, Schwartz looked back to his *Brookfield* boarding school drama script and asked, "What if Lucy becomes Ryan?" So now Ryan Atwood was a kid from a rough-and-tumble neighborhood in Chino. He gets arrested joyriding in a stolen car with his older brother Trey, and somehow—through a mechanism Schwartz hadn't figured out yet—winds up in Newport, where the representative of the wealth and opulence is now a girl named Marissa Cooper.†

> **Stephanie Savage:** The idea was to shuffle the deck so that we had the same *Breakfast Club* scenario, but different people in different chairs, from different worlds. I'm a huge *Rebel Without a Cause* person. It was always like Jim, Judy, and Plato were Ryan, Seth, and Lucy or Marissa, depending on what version. And thinking about how 1950s melodramas would have the character of the good working-class male who comes into the upper-class world with a target on his back, like Paul Newman in *The Long, Hot Summer*, where he's a barn burner and no one wants anything to do with him. But of course, he's the most moral person in the whole town, and Joanne Woodward is going to fall in love with him. So that was a great shape for Ryan. And then we had to figure out why this kid would ever come into this world.

Fortunately, the Fox network's entertainment president provided the solution.

---

* Also? Be warned that *Skin* is going to come up a shocking number of times in this book. For a show that was canceled after five episodes, its story intertwines a lot with this one's.

† "There was a girl from USC named Cooper who people called Coop," says Schwartz.

Stephanie Savage: Gail Berman was being honored by a charity, Alliance for Children's Rights, where lawyers advocated for kids who were in foster care, especially as they were aging out of foster care. Josh and I looked at each other like, "Lawyers and children in foster care? Hmmm. This could be the answer to all of our Ryan Atwood problems of how we get this kid in this house."

From the *Newport Beach* pitch document: "Sandy Needleman is the wealthiest guy in the area, a developer who builds golf courses, because if he didn't, he jokes he wouldn't be able to play golf. He's a nice man, liberal in his politics, always offering to speak Spanish with [Lucy's father] Victor."

Josh Schwartz: And then Sandy morphed into a combination of this altruistic public defender and my father. He's not the rich land developer anymore. He's this other guy, but it's his wife who has the money. He's walking a compromise, and has he sold his soul?

A WB network executive had planted the seed of the idea with McG and Savage, and Peter Roth had been tasked with mending fences between that network and its corporate sibling studio, which had been working at cross purposes under previous regimes. But the project soon proved more of a match at Fox.

Josh Schwartz: Fox at that time was really looking for a return to their *Beverly Hills, 90210* roots. They'd gotten away from that, and The WB was eating their lunch in that regard. It had been a while since *Party of Five* and *90210* had ended.

Craig Erwich (programming executive, Fox): We were making action shows like *24* and *John Doe*. There was a woman named Anne Schwartz, who worked for [Fox head of scheduling] Preston Beckman. She wrote an email saying something like, *I miss shows that were just about people like me, about young people—shows that make me feel something versus these very high-concept procedurals.*

Peter Roth: One of my fears was: How do we do a teen drama and not bring it to The WB? I do remember that there was a clear preference to bring the show to one of the Big Four networks. And as I recall also, Gail Berman was such an enthusiast of the idea from its start that there was little doubt that we would bring it there.

Gail Berman (president, Fox): When they came in to pitch us, McG's energy was very infectious. Josh was young and adorable and sweet. They had a unique presentation at that time. It had visuals, long before we all did these big decks and things like that for pitching. And I knew I had to have it.

McG: Josh was the youngest showrunner in history at that time when we finally got the show on the air. So everybody was looking for someone to vouch for this kid, and that was my role. Plus, I was the guy from Orange County, so I had to be the keeper of the flame. It was a very, very effective triangle offense with Josh, Stephanie, and me. And they clearly did all the heavy lifting. I was the steward of Orange County and that had value.

Berman liked the pitch, except for one part of it: Sandy and Kirsten Cohen's nerdy, lonely son Seth, who would find a true friend in the boy who moves into the McMansion's pool house.

Susan Rovner (programming executive, Warner Bros. Television): There were some people at Fox who did not love the Seth character. I think until we found Adam Brody, they did not understand him. I think to have our leading man be a geek was hard for some people at Fox to embrace. I think it was just, "I don't like Seth Cohen." *Big Bang Theory* and so many shows now use "geek chic." This was a first. Your leading man was not your traditional leading man. Obviously, Ryan was a more traditional leading man, but Seth was not.

Peter Roth: Seth was the son that I think Josh thought that he was—and wished that he could have been Ryan.

The inherently neurotic Schwartz didn't respond well at first to hearing this response to his fictionalized self.

Susan Rovner: Josh was sweet and a little heartbroken. I remember him being like, "Uhhh, so it's me?"

Gail Berman: There aren't a lot of Jewish characters that appear on television. So I wanted to make sure that [Seth] had a reality to him and that it wasn't just this nerdy guy that didn't have a world to him.

Josh Schwartz: I've been harsh talking about it in the past, but I think the fair version is that Gail was a hundred percent right. Seth was really annoying [in that original pitch]. We talked about when he discovers that Ryan had spent the night at the pool house, it's like Elliott discovering E.T. But the thing in the Seth Needleman version was that he wanted to fit in. So he was always like, "Yo, these are my boys! This my boy Luke!" It's much more of a fake fronting. He just was annoying, so it was deserved. I think he was into magic?

Gail said: "Well, if Ryan is our Luke Perry, who's our Jason Priestley?" And I was like, "Uh, how dare you? This is a very different show, and I'm not gonna ever watch that show."*

Stephanie Savage: Josh was unfamiliar with the *90210* paradigm, but Seth was a lot more like Brian Austin Green [as David Silver].

Josh Schwartz: But the show wasn't going to move forward with this version of Seth, and we had to have a come-to-Jesus meeting. I don't remember who said it, but they wanted a version of him that was more of a "beautiful dreamer." I had imagined, like, Jay Baruchel from *Undeclared*, and they had just canceled that show.

---

* Believe he avoided *90210* or don't, but Schwartz has always insisted that his Thursday show of choice in the nineties was *Seinfeld*.

Stephanie Savage: Which led to a very potent conversation between the two of us about what kind of a show we were making. Because in our hearts, we both loved *Freaks and Geeks*, *My So-Called Life*, *Undeclared*. None of those shows made it to a second season. And the big powerhouse shows that worked for a large audience were not as nuanced and beautiful and unique as those other shows that got crushed. So that's where the idea of the Trojan horse came from. How do we make *Freaks and Geeks* and *My So-Called Life* in a way that Fox doesn't even know that that's what they've ordered, because they have a show with guys playing volleyball and girls in bikinis?

Josh Schwartz: That meeting was a near-death moment for the show, because it wasn't going to move forward until [the Seth problem] was solved. It became, "Okay, if Seth's a beautiful dreamer, what is his passion?" That led to the whole sailing thing. And having a boat named after Summer and wanting to sail away.

Allan Heinberg, a veteran of dramedies like *Sex and the City* and *Gilmore Girls*, began talking with Schwartz and Savage about writing for *The O.C.* if it went to series.

Allan Heinberg (writer/producer): When I joined the party, Seth was more hip-hop and video game–obsessed. Stephanie and Josh and I were in McG's office, and we were sitting down asking, "Okay, how can we make Gail Berman at Fox okay with Seth as a character?" Because she was not loving him. And Josh was the one who said, "Let's make him us. He's already the Jew in Orange County outcast. So let's give him my love of all my favorite bands and let's give him your comics." Neither of us was a gamer at that time. And I don't know where the hip-hop came from, but I have this reference of Seth Green in the movie *Can't Hardly Wait*. That was the result of a Gail Berman note saying something like, "I don't get this character. I don't like him. And if this whole series hinges on the friendship between these two boys and this family taking him in, I need to love him." It's one of those notes where you pound your head against the wall, but it ends up being the magic fulcrum for the thing.

Josh Schwartz: We changed the last name from Needleman to Cohen,* which suddenly felt cooler and more accessible and less in-your-face Judaism. And they were really happy with that rewrite.

Stephanie Savage: I got a little teary, like, "This is a story. This is going to be on television."

Heinberg had joined the process so early because Fox had an unusual plan in the event it was ordered to series: an early August premiere, giving the show a couple of months on the air before the bulk of the network's prime-time schedule was hijacked for coverage of the baseball playoffs.

Preston Beckman (head of scheduling, Fox): It was developed off-cycle. The nature of our schedule, between *American Idol* in midseason and baseball in the fall, created a way for us to get a season started. We decided that what we needed to try to do was to premiere some shows early.

A different scheduling problem threatened to kill the show before it started, when production delays on *Charlie's Angels: Full Throttle* made it impossible for McG to direct *The O.C.* pilot.

Stephanie Savage: McG and I desperately hoped that this would somehow work out. We were trying to pretzel ourselves and do backflips. And then McG's agents were finally like, "Are you fucking crazy? You are the director of this $100 million movie and you will shoot the end of the movie whenever they tell you to shoot it. There's no version of you telling them they have to move the release date of *Charlie's*

---

* The name of a family Schwartz grew up with.

Angels because you have to shoot a teen drama pilot for Fox. Just fuck off. That's not happening."

Josh Schwartz: Then there came a very dark day where I was sat down by McG and Stephanie. He said, "I just can't do it." And then I was like, *Oh, we're screwed. This is the whole thing. I was supposed to have the eight-hundred-pound gorilla directing and this is what's the special sauce that I've been missing? And now it's gone and we're doomed.* Warner Bros. was so mad.

Susan Rovner: I was definitely pissed. McG was incredibly important. It was very much a combination of McG representing Orange County, and then Josh obviously being Seth. It was this marriage. It was terrifying when he dropped out on that.

Gail Berman: I felt like I had been baited and switched. I was not pleasant about it. I felt like we were on the precipice of this really great thing and then the person who had brought it in was gone. Now, remember, Josh is a young man at the time. He has zero experience. Zero. Now, McG doesn't have a *lot* of television experience, but he has an energy. And I'm thinking he's the guy who's going to be able to make this pilot great. And then I find out that he's not going to do it. And I honestly was very, very upset and angry.

Josh Schwartz: McG was banned from coming to casting.

Peter Roth, famous in town for hugging anyone and everyone, was no more pleased.

Stephanie Savage: I was told I would be allowed to come to the Warner Bros. lot, but—and this is totally serious—Peter Roth would not be hugging me.

Lisa Cochran (unit production manager): I distinctly remember calling the studio and saying, "Uh, we just lost the director." And they said,

"We know, keep going." "Keep going what?" They said, "Keep prepping." We kept picking locations, we kept hiring the crew. And this felt like forever, or maybe it was only a few days or a week, but ultimately we ended up with our new director.

When Life Gives You Limans . . .

Josh Schwartz: I was in front of my apartment on my Treo, getting a phone call that Doug Liman was interested in meeting and wanted to direct the pilot. I was overjoyed. I couldn't believe our good fortune.

Doug Liman was a director at an early career crossroads. 1996's *Swingers* and 1999's *Go* had been well-received, with strong performances from rising stars like Vince Vaughn, Jon Favreau, and Katie Holmes. And 2002's *The Bourne Identity* was a huge hit and the start of a franchise. But Liman's bluntness meant he was not going to direct any additional *Bourne* films—and, he feared, not make another movie, period. This was why Liman and his producing partner David Bartis were reading TV pilot scripts that year.

Doug Liman (director/executive producer): *The Bourne Identity* had come out, and I committed the cardinal sin of telling reporters how horrible the studio had been to me making the movie. And how I made the movie in spite of that, as opposed to giving them some credit. And Stacey Snider, who was running Universal, said she was going to make sure I never worked again. I didn't necessarily want to test whether she had the ability to keep me from working, and thought I should look into TV. And that was the climate in which I had read *The O.C.* I hadn't really thought about doing TV, but I thought, *Fuck, this would be really great.*

Stephanie Savage: Jumping on something that was already going was a good opportunity for them to get something made quickly.

Having the reputation that he had as a director, it felt like Doug's sensibility and his pedigree would be elevating things.

Gail Berman: We were lucky to get Doug. Doug was very, very happening at that moment in the feature world.

Doug Liman: In particular, what I loved about it was the character Seth. That was me in high school. And I was like, *I wish to go back in a time machine and tell the guy that was all insecure in high school that maybe it's all going to work out. It's going to get better by the time you get to college.* The whole time making the show, I always had this very protective attitude towards that character. I wished I could just shake him and tell him it's going to be okay.

The "The"

Lucy Muñoz wasn't the only name that vanished over the course of this wild development process. Before the script got turned in to Fox, there was a title change, from *Newport Beach* to *The O.C.*

Josh Schwartz: I think there was a concern that *Newport Beach* felt too much like a Saturday morning sitcom, like *California Dreams*, or maybe like weekday daytime. Just having "beach" in the title gave middle-aged housewife, soap opera vibes. And *Orange County* was already taken.

Orange County native McG was not pleased with the use of the definite article in this new title.

McG: My largest takeaway was, "Dude, there's no 'the.'" He's like, "No, it's going to be great. It's *The O.C.*" And I just said, "No, we say, 'O.C.'"

Josh Schwartz: I was like, "No, I went to college with all these white kids from Orange County who were trying to put their own spin on 'the LBC' by saying, 'I'm from the O.C.'" So that's how I heard it. I didn't know that that was historically not accurate, or even potentially controversial. And later we heard a lot of people who are like, "Don't call it that. Just call it O.C."

Schwartz and Savage were at the Wonderland offices late on a Saturday night as Schwartz did another rewrite of the pilot script, when he decided that Marissa's boyfriend, the bully Luke Ward, would punch out Ryan and then declare, "Welcome to the O.C., bitch! This is how it's done in Orange County!"

Josh Schwartz: I was like, "We've got to get this line in there." Having Luke say it felt like a way to put it out there and own it. And it was our big *Karate Kid* moment as well. Definitely influenced by *The Karate Kid*.

McG: [Josh] goes, "Trust me: *The O.C.*" And boy, was he right.

CHAPTER 2

The Casting

A GREAT SCRIPT is only one piece of the puzzle. In the hands of the wrong actors, no words on a page can be good enough. Imagine, for instance, if, during the casting of *Mad Men*, the head of AMC had said, "This Dane Cook's got a lot of MySpace followers. He should play Don Draper!" No one involved in casting *The O.C.* made such an outlandish request, but the process was a challenge.

A Rush to Find Actors

To help find their Ryan, Marissa, Seth, Sandy, and the rest, Schwartz and Savage brought in casting director Patrick Rush. Between *Party of Five* and *Everwood*, he had plenty of experience finding, as he puts it, "pretty crying white kids."

Patrick Rush (casting director): I read the script, and I was like, "You know what? I want this. This is really good." I wanted the job, and they hired me.

Schwartz and Savage already had actor types in mind.

Josh Schwartz (creator/executive producer): We had a whole board that we made that we went to Fox with, during the pitch and it had all the characters, with photos of different actors who were the prototypes. It was Jeff Goldblum [for Sandy], Michelle Pfeiffer [for Kirsten], Dennis Quaid, I think, for Jimmy Cooper. I think Kate Bosworth was

Marissa. Josh Hartnett was Ryan. I think [Jason] Schwartzman was Seth Cohen. So those are the prototypes. And then obviously the process takes over. You can't imagine anyone else but the people you cast playing those roles.

Sandy Cohen: Peter Gallagher
Sings for His Supper

The first role to be cast was the Cohen family patriarch, Sandy Cohen.

Josh Schwartz: It became a question of who is somebody who hasn't done television before. Where if you heard that they were in the show, you would think, *Oh, this must not just be a teen drama like those that have come before*, where the parents were not as featured.

Stephanie Savage (executive producer): I think Jon Cryer read for it.

Josh Schwartz: 2003 was the year the Brat Pack was going to do TV.

The Sandy wish list the producers initially gave to Patrick Rush included Jeff Goldblum, Aidan Quinn, Michael Keaton, and Peter Gallagher. Rush did not recall every detail of winnowing down that list, but could make educated guesses based on his process and a long history with Schwartz and Savage that began on *The O.C.*

Patrick Rush: The thing about working with Josh and Stephanie is that they come with a vision, which is a gift for a casting person. As opposed to producers who are like, "Well, we'll know it when we see it." That's not them. They have an idea. So you start checking avails and interest. Like, is Jeff Goldblum available and would he want to do a series on Fox? Which is probably no. You start there with the names they circled and you do your basic email checks and then you whittle it down until we were left with Aidan Quinn and Peter Gallagher. And we talked about it. I always thought the reason I love *The O.C.* is because it had humor. And Peter Gallagher just seemed a little bit funnier than an Aidan Quinn might be.

Gallagher, a distinguished veteran of the stage and screen who was looking to do television for the steady paycheck, was knocked out by Schwartz's writing.

Peter Gallagher (Sandy Cohen): I thought it was the most wonderful thing I had ever read. First of all, I just loved it as a dad. I loved my dad, but he didn't talk to me. So I always had this deficit in my heart and soul imagining what conversations I would have with a dad who talked to me. Up to that point, fathers had been portrayed just as comedy for a lot of sitcoms—stupid and clueless. It was mean.

As a native New Yorker who had recently lived through the city's greatest tragedy and its aftermath, Gallagher found a deeper meaning in the seemingly frothy soap.

Peter Gallagher: What really blew my mind was I just thought this was the absolute best story to be telling about America. Because on the heels of 9/11, we could have been gripped by a paroxysm of xenophobia. Of wanting to demonize the other: *It's* their *fault*. And I thought, what a great story about this guy, this Jewish guy from the Bronx who's living, who's in love with a shiksa from San Diego and living in a gated community. And he doesn't surrender himself or his beliefs or a sense of humor or his capacity for embracing the other. And that to me was a powerful American story to be telling: that you have nothing to fear of the other, and the real tragedy happens when all you have is fear and no communication. I saw this as the greatest seriocomic family drama anybody could ever produce. And of course, my friends were like, "I'm so sorry, man, you're doing soaps now." And I said, "What are you talking about? This is the greatest thing I've ever read. This is funny and true and illuminating."

Patrick Rush: Peter Gallagher didn't have to go to Warner Bros., but Fox asked for him to come in and test. It was weird. I was like, "Just offer it to Peter Gallagher, Jesus Christ."

Josh Schwartz: Peter, I think, had an offer subject to a onetime read at the network. And everyone's so excited, but it was still a formality. So McG's like, "Let's just read the scene." To hear Peter Gallagher reading something that I had written was such a thrill that I'll never forget it. And even though he's not Jewish, he was so clearly Sandy Cohen.

Peter Gallagher: I've played several important Jewish characters. I played Leo Frank in *The Murder of Mary Phagan* with Jack Lemmon. I feel like Jimmy Cagney. I feel like I've been speaking Yiddish since I can remember.

Josh Schwartz: He went and read and Gail Berman and [Fox casting executive] Marcia Shulman were basically flirting with him.

Patrick Rush: He was a really good sport. He had just come off of a really bad day of something he was doing on Broadway. And he came in and he's like, "So what do I got to do to get this job? You want me to sing and dance?" And Gail Berman said, "Yeah." And he broke into, like, a soft-shoe and a song.

Gail Berman (president, Fox): I'm with Peter and I'm thinking, *I'm the president of the network. I'm going to get him to sing for me.* He's just a wonderful guy. It was adorable. I was the theater nerd in the room, and I was like, *I'm not missing this opportunity.*

Peter Gallagher: I thought, *Oh, I'm not in bad shape here.* I love Gail Berman. And I love the fact that she was such a fan of the theater. She asked me to sing something, and I say, "Sure." You don't have to ask me twice. But it was nice, because it was affectionate and it was respectful and she was acknowledging that we had to have this meeting, but she wasn't going to have me jump through hoops. But while I was there, could I sing her a song? Okay!

Patrick Rush: In my heart, it was like we were done in that moment. He was ready to be a team player.

Sandy Cohen would easily be the nicest character Gallagher had played to that point in a career filled with scoundrels, cads, and outright bastards.

Peter Gallagher: I'd played so many bad guys and heels that it was really one of the first parts I'd played where I wasn't the signpost saying, "Stay away from here. Go there. Don't go here, go there."

Josh Schwartz: When you meet Peter, he's just not that guy at all. There's nothing about Peter that's anything other than incredibly warm and extremely enthusiastic, and the man just loves acting. I think the fun that he had with the role—the fun he had on the show—really popped off the screen for people.

Though the family name had changed to one that offered, as Schwartz had put it, "less in-your-face Judaism" than when they were the Needlemans, the Cohens were nonetheless overtly Jewish in a medium that still tended to imply that characters were Members of the Tribe without actually saying it.*

Lauren Gussis (writers' assistant): It was one of the first shows that had any Jewish representation at all in a way that was not grossly stereotypical. Like, I think there are shows on now that have Jewish representation and I am like not thrilled with how that goes. But I think because the call was coming from inside the house, it was a really lovely, warm, positive, openhearted thing.

---

* *Seinfeld* took 153 episodes for Jerry to explicitly identify as a Jew, when he complains to a priest about dentist Tim Whatley converting to Judaism for the jokes.

Marissa Cooper: The Most
Beautiful Girl in the World

While the producers struggled to find either Sandy's biological son or his foster son, they had an easier—if still contentious—time zeroing in on the actor to play Marissa Cooper, the literal girl next door to the Cohens, and the star-crossed love interest of Ryan Atwood.

Patrick Rush: We had tons of auditions. I remember that Kate Mara auditioned. A couple of those gals who were coming up and great. But that quintessential California sun-kissed beauty was what they were looking for.

Stephanie Savage: Josh had written a line in the script—

Josh Schwartz: "She's the most heartbreakingly beautiful girl in the world and knows it, and is a little embarrassed by it." Marissa needed to be in this world where everybody's attractive, but there's just something about her that feels alien. That feels elevated.

Savage conveniently had already worked with someone who might fit that bill: sixteen-year-old Mischa Barton, who had been acting on the stage and screen since she was eight years old, most famously as one of the dead people Haley Joel Osment sees in *The Sixth Sense*. A more obscure role brought her to Savage's attention.

Stephanie Savage: I watched *Lawn Dogs* when we were casting Sam Rockwell in *Charlie's Angels*. Sam was amazing, but there was this little girl—Mischa—who was incredible. Then a couple of years later, there was a picture of her at Sundance, now a teenager, and she was just so beautiful and lovely and outdoorsy with her scarf, in the snow at Sundance. I cut that picture out and put her in a collage on my desk of things that I liked. And then when we were doing an episode of *Fastlane* where we had a Paris Hilton–type character, Mischa came and played the Paris Hilton character.

Josh Schwartz: Mischa ran in some pretty sophisticated circles in New York, had already had the eye of a lot of fashion designers and fashion photographers and magazines, and was in that world. We were really excited about her.

Stephanie Savage: Most sixteen-year-olds coming in for pilots, their background is usually Disney or soaps or theater. They're very polished. But Mischa was coming from independent film. She didn't play to the back of the room, which was exciting, but could read as being green.

Josh Schwartz: Marcia Shulman felt like there was a similar quality to casting Ali MacGraw in *Love Story*—somebody who was a raw, charismatic star, even if they were not as experienced.

Stephanie Savage: Mischa totally had that quality of someone who was so beautiful that the way people interacted with her was actually awkward and strange, because she was the most beautiful person that people had seen. Josh and I took her to a music show. Before the show began, people came up and asked to take a picture of her. And I said, "What do you know her from?" And they were like, "Nothing. She's just so pretty." It was like, *Okay, that's someone who's living with a set of circumstances that are just very, very foreign to us other civilians.* But that was a quality that Marissa had, and that Mischa really captured.

Josh Schwartz: She was quite tall. She was a little bit uncomfortable in her skin at times. She was really beautiful and could pose on a red carpet in a way that felt like she owned it. But when you were in the room with her, she did still feel like an awkward teenager who'd just had a growth spurt and wasn't quite sure how to fold her arms. Posture was always something that we were on her about. She had a gawky teenage quality to her that was really interesting with her cover girl looks.

Mischa Barton (Marissa Cooper): I thought that she was nothing like me. So she would be a very interesting character to try to play.

Though Barton was the producers' favorite, another contender emerged: an unknown teenage actor named Olivia Wilde.

Patrick Rush: Josh and Stephanie were *very* pro-Mischa, and McG was on the Mischa bandwagon from the start. I was not. I was more excited about Olivia because I think Olivia was naturally a better actress. Not as experienced, just better.

Josh Schwartz: Olivia was really exciting. She had It. She was eighteen or nineteen, she had just moved here. She was already married to a guy who, I forget what his title was exactly—

Stephanie Savage: He was, like, an Italian prince.*

Josh Schwartz: We thought she was phenomenal and really liked her. Ultimately, though, Olivia comes from a place of real strength. Marissa was someone who needed to have a real vulnerability to her. Ryan is stepping into her life and trying to help rescue Marissa from the dark forces that are swirling around her. And Olivia was somebody who did not need saving in any way, shape, or form.

Stephanie Savage: I felt like Marissa had that quality of vulnerability of a girl who was stuck in this world where she wasn't really seen for who she was and what she wanted to be. They just saw that she was pretty and were like, "Great, you do Junior League fashion show. You date Luke. You fulfill your mother's dreams by being perfect." And she wasn't able. She had a lot going on that no one really saw or wanted to see. And Olivia doesn't seem like that. Olivia seems like someone whose version of Marissa would

---

* He was Tao Ruspoli, a member of the Italian aristocratic House of Ruspoli.

be able to get her wants and needs met, and would be able to get out of Newport, and wasn't dating Luke and wasn't doing a fashion show, and didn't get her feelings hurt because her mom was talking about her angles.

Though *The O.C.* producers were all pushing for Barton, many other involved parties felt strongly that Wilde should get the part.

Patrick Rush: All my concerns about Mischa were expressed by the network as well.

Susan Rovner (programming executive, Warner Bros. Television): I was on Team Olivia. I was not on Team Mischa. I didn't get her. I didn't understand it. At Warners, we always ultimately side with our producer, and Josh and Stephanie and McG were very, very passionate about Mischa. So ultimately, we're like, "It's your call, but I don't get it." I will say, when you see the pilot, and then you see the series, she was the right choice ultimately. I think she embodied the character and what they wanted from that character. But, yeah, I was not Team Mischa.

Patrick Rush: And in retrospect, once the show debuted, I was wrong because she was a star.

The producers took the unusual step of writing some extra material for Barton to play on camera, as a bonus screen test they hoped would assuage everyone's fears.

Mischa Barton: McG took it into his own hands to film that. I remember that day very vividly.

Josh Schwartz: She was pretty gung ho about it all. Her character, even in the pilot, is struggling with alcohol and passing out in the driveway. She didn't really shy from any of that.

Stephanie Savage: I know there was some concern that Mischa was so pretty that girls would not relate to her. And my feeling was, *Girls won't relate to her, but they'll look up to her, or they'll want to protect her.* The feeling that I had about Mischa was that I would want to watch that show every week until it went off the air, and buy every magazine that she was on the cover of, because she had that quality.

Olivia Wilde didn't get to play Marissa, but she did wind up starring in one of the other Fox/Warner Bros. teen drama pilots that season: after *The O.C.* pilot finished casting, Patrick Rush was asked to help the *Skin* producers find their female lead, and he brought Wilde to their attention. She got the job—but her time in *The O.C.* story wasn't quite finished yet. (More on that later.)

Josh Schwartz: Had it been Olivia, we would have made it work in a different way, I'm sure, ultimately. But it's hard to imagine it going the other way.

Kirsten Cohen: An Old Debt Repaid

While the other teen roles remained elusive, Rush filled out the adult ensemble. Peter Gallagher needed a partner to play Sandy's wife Kirsten Cohen (née Nichol*). Born to one of the most powerful families in Newport Beach, Kirsten had rebelled against her conservative WASPy upbringing by marrying the liberal Jewish firebrand Sandy.

Patrick Rush: You're going through the big list and checking avails and seeing who's either available or interested in being *the mom to teenagers* in a Fox show. That was an uphill battle, obviously. And then you're simultaneously doing auditions with actresses who are

---

* The family moniker inspired, of course, by McG's full name.

forty, or in their mid- to late thirties who were willing to audition, who weren't offer-only gals.

All casting directors have long memories of actors they pushed for who didn't get the part, whom they felt they owed another shot. For Patrick Rush, one of those was Kelly Rowan.

Patrick Rush: I had been casting a pilot the year or two prior at Fox called *The $treet*. That was a Darren Star pilot with Tom Everett Scott. The day we were testing the lead female role, I was literally pulling onto the Fox lot when I got the call that they were offering it to Jennifer Connelly. And now you've got a roomful of ladies coming to test for that role, and you have to send them home. So I always wanted to make it up to Kelly Rowan. But I also thought she was really perfect for that part [of Kirsten].

It was a role that for some reason attracted a lot of women of a certain age named Kelly. Kelly Rutherford didn't get it, but she would work with Schwartz and Savage years later on *Gossip Girl*, and Savage recalls Kelly Lynch testing with Fox at the same time as Rowan.

Josh Schwartz: Kelly Rowan was a really solid actress. She looked the part. She was strong. She felt smart. She read with Peter and they had a really good balance together. And she has a difficult line to walk in the pilot, because she's the one who's like, "I don't know if I want this kid living in this house." So she's taking a position opposite of what the audience wants. She was able to do it in a way that made you understand and be empathetic.

Kelly Rowan (Kirsten Cohen): It was a really good script and role. Then when Peter was attached to it, that gave it a bit of weight. They had us read together and Peter's a really good tennis partner, so when we first read together, it felt very comfortable and it made sense. I think the really successful shows, if you cast a show really well, it's magic in a bottle.

Peter Gallagher: She was a really good foil. She was pretty solid and I think it was a good yin and yang. We had fun.

Josh Schwartz: I remember after she read, [Fox Entertainment chairman] Sandy Grushow just looked at everybody and was like, "I don't see a problem here. That seemed great to me." And she's Canadian, so it's hilarious that she just naturally fell into this role of the SoCal shiksa.

Stephanie Savage: Maybe her being Canadian, is that the other part of Kirsten Cohen? She's a hard worker. She runs a company. She has a relationship with her difficult father. She was someone you needed to feel like superconfident that she in a lot of ways was running this house. And Kelly got a lot of that in a way that made you admire her and feel good that this was a house that was run well. But also, she wasn't a natural doting mom—she was someone where motherhood was a little bit difficult for her. Her own mother had died when Seth was a baby, and that made it hard for her to open her heart. So there was a lot going on in the background.

Josh Schwartz: She was the breadwinner of the family. She didn't like cooking. She worked for a very difficult dad. It was her money. But the act of marrying Sandy Cohen showed that she wasn't a typical Newpsie* who only cared about money and material things. She did do this one rebellious thing, which is marry this guy that was the opposite of her father in every single way. So she loved her father, but she also loved Sandy, which is an interesting character.

Jimmy Cooper: The Ex Next Door

Marissa's father, Jimmy, was conveniently also once the love of Kirsten's life when they were teens themselves. Instead, he wound up marrying the

---

* Sandy's derisive nickname for the tracksuit-clad Newport housewives who were always flitting in and out of the McMansion.

younger, poorer Julie in the wake of an unplanned pregnancy, living in the McMansion next to Kirsten's, and doing shady things with the finances of his many wealth management clients.

Stephanie Savage: We had a really good conversation with Andrew McCarthy, who ended up not being Jimmy. He said very interesting things about the character that we actually incorporated into the story. We had talked about Jimmy Cooper "doing the right thing," by marrying Julie when she got pregnant. Andrew McCarthy was like, "For Jimmy's parents, 'the right thing' is getting an abortion. They do not want him to marry Julie, so if he's marrying Julie, he's doing that for another reason that's not pleasing his parents. His parents want him to marry someone from his own social strata and have children in his thirties. They are not rooting for this." And I thought that was really interesting because Andrew McCarthy was the same age as the character and had gone through that echelon and experienced those values in a way that felt like what he was saying was true.

Unlike McCarthy, Tate Donovan was never labeled a member of the Brat Pack. But he had played the male lead in the mid-eighties teen adventure movie *SpaceCamp*, which made him the right age for Jimmy.

Tate Donovan (Jimmy Cooper): I thought it was a pretty good script—like, "Wow, this is not horrible for television," which you shouldn't say now, but you have to think back. I'm going to be honest: most of broadcast television is pretty unwatchable. And it was even worse back then. But *The O.C.* was very readable and the dialogue was very understandable. And it was a part I thought I could get.

Patrick Rush: He clearly won the role in the room, in a big way. There's something about an actor who just walks into the room and is ready to deliver. And he was that guy. He was present and affable and likable. Like, *Yeah, that's Jimmy.*

Josh Schwartz: He was, dare I say, the Pete Davidson of the early aughts—him and Adam Duritz from Counting Crows—in terms of getting the cast of *Friends*. He had a pretty well-documented [relationship with] Sandra Bullock. He had a [relationship with] Jennifer Aniston. So I remember when he came in just being like, *God, who is this guy? What can he teach me?* And he doesn't have any of that energy at all. He was the most charming, nicest, most unassuming guy in the world, and just brought a real charisma and likability to Jimmy Cooper, who obviously was the guy doing some unlikable things.

Seth Cohen: A Tale of Two Auditions

Finding an actor to play Seth proved strenuous in a very different way.

Patrick Rush: I've worked for Josh and Stephanie for twenty years and done a bunch of stuff with them. I now know that I have had to cast the role of Josh Schwartz eight times. I didn't know that with Seth Cohen.

San Diego native Adam Brody had decided to go into acting while working as a Blockbuster Video clerk. In only a few years, he'd racked up a fair number of credits, including playing the lead on a short-lived MTV sitcom called *The Sausage Factory*, and a recurring role on *Gilmore Girls*. His first meeting with Rush about playing Seth took an unexpected turn.

Patrick Rush: I never watched *Gilmore Girls*, so I didn't really know who he was. He came into my office and said, "I got the appointment for the role of Seth, but I would really rather read for Ryan." I'm not a casting person who would throw an actor out of my office because of that, so I said okay. He read it, and all I kept hearing was Seth's voice. I thanked him, and then I told his agent that I would really like to have him come back for Seth. I even said he doesn't have to come back to read for me as Seth; he can go straight to [the] producers.

Brody's competition for the role was close to home—literally.

> **Josh Schwartz:** We saw a lot of guys for Seth, and apparently a bunch of them all lived in the same house: Brody, Bret Harrison, Marshall Allman, and Johnny Lewis. We used to call it "The House of Seth," because all of these kids who read for Seth lived there. Then there was one guy that everybody called "Bar Mitzvah Josh," Aaron Himelstein. He was the extremely real version—like, if an even more awkward version of me had walked in to read. Naturally, I loved him, and the network was like, "No."

Despite the initial Ryan vs. Seth curveball, Brody had charmed Patrick Rush. His first meeting with the producers did not end nearly as well.

> **Patrick Rush:** In retrospect, I wish I had had him come back to read for me as Seth before they saw him. It was one of those times where I shot myself in the foot and was like, "I really, truly think our Seth is coming in today." And then Adam came in.

> **Craig Erwich (programming executive, Fox):** Adam's audition was off the wall. He was lying down on the floor at some point.

> **Patrick Rush:** Adam took . . . *liberties* with the material. He ad-libbed. He was obnoxious. He was disrespectful of the material. Josh was like, "I never want to see that kid again."

> **Josh Schwartz:** I was like, "Who is this? He came in and didn't know any of the lines? What? No, fuck this guy!"

> **Stephanie Savage:** He ad-libbed the whole thing. He didn't say anything as written. Josh and I were like, "Why did you bring that guy back? He sucks."

And what does Adam Brody remember of this process?

Adam Brody (Seth Cohen): Zero. Nothing. Not a thing. I do remember Patrick in general, I know him and like him a lot. The only audition I remember at all is the network tests with Ben [McKenzie].

Patrick Rush: I don't know if his coming back to do Seth was his way of saying, "I don't care. I don't want to play this," but it was one for the books. I'm sitting face-to-face with Adam Brody. And they're behind me. So I can't see their reactions to what he's doing. But I know my face as I'm reading with Adam is like this. [*Patrick conjures up a horrified expression over Zoom.*] I don't think Peter Roth was in love with him, either.

A good casting director trusts his hunches, and argues on behalf of them. Patrick Rush is an excellent casting director.

Patrick Rush: Luckily, because I'd spent enough time with [Josh and Stephanie], and they're truly lovely, I knew that I could fight the good fight. I said, "Would you please let me see if I can give a note to the agent to have him come back and stay on the page?" And I think just to shut me up for a minute, they said yes.

Stephanie Savage: He came back, and actually read the part as written and put some effort into it. And it was amazing.

The director swap from McG to Doug Liman proved fortuitously timed for Brody.

Josh Schwartz: It was around the same time that Doug was coming onto the show. Doug in the room looked to me and was like, "I love this guy."

Adam Brody: I was skeptical of being on a high school show in perpetuity. But I liked the script and on the plus side, Doug Liman came aboard late in the process. And that changed my calculations a bit, to be honest with you, because *Swingers* had changed my life a few years prior. So I thought, *Okay, it's worth doing it and seeing what happens, and we'll worry about the high school thing as it comes.*

Josh Schwartz: Adam was a film buff, and now he was more enthusiastic. Whether he was reluctant about the project initially, Doug's involvement definitely validated it for him.

Doug Liman (director/executive producer): In *The O.C.*, [Brody] was like the ideal version of what I had wanted to be in high school. He didn't get caught up in any of the bullshit. He's a great actor and a friggin' hard worker, and just holds the screen.

David Bartis (executive producer): Doug can be tough and he can throw a lot at you. And if you can come back from that—if you can take a punch and then get back up and do something different, do it again—that says a lot. And Adam was doing that.

Tate Donovan: I just thought he was going to be the next Tom Hanks. I was like, "This guy is just a fucking huge star."

Ryan Atwood: "Please Let This Be That Kid They're Talking About"

Ryan Atwood was by far the more conventional of the show's two male leads. Yet somehow, the producers were having an even harder go of it finding their Ryan than they had with Seth, and time was running out.

Patrick Rush: We saw Chris Pine, who was really good. I hate saying this, but it's the truth: Chris Pine was at the age where he was experiencing really bad skin problems. And it was at that point where it looked insurmountable. And as a kid who grew up with horrible skin, it just broke my heart. But Chris Pine's fine now. He's all right.

> **Josh Schwartz:** We had gone down the road with Garrett Hedlund to play Ryan, which felt like an exciting choice—like somebody who was going to be a star, as well. And then in the middle of that process, he got cast as the lead of *Troy*.

So they kept looking, including an audition for D.J. Cotrona, who would go on to star in *Skin* opposite Olivia Wilde.

> **Josh Schwartz:** No one was falling in love. We were in [Warner casting executive] Mary Buck's office for casting, and Steve Pearlman, who was Peter Roth's number two at the time in the studio, said, "Well, what about that guy Ben McKenzie," who had just come in and read for like the fifth lead of a UPN show.

Ben McKenzie was a twenty-four-year-old actor with barely any screen credits. UPN was developing a pilot that year called *Newton*, created by Craig Silverstein and David Nadelberg. The logline: "A struggling family wins the opportunity to move to a small town utopia in exchange for testing out bizarre, futuristic products that change their lives."

> **Craig Silverstein (*Newton* creator/executive producer):** Ben McKenzie tested for the role of Eli—a wannabe Holden Caulfield who positioned himself as a rebel activist out to expose the secret behind the corporate-owned town. Ben's audition was terrific. We showed the tape to Susan Rovner and Peter Roth and they agreed. Submitted him as our choice to the network. The word we got back from someone at UPN was, "We don't think he's a star." That's it.

> **Patrick Rush:** Someone in Warner Bros. casting said, "You should see this kid. He has a Ryan feel to him." If we're a Warner Bros. pilot and they like him? I'm thinking, *I'm not gonna pre-read him, we're just getting him in fast because he's going to go fast.*

If Ben McKenzie was in demand, nobody bothered telling Ben McKenzie.

Ben McKenzie (Ryan Atwood): I was seriously considering leaving L.A. I was really, really low—not just financially, but more importantly, emotionally. I didn't know anyone in L.A. I had been there a year, and I'd only gotten a guest starring role and a costarring role in an entire year of auditioning.

Patrick Rush: I remember parking and walking and seeing Benjamin McKenzie outside. I'd never met him before, and I thought to myself, *Please let this be that kid they're talking about.* It was coming off him. There was an intensity. When you meet Ben, you know immediately he's a serious actor. I thought, *He has that look, we need it. So if there's any way he could spit out the dialogue* . . . When I brought him in to introduce him, he was not chitchatty, he was not overly effusive or friendly or whatever. He was ready. My back is to them, and I'm thinking, *Oh my God, this is Ryan. Oh please, dear God, this is right. Please let them love him as much as I'm loving him.* He was so solid. He was just an actor. He had prepared. He looked like he wanted the part, and he looked right for the part. And I thought he was so, so handsome. If I remember correctly, he tested against Josh Henderson.*

Susan Rovner: That audition, I remember vividly. He owned the room. The second I saw him do it, I was like, "There's Ryan."

Craig Erwich: He really inhabited the character. He felt like that kind of man, or kid, of few words—James Dean–esque, but not a poser. He felt like there was a real soul behind him versus someone who was just playing the danger or the damage.

Josh Schwartz: I remember he was standing outside. He was smoking a cigarette. He was very taciturn and shy prior to the meeting on the way in. And then when he walked in to read, he wasn't what we

---

* In a twist of fate, Henderson wound up playing the role on *Newton* that UPN wouldn't approve McKenzie for. *Newton* never made it to air.

had imagined for the part. He felt more thoughtful and more internal, less of an obvious bad boy. He had more of an Ed Norton quality— something more cerebral.

Stephanie Savage: Which is how Ryan is written. It's the thing that makes Sandy think that this kid needs saving: his high test scores and the sassy monologue he gives about how not having dreams is what makes you smart. And he was super handsome and all the girls in Orange County would like him. So it made sense, but there was still this feeling of having to adjust the frame.

As far as McKenzie and Doug Liman are concerned, though, things did not start off well.

Ben McKenzie: It's just a bad read. I'm trying way too hard. It's ugly. And there's this awkward pause.

Doug Liman: Evidently I said to him, "Um, okay, do you mind doing that again, and this time do it better?" Which is *not* a great stage direction to give. For many reasons. I'm a little horrified when I hear that. I'm worried I might have said that to other people, who didn't end up doing it better.

Ben McKenzie: And Doug does that thing where he's like [*McKenzie does a spot-on Doug Liman impression*], "Okay. So. Uh. Okay. So do it. Less soap opera-y." I just remember being like, *Cool. So your note is, "Do it less shitty."* It's that moment in the audition where you're either going to be able to figure it out and rise to the challenge—where you're either the right person for the job in that moment or you're not. It was actually freeing, because it was honest—which is what I found Doug to be. If it works, it works. And if it doesn't work, it doesn't work. And he'll just tell you, and then you're free to go.

McG (executive producer): He was hell-bent on being the disciplined actor, very reminiscent of the greats, with the Pacino poster and the

De Niro poster. And the focus on sense memory training and Meisner and acting is reacting, and everything that goes into that. And Adam Brody was playing jazz.

Here, for instance, is McKenzie putting his theater education to work to explain the degree to which he and Ryan Atwood began to resemble each other over time:

Ben McKenzie: I subscribe to the theory that there is no such thing as "the character." There's the words on the page and there's the person playing the part, and the blend of those two things becomes this thing you call the character. And if someone else had played the role, "the character" would have been different. The way I was playing it was leaning into this side of me that has a chip on his shoulder, the kind of guy who had to fight his way up. And I did come by that somewhat honestly. I grew up in Texas, in Austin, went to public schools for the most part, I'd been to L.A. maybe once or twice before moving there. That sense that I was going to have to fight to make it, I think was definitely part of what I was able to put into Ryan initially.

Adam Brody: I just remember liking him. He wasn't like the bland actor I feared they could cast. I thought, *Oh he's got a Matt Damon thing happening*. The character is very *Good Will Hunting*-esque.

Josh Schwartz: I wasn't there the day Ben was officially cast on the show, because my uncle Joel—my mom's brother, who I was incredibly close with—had passed away from brain cancer. The whole year that we were prepping *The O.C.*, and it was like all my dreams were coming true, I was also dealing with the tragedy of this guy that was one of the closest people in my life and a mentor to me. The line that Sandy says to Kirsten about how if we compromise now, what will we do when we're older—that was something he used to always say to me as advice. And his favorite song, that brought him a lot of solace when he was sick, was Jeff Buckley's "Hallelujah." So a lot of my connection with him obviously infused its way into the show. His funeral was the day that Ben was cast on the pilot.

Summer, Julie, and Luke*:
Three Stealth Cast Members

The main ensemble had been filled, but there were three guest-starring roles in the pilot that had the potential to become significant parts of the show down the road. And thanks to the actors chosen, all three of them did.

Josh Schwartz: It's a budgetary thing. In network television, the whole game is you don't have enough money or enough days, ever. So you're always looking for ways to cut corners. One way is cast someone as a guest star and then pray that they don't get cast as a series regular on something in between your ability to upgrade them.

The smallest of these in the pilot, but potentially the biggest for the series, was Summer Roberts, a plastic surgeon's spoiled daughter, Marissa's best friend, and the oblivious object of Seth's unrequited love since early childhood.

Rachel Bilson (Summer Roberts): My best friend Olivia[†] got the audition for Marissa. I read the sides, and I was like, *Oh, that's such a good part. I want to audition for that.* And then for whatever reason, I received the audition for Summer.

Bilson had grown up around showbiz—her father Danny Bilson was a producer who had cocreated TV shows and movies based on comic book characters like the Flash, the Human Target, and the Rocketeer—but had not acted much professionally to that point.

---

* Schwartz: "Felt like every other kid at USC was named Summer or Luke."

† Not Olivia Wilde. A different Olivia.

Rachel Bilson: My parents were like, "Get through school. And then once you graduate, if that's what you want to do, then fine." I did theater in high school. Rami Malek and I did plays together, and he was my good friend. Our senior year, we did *The Crucible*. My dad, after watching it, was like, "You're good at this. Do you want to try this?" So it was after high school that I started auditioning and decided I really wanted to pursue it.

Josh Schwartz: Rachel really had three lines in the pilot, one of which was, "I gotta pee."

Patrick Rush: She wasn't even a guest star in the pilot. That was a costar role—that was not a big role. And the fact that someone can make magic out of "Ew!" and "Coop, I have to pee."?

Josh Schwartz: As scripted, that part was a more classic, obvious blond California girl.

Rachel Bilson: And he got a short half-Jewish brunette.

Josh Schwartz: She was like this little dark-haired terrier. But she was really funny and was so unexpected and so different from Marissa and Mischa. So it's not as we scripted it, but how do we not cast this person?

Rachel Bilson: It's because I made him laugh. I said I had to pee, and he laughed, and that was it.

One advantage of being initially hired as a guest star: the casting process is much less rigorous, so Bilson didn't have to go through as many rounds of it, in front of as many different people, as Barton, Brody, or McKenzie had.

Rachel Bilson: Dude, I had it so made. I was able to skip all of the testing. I probably wouldn't have gotten the part, but because I was originally a guest star, it really worked in my favor.

Stephanie Savage: We always were hoping to have these characters in the cast. And then once it was Rachel and Melinda, and we knew them and saw their work, we knew we must make this happen. Which we were able to do. But from a studio or network perspective, it's like, "If Rachel went away, can Marissa get a new friend?"

McG: She made chicken salad out of chicken shit, to say the least. And she blew up.

Marissa's mother, Julie, was designed as a spiritual opposite of Kirsten Cohen: a judgmental, materialistic woman from the wrong side of the tracks who took to the Newport lifestyle far more easily than a native like Kirsten had. Melinda Clarke had been acting for over a decade by this point, including a stint working with her father on *Days of Our Lives*, a mid-nineties syndicated action show called *Soldier of Fortune* that briefly costarred future NBA Hall of Famer Dennis Rodman, and a recurring role on the original *CSI* as dominatrix Lady Heather.

Melinda Clarke (Julie Cooper-Nichol): I was up for the role of Number Six on *Battlestar Galactica*, against Tricia Helfer. In the meantime, I had auditioned for *The O.C.*, first for Kirsten and wanted that role, and then they brought me back for Julie. All of a sudden Patrick said, "They want to offer it to you." And *Battlestar Galactica* said, "No, we're not going to let you out." There was something in my gut that made me say, "Please let me out. Tricia is the role. This is not my role." And eventually, they said okay. But Patrick was holding them off. They were going to move on to the next choice. And they had a couple of them.

Patrick Rush: Melinda as that character is my spirit animal. That's who I want to be.

Melinda Clarke: It's not my world that I grew up in, but the first thing I wanted to do is make sure they knew I was from Orange County. I was wearing red Theory pants and a white top. They wrote [an audition] scene for Julie that was never in the show. If you read it, it just read as a complete bitch. So I pulled out a friend of mine who I based Julie on, who's an actress who's going to remain nameless, but everything that comes out of her mouth makes you ask, "Was that rude? Was that mean? That was so harsh!" But she says it with such a smile that you don't really know if it was an insult.

Just as Rush felt he owed Kelly Rowan a favor for what happened on *The Street*, Stephanie Savage still carried around some guilt regarding the casting of the boss character on *Fastlane*.

Stephanie Savage: We wanted to hire Melinda for the female lead on *Fastlane*. Part of the issue was that Melinda was, I think, thirty-three and [Fox felt] that was too old, because you'd be nearing forty by the time you got to the end of your contract. And this was to play someone *who ran a secret wing of the LAPD* that did undercover investigations, and they didn't feel that the woman who had this job should be over thirty years old.

For Julie, age was also a factor, but in a different way: Clarke was technically old enough to be the mother of a sixteen-year-old, but just barely.

Josh Schwartz: She was probably mathematically too young for the part, but she could play older. She was a mother at the time. She had a really young daughter, and she just got it. She was from Orange County. She just understood those women and the Juicy tracksuits and the Froyo and the humor. And she also was just really fun opposite Mischa.

Melinda Clarke: She was that original *Real Housewives* kind of character.

Gail Berman: Melinda probably would have had a little bit of a harder time [going through the regular casting process], I'm guessing, but I loved her, too, when I saw her. Maybe we would have been looking at people that had more of a name at that moment. But obviously [she and Rachel] were so perfect for their roles.

Stephanie Savage: And then honestly, [the executives] were thinking, *If Jimmy and Julie get divorced, can Julie just leave the show?* Which, once we knew Melinda, we knew that could never happen. Even if they do get divorced, she's staying here.

Finally, there was Luke Ward, Marissa's water polo–playing boyfriend, and thus Ryan's mortal enemy. Chris Carmack was a former model with the right look for the part, even if he—like Adam Brody—had originally wanted to play a different role.

Chris Carmack (Luke Ward): I first auditioned for the character of Ryan. And I went in and I must have made an impression because they called me back but for the role of Luke.

Patrick Rush: We probably had two sessions for that role. The role of Luke wasn't the focus. We needed that quintessential square-jaw California surf boy from the O.C. And Chris walks in and is that. But I give him credit like I do with Melinda and Rachel—he made something more than was on the page. I remember after the show got picked up, going to McG's office, and they had posters up and it was Ryan and Marissa and Seth. And then they had Luke. How did he get a poster? Good for him. He took a role that wasn't that much and became a great foe.

Chris Carmack: I believe there was a joke in the pilot where somebody mockingly calls Luke "Abercrombie." And at the time I was actually featured on Abercrombie Girls, because I had done a modeling campaign for them. Because of that joke and the fact that I was on these Abercrombie billboards, I thought, *Well, maybe this gives me more of a shot.* I don't know if that played in at all, but I did get the role.

Kaitlin Cooper 1.0

There was another minor character in the pilot who made a handful of additional appearances over the course of the first season: Marissa's little sister Kaitlin.

Josh Schwartz: I guess we should also say we had Kaitlin Cooper at the time, cast with a young child named Shailene Woodley.

Melinda Clarke: There's certain kids that are just meant to do this.

Tate Donovan: Oh, I know. Tiny. Amazing.

Josh Schwartz: She was just really funny when she said, "China has alopecia."

Lisa Cochran (unit production manager): She was incredibly quiet—church mouse quiet. And she was so young. She spent a lot of time in school with the studio teacher.

After weeks of auditions and meetings and debate, the ensemble was set, and the producers were excited.

Josh Schwartz: We got to be like, "Ed Norton is Ryan, and Tom Hanks is Seth, and Gwyneth Paltrow is Marissa." We had a really exciting cast that felt like potential movie stars. And then we had people like Gallagher and Tate who'd been in movies. So we were feeling really, really good about our cast.

They were right to feel good, as they would find out when everybody got to work on *The O.C.* pilot episode.

CHAPTER 3

The Pilot

A PILOT EPISODE is as much a sales tool as it is a piece of storytelling. Before you get to make your TV show, you have to make a pilot to convince the network to buy that show. With *The O.C.*, this was happening faster than usual. Fox's hope of premiering the series in August meant that network executives would make their pickup order based on a sizzle reel from the first week of shooting. Doug Liman had never directed for television before, and had arrived very late in the process. Josh Schwartz was young and inexperienced. There was a lot of learning to do, and not a lot of time in which to do it.

Chemistry 101

While many of the actors met either during the casting phase or as the pilot went into production, two of them already had a shared history.

Rachel Bilson (Summer Roberts): I knew Brody before, because he had casually dated one of my friends. *Casually.* I think I thought he was cute and funny, but he was dating my friend, and he was around, and I don't know if I thought much beyond that. I was dating someone when we started the show, so it wasn't immediately, *Oh, I like this guy.* That grew into itself, but I always thought he was cool and funny. I also thought he was a little bit of a dick at times, but that's just his sense of humor before I really knew him. And then I realized that was just his charm.

Adam Brody (Seth Cohen): [Bilson was] super funny, super loose. Obviously, we got along very well, so just very comfortable. And I think the dynamic was fun. I knew her only a little before. My first strong memory of her is shooting an early episode, sitting next to each other and talking for a while, and she showed me her iPod and explained to me what it was and how to work it.

Schwartz and Savage had fought for Mischa Barton in part because they felt her beauty would turn heads even in Newport Beach. This soon proved correct among the cast, as well.

Melinda Clarke (Julie Cooper-Nichol): Mischa was stunning. There's some people when you meet in person, they're just, you're even more blown away by how great their presence and their beauty and what they exude. I had a director once say, "Melinda, we love you, but when we light you and frame you, it comes alive." But I can pass for a normal person. But there are certain people who off-screen, are even more beautiful and stunning. That was Mischa.

Rachel Bilson: [Mischa] was great. She was so young, but knew way more than I did. And really was like, "How close is this shot?" And, "Let me see the frame," and all that. And I'm like, "Whaaaat?" She was beautiful and kind and sweet. And we had a lot of fun.

David Bartis (executive producer): We didn't really know Mischa. We knew she'd been a model who had started acting, but we really didn't know her. We didn't know what she could do, really, until we started shooting. And I think it's fair to say that was a little bit of a wake-up call. She had been given quite a bit of heavy lifting, and I think it was hard for her.

Barton, though, was mainly concerned with how the exact nature of how the character felt was like a moving target as filming began.

Mischa Barton (Marissa Cooper): I do remember getting a little bit dismayed as we got into the territory of, "Could she be more ditzy?" Or, "Could she be more Southern California?" Being British and a

New Yorker, that's just very far from me. So I struggled at first setting the tone with her as this like, SoCal, beachy, preppy thing. Though I could maybe relate to the preppy more. We tried a lot with how much of a party girl she was, or she wasn't. And I do think it took a minute to land on the character.

Other actors had to adjust to the new job in different ways.

Melinda Clarke: My first day on set was the party scene. I get on the bus that's taking us from base camp to this big party scene, and I see Ben McKenzie in a tuxedo and Adam Brody more slouchy. I thought Ben was Seth because of the way he was dressed—really clean-cut and quiet—and Brody exuded more bad boy, so I thought he must be Ryan.

Lisa Cochran (unit production manager): When we were doing the pilot, Ben was sleeping on a friend's couch. And his car did not work. I got a phone call from his agent asking if there was any way we could give him transportation back and forth. Which the studio does not do—you're in town, this is your home, you drive yourself to work. And then I realized that he had a car that couldn't get him to Malibu.

Ben McKenzie (Ryan Atwood): When I ended up in L.A., I bought a car for $500 out of the back of the *PennySaver*—a 1986 Cadillac DeVille with 228,000 miles on it. The radiator was completely shot. I was living in the Valley, so if I had an audition in Santa Monica, I'd purposely leave when traffic was at its lightest. Because if I got stuck on the 101 or the 405 in bumper-to-bumper, that fucking thing would overheat and I would be screwed. I'd have to pull over to the side of the road and let it cool down and go on.

Lisa Cochran: So we ended up renting a car for him.

Ben McKenzie: They rented me the worst car ever. It was pretty funny. Not worse than the car I was driving, but the worst car that had been built in the last ten years. One of those cars that they gave it a name like "Echo," just so you know how far down on the totem pole you are.

McKenzie was also not prepared for some of the basic perks that come with being one of the stars of a show, rather than a guest star with a couple of lines.

Ben McKenzie: You didn't get a stand-in for parts that small—you would just stand in for yourself. But obviously, as the lead of a pilot, you'd have a stand-in. I finished a rehearsal, and I just stood there, and this guy, who looked weirdly a lot like me, came up to me and was like, "Do you want me to . . . You know . . . Can I, like, get you anything?" Because I wasn't moving. Everyone thought I was method. But the truth is, I was just so inexperienced. I didn't know I could leave. I was like, *Oh, shit, that's actually cool. In fact, I will go have a snack. Thank you. That works.*

Orange County native Melinda Clarke wasn't wild about how she was being styled to play a quintessential Newport Beach mom.

Melinda Clarke: They wanted tan, they wanted nails, they wanted very heavy makeup. But that was also just a reflection of the time, which was the style. But they were dressing me like in Jones New York, or they were dressing me very like what I consider women in their sixties in Orange County. I really fought it. My experience is when you go to the beach in Orange County, in Newport Beach, the women are trying to look like the teenagers, and the teenagers are trying to look like the moms.

Liman Law

Doug Liman had arrived midway through the casting process. It was a striking shift from McG, and a memorable experience for everyone who worked with him.

Patrick Rush (casting director): What was weird was the juxtaposition between the McG energy and Doug Liman. They could not be more opposite. McG's literally jumping on tables, giving people direction, and he's excitable, his energy is great and he's just a force of nature. And Doug Liman is just not that. He is a very quiet, serious guy.

Stephanie Savage (executive producer): He was prepping *Mr. & Mrs. Smith* at the same time, which was our friend Simon Kinberg's movie.

Josh Schwartz (creator/executive producer): I actually didn't know Simon at the time. He was my mortal enemy, having nothing to do with Simon himself, just because of how clearly Doug was more interested in directing *Mr. & Mrs. Smith*.*

Stephanie Savage: It became clear talking to him that he wasn't going to have much time to prep the show because he was so involved in *Mr. & Mrs. Smith*. So if he signed on, it would basically be us prepping the show, and then he would show up to shoot it. His vérité style would suit him well, because he would shoot it like it was a documentary—whatever was happening was happening, he would capture it on film—but was a little bit daunting to us. That would mean we'd have to make a lot of decisions without him, like picking locations.

Josh Schwartz: Doug's process is by its nature a bit more chaotic—I think for the creative good. At the time, we may have been mystified at certain points, but he's somebody who shows up and figures it out and is very open to having a plan, and then being like, "Nope, I was wrong. I want to shoot it over here." And everybody moving on the

---

* Between the *Mr. & Mrs. Smith* issue and Garrett Hedlund exiting the casting process to costar in *Troy*, Schwartz jokes, "Brad Pitt is actually the unspoken nemesis of *The O.C.*"

fly. That's just part of his process. There is something to it that keeps you feeling alive and real because it's not overly rehearsed. It's not been set in stone. Everyone's invested in figuring it out enough together.

Peter Gallagher (Sandy Cohen): I remember, when we were shooting the burning house scene in episode two, Doug telling the camera operator—and it was all handheld—"Here. Start over there. Put your camera over there on that building." "Well, that's not where the scene is." "I know. Start over there and find the scene. Okay, action." And all of a sudden, there was a vitality in that camera with the guy. The operator was really finding the action. And that gave it an immediacy. And I thought, "Oh my God."

Doug Liman (director/executive producer): I look for something that lives in the world of a heightened honesty. That's where, as a filmmaker, I like to live. I'm not Noah Baumbach, who's all honesty. And I'm not McG, who does not care about honesty.

Josh Schwartz: It's certainly not an approach that you would expect of a teen soap on the Fox network. It was much more of an indie film approach, which is what he brings to the movies as well, regardless of the budget.

Peter Gallagher: I would have loved working with McG. But I think everybody was expecting us to be really glitzy and really empty—like, if you look close enough, there's nothing there. I think that was the anticipation.

Doug Liman: Raw is my thing, just because I put the camera on my shoulder. Unfortunately, I'm a little bit too good at raw. My career has been working on how to do less raw. People don't go to the movies or watch TV to just see their own life reflected. But there are times when my extremely good ability to capture life in a very raw, honest way plays well. And that was definitely one of them.

But there were times his avant-garde style didn't mesh with what the producers were looking for.

Mischa Barton: I love Doug. I remembered Doug controlling the camera, and cutting my head off in one of the first takes of the scene where I come down the driveway, and the producers got so mad at him, because they thought it was a really good take.

Liman's technical style was not the only aspect of the director that required adjustment from the cast and crew.

Lisa Cochran: Doug was a very unusual person. We put the tech scout together and I got a call from his partner, who said, "He'll meet you at the first location. Can you send the itinerary?" And I said, "No, we need him in the bus." We had a forty-passenger big bus. I said, "Maybe he could meet people he hasn't met yet on the bus." So Doug is sitting in the row directly across from me. We hand him the script. He looks at the script, he fans the pages, takes the script, puts it against the bus window, puts his head on it, and he fell asleep and woke up when we got to the jail location. I looked at the first AD in the row behind him, and the first AD looked at me with this look on his face, like, *What am I supposed to do?* I said, "We'll talk him through the changes when we get to the jail."

Josh Schwartz: Every day, Simon Kinberg would come to set with Akiva Goldsman, who was the producer of *Mr. & Mrs. Smith*, and they would have a meeting about the movie at the end of the day's shooting. For the most part, we had Doug's attention. Then one day, we were shooting in the middle of the water, when Seth takes Ryan out on the *Summer Breeze* for the first time. We're all on a crew boat, attached to the *Summer Breeze*. Doug finds out that he is late for a *Mr. & Mrs. Smith* meeting, and all of a sudden he just jumps off of the boat at sea and swims to shore to go to the meeting. And is basically like, "The actors know what they're doing, and the DP knows what he's doing, and you've got this." That was incredible.

Doug Liman: That was true. I had to get back, and it just seemed like the fastest way. And obviously it worked out. *Mr. & Mrs. Smith* came out great. So I'm glad I didn't miss the meeting. Not that I remember what it was about.

David Bartis: I don't remember if he was really late for the meeting, because Doug will jump off a boat any excuse he can get. I have seen him jump off of more than one boat.

Liman's investment in the Seth Cohen character began manifesting itself in a surprising way.

Doug Liman: The hours are so long, and we had built the house on the soundstage in Manhattan Beach.

Lisa Cochran: We wrapped after going late one day, and they called me up in my office and said, "We need you to come down here." I went downstairs to the stage floor, and they said, "Doug Liman is going to spend the night here," because he didn't want to drive home. So I said, "Well, where is he?" And they said, "He went into Seth's bedroom set."

Doug Liman: I oftentimes would just sleep in Seth's bed, rather than drive all the way home and drive all the way back in the morning. Like, *Well, it is a house. I can just sleep here. There is a bed.* I felt the connection to this character, so that felt like my room.

Lisa Cochran: So I walk around the corner into the beginning of the set, and there's a pair of shoes on the carpet. I go about three feet further, and there's a pair of jeans on the carpet, and that's when I stopped. I said, "Doug, are you in here?" He said, "Yes." I go, "Doug, you can't sleep in here. Set construction's going to be in in about an hour and a half. You cannot be sleeping here. Please get dressed. If you really want to stay here, I'll give you a dressing room." He said, "Okay." Peter Gallagher had already wrapped for the day. We walk over to Peter's dressing room, door is open, so I walk in. The room's dark in there, but it had a couch, and in the closet, there was always a pillow and a blanket. I said, "Here, Doug, make yourself comfortable on this couch. There's a bathroom here. Everything's fine." He gets on the couch, he puts the blanket over him. I turn around to leave, and the bathroom door opens, and Peter Gallagher is coming out of the bathroom, zipping up his pants! I froze. I looked at him and I looked back at Doug. Doug did not care. Peter apparently took his time getting ready to leave. Peter turned around, looked at Doug, looked at me, and with a smile, said, "How do you think I got the job?"

David Bartis: It has also happened many times where Doug has slept on set.

Doug Liman: And there's a backyard with a swimming pool, so I would jump in the pool in the morning. That was my shower. The crew would come into work, and I'd be in the pool.

Liman's candor also required some adjusting.

Josh Schwartz: He's pretty succinct. I think he expects the actors to show up and have thought about it, and then he just throws them into it. And if he doesn't like something, he's extremely blunt about it. But because his personality is overall very sweet, it's not like he's doing it in a way that feels mean or manipulative. He can just only be really honest.

Norman Buckley (editor/director): The first thing I showed Doug, he said, "It's horrible. It's the worst thing I've ever seen." At that point, I felt very confident in my abilities as an editor. So I wasn't particularly affected by that remark. Then I showed him the scene of Summer arriving at the party in Malibu. And he was like, "It's perfect, don't change a frame." So right off the bat I thought, *Okay, he's going to tell me exactly what he thinks about things.* Which is great in a way, because you cut through all the bullshit and you get right to the work.

He was very complimentary of the things he liked, and he was not complimentary at all of the things that he didn't like.

Tate Donovan (Jimmy Cooper): Doug Liman is a seriously odd duck. And is not great with actors, so I think he had a hard time with some of the young kids, being way too blunt and saying harsh things to them, and them being like, "They're going to fire me." All an actor really wants to hear from a director is, "Wow, you're amazing. That take was incredible." And he's not like that at all. And I actually liked how direct he was, like, "That wasn't good. Do it like that." No bullshit.

Liman did win several fans among the cast, though, several of whom would work with him again on later projects.*

Rachel Bilson: Doug, I could not love that human more. He's so passionate and just goes for whatever he wants, and he sees his vision. You have to respect that. He takes guerrilla shooting to the next level. I did a movie with him, and I was asleep on an airplane, and I woke up with his camera in my face that he wanted to use in the movie. I was like "What's happening?"

Adam Brody: I think he's brilliant. He was so nice to me then, and has been in the years since. I'm forever grateful and love him.

Peter Gallagher: Listen, I can see how he could drive people crazy. I just love him. He is so smart and he's so bold. And I can understand why sometimes his language, or his affect, is not cuddly. But I've had some really delightful times in my life with people who think a little differently and are a little different. He's not mean. He's not unkind. He doesn't use his intelligence or his power to wound people. He's just working. If I ever thought that any of that was combined with a desire to wound, my estimation wouldn't be as high, or my affection as great.

---

* Adam Brody wound up in *Mrs. & Mrs. Smith*, Rachel Bilson costarred in *Jumper*, and Peter Gallagher spent five seasons on the Liman-produced spy drama *Covert Affairs*.

Mischa Barton: He's sarcastic, and I enjoy that type of humor, and that kind of a person. So I got along with him. I thought he was a welcome breath of fresh air, actually.

And regardless of the personality conflicts, Liman's work impressed everyone.

Josh Schwartz: Doug came up with probably my favorite shot in the pilot. Ryan is leaving to go back to Chino with Sandy. It's scripted that he's in the car. Sandy backs down the driveway and Ryan sees Marissa in the driveway going away. The sun was going down and there wasn't a lot of time to get the scene. We already had a shot of Marissa on the corner, but Doug really had a shot in his mind. He grabbed the camera, jumped into the backseat of the car, and got this shot that's Ryan's point of view of Marissa, as the sun is setting. And to me, it was one of the more beautiful shots in the show, a really haunting image, one that we return to over the course of the series and something that he just brought to you. Another director probably would have been like, "We got it, let's move on."

David Bartis: That's also very typical Doug. On everything we've ever shot, he's picked up a camera himself, because he'll have something that's hard to convey to somebody else. And it's easier for him to just pick up the camera and shoot it. There were a couple of scenes that really elevated the pilot, and that was one of them. I think everybody was on Ben's side by the end of that scene. It's a classic Doug shot setup. He just makes you feel like you're with the characters.

No Smoking, Please

Ryan looking at Marissa through the car window was actually the second of two memorable pilot moments between them filmed in the shared cul-de-sac of the Cohen and Cooper homes. In the first, Marissa finds this strange boy smoking a cigarette, and asks who he is. "Whoever you want me to be," he quips, trying to go full James Dean. She asks to bum a smoke, and he lights it by pressing the tip of his cigarette to hers—a metaphorical prelude to the many actual kisses these two would share.

Ben McKenzie: That was definitely one of the most memorable nights of the entire show for me. It was a pivotal moment in the pilot. We had rehearsed it many times, and we were trying to capture that magic, which is difficult to capture continually. You can rehearse it, but you can also rehearse it too much. Doug was very good at getting us to try different things in different takes, so that every time, it felt new.

Susan Rovner (programming executive, Warner Bros. Television): The moment that I knew honestly that this was something different is the cigarette kiss between Ryan and Marissa. That's honestly even more iconic for me than "Welcome to the O.C., bitch." Looking back on teenage years, there's something so relatable about that moment where there's a literal spark between a boy and a girl. And the danger of the bad boy and a girl next door, and what does that mean?

Josh Schwartz: When Ryan lights the cigarette for her, there was no wind on Ben's side. But as soon as the camera turned around on Mischa, there was this gentle breeze going through her hair. That's star power.

The final version of the scene proved useful for Mischa Barton, who was still trying to get a handle on Marissa, especially as Schwartz and Liman were encouraging her to try several different takes on the character throughout the pilot shoot.

Mischa Barton: There was so much pressure on that scene to get it right, for all the obvious reasons. Having just watched it back with Rachel and Melinda, it's funny to see her being so sarcastic at times in the one they used. That was very much in the early days of trying to set the tone of who Marissa was going to be, and there was a lot of experimentation with that.

It was, however, a difficult moment to get approved by Fox's standards and practices department.

Ben McKenzie: The cigarette lighting was a really nice touch—which we would, of course, never get away with now.

Josh Schwartz: It was pretty much unheard of for anyone on TV at that time to smoke a cigarette, let alone a teenager. Dave Bartis took me to lunch with the broadcast standards guys at the network, and basically the whole meeting was about getting the cigarette approved. The way we did that was the last line of the scene: as they're walking up the driveway, Sandy says, "There's no smoking in my house." He stomps on the cigarette, and that's the last time Ryan is allowed to smoke.

David Bartis: They didn't want to set a bad example, and they didn't want viewer backlash from their audience. I think all of us felt like, "We don't want to promote smoking. We're not advocating for smoking, but we're also trying to do something that feels honest and authentic to the characters whose stories we're telling." It wasn't going to ruin the pilot if it wasn't there. But our strong feeling was that it would resonate with the core audience if it was there.

Josh Schwartz: Later, when they wanted to do commercials for the show, they wanted to use that scene because it's a provocative scene. But they couldn't use the cigarette, so they had to reshoot it on a stage with Ben and—I forget if he had a French fry, or maybe a straw. They were trying to figure out other things. And I was like, "See, it doesn't work without the cigarette!"

Welcome to the Catchphrase, Bitch

The shoot began with several nights at the location for the beach house party where Ryan runs afoul of Luke, leading to the famous "Welcome to the O.C., bitch!" scene where Luke beats up Ryan in the sand.

Chris Carmack (Luke Ward): I grew up with an older brother, so I had done plenty of [fighting] before. I was studying to be an actor. I'd done stage combat and all that stuff. So I wasn't too fussed about the scene. Also, I was twenty-two years old and nothing hurt. And now I'm shifting in my chair eight times while I'm talking to you. Everything hurts.

Josh Schwartz: We spent a lot of time trying to come up with funny things for Brody to say as he was being picked up and carried around and beaten up. And in the end, no one cared what Seth had to say. They were only ever going to remember "Welcome to the O.C., bitch!"

Chris Carmack: The line was presented to me with great fanfare. It wasn't like I was reading the script and came across this line and made up my own mind about it. Josh was like, "You get the line!" There was a preconceived idea that it was going to be an iconic moment for that show.

David Bartis: We all loved it, because he nailed it. It definitely felt like an iconic moment.

Peter Roth (president, Warner Bros. Television): I've experienced a "Welcome to the O.C., bitch" moment in my life. Who has not? Where you were new to this scene and, "Who the hell do you think you are? Get up. Get out of our space. You're in rarefied territory. We don't want you."

For Carmack, the biggest challenge of the scene wasn't the line itself.

Chris Carmack: Television—our show included—tends to propagate this myth that Southern California beaches are warm in the summer, dude. So everybody is in bikinis and open shirts and shorts, and it's effing freezing. We were just trying to stay warm, huddled by the fake fire on the beach.

Which Was the Style at the Time

While the pilot as a whole still feels modern, a few aspects of it definitely belong to the early 2000s.

Josh Schwartz: Ryan uses a payphone. So now when people will watch the pilot, it's always funny to explain to young people that those used to be readily available to the public. While we were shooting it, Ben improvised putting the phone in his mouth, and I was screaming, "Fuck! Do not put that in your mouth! Oh my God!"

Stephanie Savage: The fashion show [in the pilot] has been criticized for not having great fashion—even by us. But pilot season coincides with awards season. Even if you have money to buy something, no one wants to deal with your desire for red-carpet looks. And when you're a pilot, there's no real guarantee that your show is going to be on television, or that anyone will see it. So really, no one wants anything to do with you. We had a very hard time even just getting enough outfits together to do a fashion show. We're also not saying that like this is a great fashion show. Like, this is a junior league fashion show, in Orange County. It's okay if it's just girls and cute, colorful dresses. It's not a *Gossip Girl* fashion show or fashion show where we're trying to say this is a New York Fashion Week event. It's something different. And that ultimately it's going to be fine if they're not wearing the latest and greatest red-carpet looks.

Jane Espenson (writer): The pilot was being filmed as we were starting work in the room, so none of us writers had seen things like wardrobe. One of the higher-level writers got to briefly visit set and returned a little concerned with the short bright print dress that Summer wore in the charity fashion show. He reported to the rest of us that it was from "the Ruth Buzzi* collection," a phrase that has always stayed

---

* Buzzi is best known for playing a variety of old and/or tacky characters on the sketch comedy series *Laugh-In*, which aired its final episode thirty years before *The O.C.* pilot began filming.

with me. But it turned out that the show's looks were beloved and iconic! Thanks, Ruth Buzzi!

The fashion show was not the only scene where it was hard to secure the appropriate clothes to reflect Newport Beach, including a signature piece of Julie Cooper's wardrobe.

Stephanie Savage: Originally, we were told, "You can't have a Juicy jumpsuit, because it's too expensive. Just get a pink non-Juicy jump-suit." We had used a Juicy jumpsuit in the *Fastlane* pilot. I was like, "I know that's in a Warner Bros. locker somewhere," and I made them find it. So it's the same jumpsuit.

Other characters' looks would evolve significantly from what they wore in the pilot.

Stephanie Savage: [Later], we put Seth in a lot of Members Only jackets and Fred Perry polo shirts. In the pilot, Brody's shirts are really big on him. That felt like that was telling the nerdy outsider story. Then throughout the series, he got a much more fitted silhouette, with his skinny jeans and his tight Penguin shirt. And I really liked the idea that Marissa's style was not the typical O.C. style—that she was a little bit more classic and Summer was really rocking the Y2K fashions. And that fell away, the deeper we got into the show—they were all wearing spaghetti straps.

As the show grew more popular, and as Mischa Barton continued to work in the fashion industry, it became much easier for the show to put its characters in the right outfits.

Stephanie Savage: Mischa, before the show even started, was a Chanel ambassador. She helped us get handbags. Then their prom dresses [in Season Three] were much more indicative of where the show wanted to be, fashion-wise, versus our original fashion show. And the dress we got for Mischa was a Chanel dress.

California, Here We Come: The Sound of the Pilot

The soundtrack of *The O.C.*, loaded with emotionally wrenching indie rock music, would quickly become as big a selling point as the actors' charisma or Schwartz's writing. That started with the use of "California," by the band Phantom Planet, over the montage of Sandy driving Ryan from Chino to Newport Beach. Though it would eventually become the series' theme song, "California" was not written with future TV ubiquity in mind.

Alex Greenwald (Phantom Planet): It was the year 1999, and I had just moved out of my mom's house and I had my first place, which I shared with four girls, and they all had jobs during the day. My buddy and the drummer of Phantom Planet at the time, Jason Schwartzman,* was like, "I got a song idea. Can I come over and we'll flesh it out?" We sat on one of my roommate's really big, ugly purple couches, and he had this idea that had the beginnings of that riff, the motif of the [*humming the opening notes of "California"*] "duh-duh-duh-duh." As we played it together, it formed. And he kept saying, "I hear, at the end, if we're singing this melody, 'California, here we come.' Is that weird?" And I was like, "No, why don't we just reference that old Al Jolson song?† And sing, 'Right back where we started from.' And then it just popped in my head for the chorus to go, 'California, California here we come.'" It's not the most brilliant thing, and it's definitely referencing what's been said in the verse already, but it just worked. It even had a physicality to it. It's this triumphant march back home.

Stephanie Savage: In the show, the driving song was originally Interpol's "Untitled."

---

* Yes, the *Rushmore* actor, who was also one of the early models for Seth Cohen.

† Once the show became a hit, the estates of Jolson's cowriters sued for, and received, a shared credit on the song.

Josh Schwartz: We had to make a trailer for the presentation of the pilot based on the first two weeks of shooting. That's where we used "California." And then everybody responded to it so positively that that's how it became the main title song.

Alex Greenwald: My manager calls and says, "There's this show that's going to be the new *90210*, and the creator of the show wants to use the song 'California.'" I came from the Nirvana world of, if you give your song to a corporate entity of any kind, you're selling out. So my initial answer was no. My manager is like, "Don't be stupid. What are you going to do with that song now? He seems to think he saw your debut of 'California' in '99 when you played it first live. Can he call you and just talk to you about it?" And I was like, "Okay, sure." So he calls me and it wasn't Hollywood bullshit. And now I don't feel like I'm selling out to something weird.

Josh Schwartz: It was a song that was out and on the radio—it was on [local alt-rock station] KROQ. It seemed in L.A., at least, to be a pretty well-known, great song, but from a couple of years prior.[*] So we thought, "Oh, we'll put this song in. All the executives will know it. They'll lean in." And they did lean in, but they were all like, "What is the song? I love it." We were surprised to realize that it hadn't quite penetrated outside of, I guess, people in their twenties living in L.A. at the time.

Peter Roth: I knew that we had a winner when after the fourth episode, my young nephews said to me, "Oh my God, that is the coolest song, Uncle Peter."

Adam Brody: That Phantom Planet song is so good. When it plays with the road montage, the show works already. You're sold once the notes come in. You haven't even been to Orange County. You've only

---

[*] It had even been featured on the soundtrack to the Colin Hanks movie *Orange County*.

been in Chino and stolen a car and been to jail. Now you're driving out of Chino, and that song comes in, and it's already magic. That song does so much.

Though the pilot has a few songs ("Swing, Swing" by the All-American Rejects, "Hands Up" by Black Eyed Peas) of the type that kids in Newport Beach might have been listening to that summer, most of the soundtrack was filled with tunes that the creative team loved.

Josh Schwartz: There was Joseph Arthur's "Honey and the Moon." That was always the last song of the show. And I think that helped us orient the sound of the show—what we wanted the music to be. We didn't necessarily want it to be music from Orange County. It had its own very successful music scene, very different from what we were going for. Stephanie had pitched "Into Dust" by Mazzy Star for Ryan carrying Marissa. Most of my inspiration came from movies, like Cameron Crowe and John Hughes movies. Those are the things that really instructed me in the best way to use music against picture.

A Home Run

After all the tumult and arguments and last-minute changes, the pilot worked beautifully. The emotional moments all landed, the jokes all got laughs, the soundtrack induced chills. The director switch that had nearly killed the show before it got started instead provided the secret ingredient to make Schwartz's blend of melodrama and self-aware comedy work.

Doug Liman: Probably the difference is that McG would have started with some kind of style sheet. And imposed that over how you make it look pop culture in a way. Whereas I just start with character. And I'm going to find the style from the story, and not impose it. Or they go hand in hand. But it's not just abstract style for me. I'm not coming in with pictures from magazines and being like, "I want it to look like this or look like that," as much as having a gut reaction to picking locations and wardrobe and lighting and trying to just go from there.

McG (executive producer): My version would have been more polished and luxuriant and colorful, in keeping with the vernacular of my filmmaking style at the time. Doug was infinitely more gritty and handheld and not nearly as chromatic. And I think we were the beneficiaries of that as well. In success, you don't make a straight line crooked. Thank God Doug did the pilot.

Adam Brody: What I really like about it is how melancholy it is. It's a fairy tale—Ryan goes to a magical place—but it's sad. He's lonely and basically an orphan. And Seth is very lonely and Marissa's very lonely. And I think that's what made everyone coming together and finding each other so wonderful and warm and affecting. They're such lonely characters that you want them to be together. You want Seth to have a brother, you want Ryan to have a family. You want Marissa to have an advocate—someone in her life that cares and really sees what's going on.

Because of the accelerated time line, Fox executives had already ordered *The O.C.* to series midway through the pilot shoot, pleased with the sizzle reel featuring footage of scenes like the cigarette kiss, and Luke fighting Ryan.

Stephanie Savage: We were in Malibu. Someone at Fox, probably Gail, had just called to say they were picking up the show. I told the crew at lunch. That was a stunning moment. You would never get the chance to tell a crew that your show was picked up while you're still shooting the show. It was hoots and hollers and people jumping up and hugging each other. It felt like winning the Super Bowl. Everyone worked really hard on that show. It was a lot of night work, not warm on that beach in March, a lot of moving pieces. So it felt like that was an incredible accomplishment, and we were going to go directly into production. We weren't really even going to have a hiatus. It felt pretty spectacular.

Adam Brody: There was big applause, and it felt like green lights the whole way, and the wind at our backs. And that made us all excited, too. We all felt that it was special—that we were doing something, and that it was coming together in a magical way.

The finished product confirmed that Fox had made the right choice.

Craig Erwich (programming executive, Fox): *The O.C.* pilot to this day is probably one of the top five pilots I've ever been involved with or ever seen. It was incredible. We had set out to get back to our roots and deliver a show that had an emotional core to it and made people feel something and root for the characters and care. That's what that show was.

Gail Berman: It was a home run. It was exactly what I said I wanted to do, the kind of show I wanted to do, the kind of soap I wanted to do when I was at Fox. I thought it was terrific. I loved it.

Fox prime time, here they came.

CHAPTER 4

The Summer of Summer

BACK IN 2003, TV still largely functioned on the same annual schedule that had been in use since the days of *I Love Lucy* and *Gunsmoke*: shows premiered in early fall, and aired new episodes intermittently through the spring. The networks had begun experimenting with the idea of year-round programming, and cable channels like HBO were making inroads in that area, but summer was still mostly for reality TV. Fox's plan to debut *The O.C.* on August 5, and run seven episodes before the baseball playoffs began, meant that the series would largely have the scripted space to itself for two months. It was an exciting time for the cast and crew to learn more about one another, and about the show they were making together, and for audiences to gradually discover that something special was happening in this fictionalized Newport Beach.

Obscure No More

The pilot was filmed in March, and everyone moved right into production on Season One. This gave the cast one final burst of anonymity before the premiere. It did not last long.

Adam Brody (Seth Cohen): In some ways, it felt like a hit before it came out.

Josh Schwartz (creator/executive producer): Nobody knew what the fuck we were doing. We went to a concert with Ben and Adam, and we're like, *Oh, this is the last time. You can never walk around with these guys without people knowing who they are.*

Chris Carmack (Luke Ward): After the pilot aired, I was doing my laundry in the laundromat. And it started with somebody recognizing me in the laundromat, saying hi. And then people started walking by and looking in. And then people started coming in, yelling, "Oh, my God, it's Luke." And people on the sidewalk were coming in. Eventually, I said, "Oh, forget this." And I grabbed my wet laundry, threw it in my laundry basket, and then walked home.

Doug Liman (director/executive producer): There was a premiere party that night after the first episode aired. After the party, Ben and Adam and I went to the 7-Eleven nearby and got nachos. We're just sitting in the parking lot with our Big Gulps and our nachos and I was saying to them, "All this? This might be the last time you guys can do this." And sure enough, within a week, they couldn't go anywhere without being chased by a horde of teen girls. This was really the last quiet before the storm: sitting at that 7-Eleven having nachos.

Adam Brody: For what it's worth, I've been into many 7-Elevens, and they don't seem to recognize my stature.

THE KID STAYS IN CHARGE OF THE PICTURE

Schwartz was twenty-six when the pilot was filmed, and turned twenty-seven the day after it aired. There was little precedent in 2003 for an untested writer that young to be handed the reins of a network prime-time drama series. But the kid from Providence quickly impressed everyone who worked with him.

McG (executive producer): I think Quentin Tarantino's the heavyweight champ, but Josh Schwartz is the cruiserweight champ of the synthesis of high brow and low brow. *The O.C.* was a teen soap opera that would honor the tropes of the genre, there's no doubt. But then for those paying attention, we would talk about Thomas Pynchon and magical realism. And what was vibrating on a musical level was also very, very sophisticated. Even the snobbiest of the snobby appreciate what Josh was up to sonically in the show. Which gave us a patina of excellence and not cheeseball.

Patrick Norris (director): When I met him, I was fascinated at the idea that this kid was writing a show, and he was high energy and very explicit about how he saw the show evolving per episode. I don't know if he knew anything beyond the episode that we were doing at the time, but he definitely knew what he was doing in the moment.

Yvette Urbina (programming executive, Fox): He called me when the show first started, and he said, "Is this what writing is in a room? Is this what it is to be in charge? I don't like this. They want me to discuss my ideas." And I was like, "It's okay. You'll get used to it."

Lauren Gussis (writers' assistant): I was the youngest person there. I was a child when I was working on *The O.C.*, twenty-four years old. Josh was a year older than me, so that was a whole thing: *I cannot believe that this person who is essentially my peer is in charge.*

The accelerated schedule meant that Allan Heinberg had to set up a writers' room during the filming of the pilot, to get things rolling in the event Fox ordered the series.

Allan Heinberg (writer/producer): It was really fun. We had to put together a bible to basically sell the summer season before they would commit to the series, while we were shooting the pilot.

Josh Schwartz: I remember very quickly [in the pilot], we were never ever getting to Allan's trailer, due to the demands of production and Doug's process. We just had to be on set every minute of every day.

Because Schwartz was so young and inexperienced, Fox wanted a veteran to backstop him in the traditional but unofficial role of "showrunner"— aka the person who keeps the trains moving and usually has final say on everything.

Josh Schwartz: [Stephanie] wasn't going to be the showrunner. She hadn't run a show. Finding a showrunner that we could work with became like the drummer from *Spinal Tap*. We met with a lot of people, and I was like, "They seem great." And Stephanie's like, "The second you turn your back, that person is going to stab you and take the show from you. You cannot hire that person."

Stephanie Savage (executive producer): This is no offense to anybody, but Josh was literally the youngest person who was ever going to have their own drama on television, and the level of resentment and suspicion—as much as people would try to be kind and pleasant in the meeting, it just oozed off of them. They were just so angry that this was happening to someone that wasn't them. Finding someone who wasn't going to be poisonous in that way turned out to be quite challenging.

Josh Schwartz: Now I'm incredibly attuned to any level of disdain towards me, but at this moment I was oblivious. Clyde Phillips was [briefly] attached as our showrunner, but then he dropped out,* so we made the pilot without anybody in the role.

---

* Phillips (later to become well known as the showrunner of *Dexter*), wasn't one of the poisonous ones. "We really liked Clyde," recalls Schwartz, "and then Clyde ultimately decided he didn't want to drive to Manhattan Beach every day from wherever he lived." While Phillips admits he would not have enjoyed that commute, his main concern was the salary he was being offered compared to what he had recently made on a canceled Fox teen drama called *Get Real*. "Craig Erwich called me, and I said, 'We don't have a meeting of the minds financially here.' It was pretty straightforward."

Finally, salvation arrived in the form of Bob DeLaurentis, a veteran TV producer who had recently finished working on a show named after Schwartz's hometown.

Josh Schwartz: Dave Bartis recommended Bob DeLaurentis at first because Dave had worked at NBC when Bob was running a show called *Providence*.

David Bartis (executive producer): Bob was a great candidate because he knew the mechanics of running a show, but also, it's the last show that Bob would write himself. He's not going to be going in there telling Josh how to reinvent the show. He would just support Josh in producing the show. And that's what Josh needed.

DeLaurentis liked *The O.C.* pilot script, but was planning to work on a film script or a book. He rejected his agent's first two attempts to broker a meeting with Schwartz.

Bob DeLaurentis (executive producer): He called me a third time and threw everything at me: the writer's sympathy package. I went and met Josh. We connected immediately.

Josh Schwartz: Bob came in and was just the most down-to-earth, warm, kind person. He was like, "Look, I get what you do. I get what I would be here to do, they'd be two different things. And I'd show you how it all works." It just seemed like a really great fit.

Yvette Urbina: Bob really understood that his job was to shepherd Josh's vision and teach him and help with the production elements that Josh didn't like.

Bob DeLaurentis: The very last thing I wanted to do was take over anybody's show. The big question I asked Josh in that meeting was, "What do you want to do?" Because he had not done it yet. And he said, "I want to write." And I said, "Okay, well, we'll set this up so that you get to do what you want to do and I'll figure out the rest."

Lisa Cochran (unit production manager): Bob was wonderful. Bob was the calm voice.

DeLaurentis quickly began fighting the good fight on behalf of his new colleagues as everyone figured out exactly how *The O.C.* would function, stylistically and logistically, on a weekly basis.

Bob DeLaurentis: There was a fundamental difference, I think, in the way we saw the show. I think Warner Bros. saw the show as a soap, and soaps are made in Hollywood rather inexpensively. And Josh had a point of view, which I wholeheartedly backed, that this was a show that needed to get outside. We needed to see the glamour of this world. It was a show about a kid who was crossing the tracks to this luxurious community. And without seeing the community, you didn't have the fabric of the premise.

Norman Buckley (editor/director): For those first episodes, we were trying to find the form of the show—the balance between the comedy and the drama. If you look at the pilot, the pilot is much more dramatic than the show ended up being. It's a much more grounded story and has a little bit more verisimilitude than what the show ultimately became. And I remember that transformation happening over the next six episodes.

Allan Heinberg: It was bliss. It was no sleep. We were breaking and writing outlines and drafts, and Josh was revising all the drafts. Because it was his voice, the show needed to sound like Josh. So I remember nonstop Josh writing, writing, writing, rewriting.

Bob DeLaurentis: We treated Josh as the tiger in the cage; I always joke that we opened the door just long enough to throw the outline in and slam the door shut. And that's certainly what the first half dozen episodes were like: "Josh, here's the outline. Go."

Allan Heinberg: As you may remember, the Cohens' driveway and Marissa's driveway were next door to each other.

Lisa Cochran: One of the homes was sold in the interim. And that new owner had no interest in us being around. They didn't want us to be inside. Mark Burnett's ex-wife had bought the house.

Allan Heinberg: I remember Bob saying, "No more of those scenes, because we can't afford to keep going out there." Which I think we took hard for a minute. Because that's where Ryan smokes in the pilot and we thought it was iconic. We had to reevaluate, because we had planned to do one of those an episode, and those had to go.

Adam Brody: I loved that it was a real location. When Jimmy and Kirsten talk about the kids out there, those are real Santa Anas blowing up around them, and it adds this texture to it that I found really affecting.

Allan Heinberg: One of the rhythms we got into fairly quickly was that there was some gala every episode, and that brought the entire cast into one setting. That became more and more challenging, because those are expensive and hard to orchestrate and hard to shoot. But it was part of the magic formula of that first season: you bring everyone together out of their separate storylines at an event where shit would get out of control, hopefully in an entertaining way.

Coming up with new gala ideas was particularly easy for one member of the creative team.

Josh Schwartz: Have you seen *Gossip Girl*? Savage has an endless supply of gala events at her fingertips. But some of them were sourced in actual events, like the cotillion ball, or the Man of the Year award.

Boats would prove difficult, for both the actors and the producers.

Kelly Rowan (Kirsten Cohen): I get cold really quickly, which is ironic because I'm Canadian by birth. I remember being out on these boats at two in the morning, just freezing my ass off. So you've got your high heels and then on the side, you've got slippers. And if it's going to be a while, you've got sweatpants underneath your gown. These are the secrets of the trade to make yourself comfortable.

Lauren Gussis: The first season of the show was crazy. It was like, "Oh, we're going to do a sailing regatta." And then it would come back, "Y'all, we cannot afford to do a sailing regatta." "Okay, it's a golf tournament."

Josh Schwartz: We had a whole "boat life" pitch where Ryan worked at the gas docks, where the rich kids would bring their boats in. Ryan would pump gas for them and they would all give him shit. Boats are a big part of life down there, but it was too logistically challenging for us to figure out.*

Stephanie Savage: Shooting Seth on a boat for four seconds in the first episode nearly broke us.†

Josh Schwartz: We had a party [in a later episode] that took place on a boat. In our minds, it was going to be on a luxury yacht. And when we started shooting it, there was barely enough room for people to walk around each other. But I guess that is actually probably more truthful to what a Newport event would have been like, on that size boat.

---

* When Savage saw Netflix's *Outer Banks* debut in 2020: "I was like, *Oooh, gas docks!*"

† Instead, Seth would more often be seen on his skateboard. "It's much simpler to shoot," says Savage. "And Adam also was a skateboarder and a surfer. He actually went surfing during the pilot and twisted his ankle. And leaving the fashion show to go to the beach party, he literally hops like a bunny into the back of Holly's Jeep. And that's because he cannot bear weight on one of his feet because of his surfing injury."

The Not-So-Model Home: A Metaphor

Second overall episodes are among the toughest to make in the life of a TV show. Sometimes, there's pressure to simply repeat the conflicts of the pilot for the benefit of potential new viewers who missed the premiere. Other times, the creative elements that come together so easily for one episode quickly get out of balance on the next. With Doug Liman returning to direct in the midst of more *Mr. & Mrs. Smith* preproduction, the hope was that "The Model Home"—in which Ryan runs away from the Cohen house rather than be sent back into foster care, and Seth and Marissa stash him in an unfinished Newport Group housing development—would avoid the usual stumbles.

That was not to be.

Josh Schwartz: Doug crushed the pilot; I cannot ask for a better director of the pilot episode of the show. But if I'm being completely honest, Doug, given his schedule of making this giant movie, [it wasn't a great idea] to jump into a show that he was not able to [sufficiently] prep, that was going to shoot in eight days, but also have to shoot the same amount of pages as the pilot did in fifteen days.

Stephanie Savage: And for the second episode, you're shooting on your sets for the first time.

Josh Schwartz: The first time I saw the Cohen backyard on film, I lay on my floor in the fetal position. We were trying to do something pretty atypical, which is build an infinity pool on set, with a ground. And it looked like a putting green. Our sets just looked really fake and really bad, and we didn't have the time to figure it out. Doug was so consumed with the movie, he wasn't able to give it [enough of] the time it needed.

Liman did not feel the condensed schedule was a challenge.

Doug Liman: I made *Swingers* in eighteen days, and that's a whole movie.

Susan Rovner (programming executive, Warner Bros. Television): At Warners, it was often the case of that person above me on the org chart was unhappy with the second episode.

Josh Schwartz: When people saw the first cut of "The Model Home," I'll never forget, Peter Roth called us and said, "I am gravely disappointed." And I was like, "Wow, this is the shortest run in Hollywood anyone's ever had. One episode and we are dead by episode two."

It's a Dog Eat Doug World

Liman had a separate reason to be distracted during the shoot, and it involved the FBI.

Josh Schwartz: We're shooting the scene where everybody is in the driveway, and it's twelve series regulars, and a lot of coverage. Everyone's waiting for Doug to yell action, and he's not yelling action. And I look over at the monitors and Doug is on his cell phone and he's having a conversation, and I'm like, "I think they're waiting for you to call action." He's like, "Oh, action." And he's still on the call. So at a certain point, I ask, "Doug, what is happening that is more important than twelve of our actors standing in this driveway shooting the scene?" And what happened was, his dog had been kidnapped three years prior. And now the kidnappers had finally reached out to Doug and said, "We have your dog. And this is the amount of money that we want." He was being extorted to get his dog back. There was a sting operation going down where someone was meeting these people in the park as Doug.

Stephanie Savage: There were snipers in the trees.

Josh Schwartz: And the FBI was going to come out and grab the dognappers and get the dog back. This was all happening while we were shooting. He tells me the story, and I was like, "Yeah, that's more important than what's going on here."

David Bartis: We're all in video village waiting for Doug to get the phone call from the FBI. It was crazy.

Doug Liman: I got a ransom call while we were shooting, and it was a Monday and they were like, "We'll meet you Friday at noon at a dog park in Washington, D.C." And I'm like, "I'm shooting this episode till next Wednesday. I can't leave. I'm directing something. Somebody has to die in your family for the director to leave set." My dog had been gone for three years. This call came out of the blue, and there was nothing more important to me than seeing if the kidnappers actually had my dog. But I couldn't leave the set. And they thought I was bullshitting them, because they're dognappers—they don't know shit about the TV business or directors. So they moved the time line up to Thursday evening. I had to send a friend. In between takes on that Thursday, we're shooting in the house. I would call in between takes and see what's going on. It dragged on for quite some time, and the whole crew would wait and watch while I made another call. Then one of the times I called, my girlfriend at the time was one of the two people who went to the meet, and she said it was Jack, my dog. And I burst out crying in front of everybody. But that's the thing. It goes from reading the script and thinking, "I like this script and I like these characters and Stacey Snider said I'll never work in film again," to six months later and like, these people are your family. You're crying in front of them and they're all hugging you and holding you.

There was a happy ending for Liman and his dog, and also for "The Model Home," which was saved by a less-heralded director. The British-born Ian Toynton, who would officially helm twenty episodes of the show over four seasons, did some uncredited work on this one.

Josh Schwartz: Ian Toynton had been directing the episode after that, "The Gamble." You're dealing with a disaster of a second episode in terms of how people respond to that, but the train doesn't stop. You're rolling into your next episode of shooting. And in the middle of everything, we watched some scenes from "The Gamble." And it was just, *Oh, this is the show. This is the way we intended it to feel. And our sets look great and everything feels like the show.*

Even the reshoots weren't entirely without drama, as Ben McKenzie found out when he and Chris Carmack had to redo parts of Ryan and Luke's model home fight on a miniature re-created set on the stage at Manhattan Beach.

Ben McKenzie (Ryan Atwood): I was supposed to pretend to trip and fall through this window. I wasn't selling it enough, so they asked me to do a little more, and they asked Chris to push me a little harder. It wasn't his fault, but I tripped and fell back through what was an actual plate glass window, as opposed to fake candy glass. I could have gotten seriously injured, or shut down the show, if my face had gotten cut up. And it was just miraculous; I had nothing on me. I was wearing the hoodie and jacket, and I just scratched that.

Chemistry 102

Once the series was picked up, actors who might have otherwise only known each other for a couple of weeks were now committed to spend several months, and potentially years, together. It was bonding time, which Peter Gallagher decided to jumpstart by inviting his new colleagues to his house in Connecticut for what came to be known as "Camp Gallagher."

Peter Gallagher (Sandy Cohen): It was right after the first upfronts*

---

* The upfronts are annual presentations made by TV networks to ad buyers, at which they unveil their upcoming schedules, present sizzle reels of their new series. Casts from new and old shows are flown to New York, usually just so they can walk across stage and wave to the crowd. (In this case, though, Gail Berman asked Gallagher to sing to the audience.)

when we got picked up. Adam still talks about it. He was like, "You live in a park" which was just being in Connecticut for us.

Adam Brody: All of us stayed at his place a night or two and had a great time.

Peter Gallagher: We played Capture the Flag. Tate Donovan and I ended up in jail and Mindy [Clarke] just became a she-devil. She became drunk with power, like she was never going to let us free. I remember at one point running across that field at full speed, right into Ben. I thought, *Oh, my God, I've killed him.* It was really full-body contact at full speed, and we were both fine.

Ben McKenzie: [*stifling a smirk*] All right, Peter. I played Texas high school football with Drew Brees. You didn't hurt anybody. You know, I love Peter. He fancies himself a very tough man. So I'll just let him believe that. I'll be all right.

Adam Brody: Peter was a little older. So he was a bit more of the father figure, the veteran. Kelly was so sweet and young and a peer. She was thirty-seven, so, yeah, not my mom. But so great. Never, never had a bad moment with Kelly. Ben and I would always love teasing her. We all had a lot of fun together and a great rapport, and Peter as well.

Rachel Bilson and Melinda Clarke were still technically guest stars at this point, and would not be officially made series regulars until midway through Season One.* But they were considered members of the family from early on, and the writers began referring internally to Ryan, Seth, Marissa, and Summer as "the Core Four."

---

* Chris Carmack got an earlier promotion than the others. "When we did the pilot," says Stephanie Savage, "he was not a series regular for all the reasons that you would think: he's the villain, and how long is he going to stay in the show, potentially? And there was a discussion about making him a series regular versus making Rachel a series regular. And I think the studio and the network thought that we needed to make sure that we had him for the series."

Rachel Bilson (Summer Roberts): I was always treated pretty fairly by the cast. I remember magazines and stuff coming out, and it was just the three kids, and feeling, *Oh, man, I'm not a part of that*. But that was just youth and ego probably.

Lisa Cochran: Rachel was logical. Funny. And God bless her, she was willing to wear very short skirts. [*laughs*] There were some of the outfits that she was put in where it was, "Where are we mic'ing her? How do we put the pack on her?" She was a trouper. I believe that many departments would say that Rachel was the favorite. She was just natural.

Peter Gallagher's role as father figure continued long after Camp Gallagher had concluded.

Allan Heinberg: Peter was a key collaborator. He would sit down with you and get into it and tell you stories and things about his life. I have really fond memories of those moments with Peter, where talking about the script in the scenes would make the scenes better.

David Bartis: Peter was a mentor to a lot of the actors. He was there to say, "Hey, you know it's nice if you stay and read sides with colleagues even when you're not on camera"—in a very gentle way. Peter offered a lot of really positive advice to the actors on the show. I think that made a big difference

Tate Donovan (Jimmy Cooper): When I first worked with Peter, I was a little taken aback. In the scene where we're playing golf,* and he explains to me how screwed I am, he came in guns blazing and changing shit: "I want to say this line," and "Can you not say that line so I can do this?" And I was like, "Who the fuck are you, man?" To

---

* "We shot a lot of Sandy Cohen's golf stuff at the Trump golf club," says Josh Schwartz, "which was also in Palos Verdes and which was very cheap to shoot at because one of the holes had fallen into the ocean. So a lot of those scenes where Sandy plays golf, we got a great deal."

his credit, he just completely ignored me. I became very uptight, but it worked for the scene when I watch it now. I am genuinely pissed at the news that he's giving me, and it was sort of what happened in the scene. That happens a lot when you act: you're not in control, and your emotions get caught up in the scene that you're doing. It's like why a lot of costars fall in love with each other.

Melinda Clarke (Julie Cooper-Nichol): When you get Tate, Peter, Kelly, and [me] in a room, my cheeks hurt, everything was just so funny, especially in the Cohen kitchen. It was going to musical theater camp every day. It wasn't like going to work. It was a very social, happy, fun, gregarious set.

Whose Line Is It, Anyway?

Adam Brody settled into the rhythms of production very quickly.

Lisa Cochran: Adam to me was more of an introvert. He was really quiet off camera. He would sit and read.

Adam Brody: The set was really comfortable. I've never got more reading done at work than on that show. This was before phones, or before social media.

Peter Gallagher: Oh, my God. I just loved working with him. I wanted so many more scenes with him. He was really good. It was fun to do comic scenes. Everybody was awake.

John Stephens (writer/producer): There are actors who, when you see them, they immediately have a spark. I know that sounds like a cliché thing to say, but it's true. You can't stop looking at them. And Adam had that. Besides being extremely good-looking and all the rest of that stuff, he had something where he came alive when you were watching him. And he also did two other things that fascinated me. Sometimes, people try to flatten out their intonation, and then it becomes very general. Adam was very specific, and you heard his voice in his intonation—it was unique. And sometimes, we see actors live inside lines, and they move around them in a way that brings more life to the words than are actually there. I can't describe it any better than that. But there was this energy level behind all of his stuff, which was super exciting.

Adam Brody: Josh and the rest of the writers, really digging into the humor of it and finding their comedic voices for us, was part of the thing that made it so enjoyable.

While filming the pilot, Brody improvised a few lines—most memorably, Seth spotting drugs at the party and declaring, "Oh, hey, cocaine . . . that's awesome." Where his deviations from the script at an early audition had angered Josh Schwartz, his riffs during filming were so well-received that he kept doing them in later episodes.

Adam Brody: I think it was my worship of Vince Vaughn at the time. It's just, *That's what you've got to do.*

Stephanie Savage: Brody was very smart about how he did his ad-libs, knowing that we could cut around them. It would be his scripted dialogue, and then something improvised at the end of the scene or the beginning of the scene, knowing that we could shape that. I think he felt very free, because we would protect him. He could say anything, and you didn't have to worry that if it didn't work, it would go on the show. But also—certainly at the beginning—he was very respectful of the dialogue and Josh's voice, and wanting to bring that character to life by saying what was scripted for him.

Patrick Norris: He'd say something and the other [actor] would have a look on their face like, *I'd like to buy a vowel? What the fuck? Where are you going with this?* But he would be committed. And because of him being committed, they would have to respond.

Ben McKenzie: Adam's hilarious. He had such confidence—certainly outwardly. I'd be curious to hear what he says about that.

Adam Brody: I was very confident. That wasn't a projection.

It had, however, taken him some time to develop that confidence.

Adam Brody: I'd been acting for four years at that point, but really only on visible stuff for a couple of them. But even in those two years, it gave me the confidence to go, *Okay, I think I'm truly part of this industry of my peers, at least in this age group. And one job is not going to change that or not.* That gave me more of a take-it-or-leave-it attitude, even though I was very happy to be on the show. And once the show was working and once they were writing us so well, it was magic and I loved it.

Ben McKenzie: And he was so funny. Really, genuinely, excellent comedic timing. He was loose. A lot of actors who are comedians are trying to find a rhythm. And if you're the straight man—which I effectively was most of the time—they want you to hit the same beats in the same way. And Adam could roll with whatever. He was good.

The person least impressed with Adam Brody's improv skills? Adam Brody.

Adam Brody: I'm no Groundling. I'm no fuckin' Upright Citizen. I have gotten much too much credit for this only because it was by and large a soap opera, so a little off-book comedy goes a long way in a dramatic scene. I would be annihilated on an improv stage or even in a broad comedy with a bunch of really talented improvisers. I'm mediocre at absolute best, and at worst terrible. My ability to come up with things on the fly is truly very limited. When I say, "Oh, cocaine, awesome," that's not a clever line. It's funny because someone's saying something ironically in a soap opera. But it's not as if that was a clever line, or hard to come up with.

Rachel Bilson: He's just saying that because of the pressure that he puts on himself. But in the moment, he's hilarious. And his fucking improvs, every single one, I think, made it on camera. Everyone laughed and loved it, and they all wound up in the show.

Adam Brody: In reality, anyone could have done it. Anyone *did*. Peter, Kelly, Melinda, everyone started doing it. Rachel. It was not like it was exclusive to me after the first handful of episodes.

Stephanie Savage: Any episode that ended with a Seth and Summer scene, there's a good chance that the end of that is improvised. When she brings home Pancakes the bunny [in Season Four] and goes, "Pancakes is my daughter," that was all completely made up.

Peter Gallagher: I remember the scene with the Newpsies coming in the front door referring to Ben, and then [Sandy] saying, "Well, I'll just have to go find an Asian kid or a Black kid to bring home." That was improvised. And they kept all that.

Well, almost everybody followed Brody's lead.

Stephanie Savage: Ben didn't want to ad-lib. Ben wasn't like, *Well, now it's my turn to try and say something funny.* Ben learned his lines and delivered them well, and Brody was very smart with how he ad-libbed.

Rachel Bilson: I had to attribute all of my confidence as an actor and doing scenes and everything else [to Brody]. He really taught me how to do it. And it was the best lesson. Working with him was a gift because of how much confidence he gave me in just believing, and just doing what you want to do and really going for it. And it was always fun doing a scene with him.

Brody can at times be his own harshest critic.

Adam Brody: I fucking hate myself in it. I absolutely hate myself. And maybe that's something that I need to work on, or that's some growth that I still have yet to do. For whatever reason—my tastes, my maturity, my styles or whatever—it's hard for me to stomach my own perfor-mance. By the way, that's not specific to just that show. That's specific to anything except what I'm working on right now.

Or maybe he's not so harsh? After our initial interview, Brody rewatched the first five episodes of the series for the first time in forever, and came away with a more generous interpretation of his old work.

Adam Brody: I felt a little better. I still would do everything differently, but that's a sign of growth. But the more context I see, the more it's of a larger piece. And it certainly fits and adds to it. As I get used to it, it's much easier to take, and much easier to appreciate. I'm not impressed with myself, but it's not as cringey as I thought it was. And I can see myself trying stuff, too, and that's interesting, too: to see your own evolution.

The Mischa Machine

Mischa Barton was seventeen when filming began on Season One. All the other "kids" on the show were in their early to mid-twenties. At that age, the five-year gap between her and Rachel Bilson felt vastly wider than the decade separating Kelly Rowan and Peter Gallagher. She had recently graduated high school, and her mother Nuala Quinn-Barton was a con-stant presence on set—in part because Nuala was also her daughter's man-ager.

Lisa Cochran: Mischa didn't have a BFF on set. She was quiet. I think that she was always wrapped up in whatever she had going on. She would be doing voiceover, or she'd be on calls or interviews she did. She had a lot of press going. And yes, Nuala really managed her.

Stephanie Savage: She was very sweet. She definitely seemed her age, even though she grew up in New York and ran around with Ally Hilfiger. She'd been a model since she was a little girl and acted since she was little. But there was something very innocent. The things that she laughed at were really young, funny, goofy things. She painted the toenails of Jamie, our cameraman, and thought that was just hilarious. She was not a sophisticate in that way. She was a Chanel ambassador when she started the show and she had good taste in music. And so there was some sense of elevation, of that she was dabbling in this sophisticated world, but her personality was very sweet and goofy and young.

Lisa Cochran: She was a dog lover. She always had dogs in her dressing room. Sometimes, she would wrap her dog up in her robe which she was wearing, just to be comfortable while on stage, because stages can be cold. [One time], she rolled it up and then she turned around and tossed it to the costumer. Well, the costumer didn't know there was this teacup dog inside. And all of a sudden you hear, "Yipe!" It had hit the floor, and of course, everybody immediately jumped in. The dog was fine, by the way. There was nothing wrong. And she did have another dog, that I just don't know if it was socialized. A poor PA did not know that dog was inside, and walked in there to drop the next day's call sheet, and that dog was laying on the couch, woke up, just charged this poor PA, and the PA made it out and closed the door just in time.

Adam Brody: I didn't feel like, *Oh, here's someone who's in over their head.* And she's perfect for [this character]. She's so good in it. That character is so likable. You feel for her, and you very much want them to be together, and she's such a sad person.

Josh Schwartz: I think Mischa took off because she was not your typical network TV actress. She felt like she had an otherworldly elegance to her. She was a fashion icon, right out of the gate. She just was a really exciting on-screen presence. And I think men and women were just very taken with her.

Mischa Barton (Marissa Cooper): I think [Marissa's] an empathetic character. She cared for people, and I think that came across with her, and so people felt for her. She's also just complicated and struggling through her teen years, through depression, and substance abuse, and body image, and you can tell that she's grasping at straws with certain relationships in her life. And I think a lot of people relate to that.

Marissa spends most of the summer episodes torn between her soulful attraction to Ryan and her loyalty to forever boyfriend Luke. In the sixth episode, when she thinks she's witnessed Ryan flirting with another woman,* she decides it's time to finally have sex with Luke.

Chris Carmack: That was my very first in-bed love scene I had ever shot. I was not particularly uncomfortable with it. I have done photo shoots with people draped over top of me, or me draped over top of them. I've been in theater school, so we had done movement projects in our underwear rolling over the top of each other. I was fine. I wanted to make sure that Mischa was comfortable. I do very fondly remember this moment. She was so young. So her mom was always on set. And I remember we were in bed together scantily clad under the covers, and there was a crew around us, which was strange. The lights are bright, it's hot, it's not nearly as romantic as it is on-screen.

Filming a sex scene can be awkward under the best of circumstances. This one was about to get particularly awkward for a moment.

---

* In the initial pitch for that episode, Ryan sleeps with this woman (Caleb Nichol's trophy girlfriend), but Schwartz pulled back on that because, "Although we liked the idea of Ryan as a bad boy ladies' man, it was going to undermine the Ryan-Marissa story if he was just sleeping around with random ladies."

Chris Carmack: We did our rehearsal, and I rolled over in bed and looked next to me, and there was Mischa's mom standing right behind me. And I said, "Oh, hey, Mom." And the whole crew died laughing. I didn't know that she was there in this uncomfortable moment. She was looming over the bed and the crew is watching—*What's going to happen?* So that was a funny moment. But everything was fine. And good for Mischa's mom, for looking out for her daughter. I think she deserves some respect for that.

Lisa Cochran: Mischa is a machine. She was incredibly busy. I can recall her working late on Friday night, and she had to be in Miami for a Neutrogena shoot for Saturday and Sunday, and then she'd be back for her call time on Monday. Her dance card was booked during that shoot. She had campaign after campaign going with her name attached, which I'm sure served her well. But still she was a young girl and I'm a mom so I found myself being very protective of them. Nuala needed the production to work with her. I never had any problems with her.

And in the midst of all this, Barton also had to figure out a character who remained somewhat elusive to her.

Mischa Barton: She was always changing and going through so much. I always felt I didn't have a handle on where that character was going to go. But when you're working that often—and I was—at some point, you've just got to roll with the punches, and there's nothing you can do. There's not enough time to continually prepare. Unlike that first scene in the driveway, or the first party scene where she shows up drunk, there just wasn't time to think about it that much anymore.

Selling Summer (as in the Season)

The O.C. premiered on August 5, 2003, opposite reruns of scripted shows like *According to Jim* and *Gilmore Girls*, plus new reality TV episodes of NBC's *Last Comic Standing* and a short-lived CBS dating show called *Cupid*.

Gail Berman (president, Fox): It was perfect. It's a summer show. It evoked summer. Wish fulfillment in location, wish fulfillment in family.

The series debuted to 7.5 million viewers—a fairly massive number for the fractured TV viewing world of 2023, less so in the days when the broadcast networks were still king. The Associated Press described the initial ratings as "not impressive, but no disaster, either."

Josh Schwartz: The show premiered. The next day was my birthday. The show did not open at the number everyone thought it was going to open at. It opened low. Sandy Grushow [from Fox] actually reached out and said, "It's going to be fine. It's going to be okay." And I just remember being like, [*in a squeaky, pained voice*] "When is Peter Roth going to call me and tell me it's all okay?!?!" My assistant at the time, Kristen Campo, took me to lunch at the Hamburger Hamlet, and that was where I had a cheeseburger and tried to buck up.

Preston Beckman (head of scheduling, Fox): So the rating was eh. But I said to Gail, "Look, it's the summer. We can do whatever the fuck we want to do with our schedule." Back then, there was still a difference between cable and broadcast. Cable was running shows three or four times a week. So I said to Gail, "Why don't we run *The O.C.* three times a week? We can expose as many people to it as we can. And maybe that will help. It's the summer; we can do things like that." So we reran it Mondays and Fridays.

The experiment quickly began to pay off.

Preston Beckman: The rating jumped up the next week. I think when people saw it, they liked it. Because the third week, again, the ratings went up. So when it went up the second week, we got a lot of positive press, because shows usually premiere and then start to dip. So it started to look like, "Hey they're on to something."

McG: We'd call them at six in the morning and try to get the fast national ratings to see how we were doing. It just went up this week, up next week, up the next week, up the next week. And we started hearing about viewing parties at high schools and colleges.

The New (Old) Guy in Town

The sixth episode introduced a major character to the adult world of the show: Caleb Nichol, Kirsten's icy, powerful real estate magnate father.

Josh Schwartz: We were really interested in this real-life figure from Orange County who was a loose inspiration for Caleb's character: Donald Bren, who basically built Newport.* We needed somebody who could convey that level of authority. Obviously, he was gonna be the oldest character in the show and not a natural crowd-pleaser for the Fox audience on paper—Seth's grandpa.

Australian actor Alan Dale landed the role.

Alan Dale (Caleb Nichol): My favorite character I ever played, apart from playing King Arthur in *Spamalot* on the West End. I thoroughly enjoyed playing him because he was so naughty and fun and serious, too.

Josh Schwartz: Alan Dale was someone that Patrick Rush put on our radar. He had just been on *24*, he'd been in a bunch of stuff where he was the president, or somebody in authority. And he had a bit of a twinkle in his eye that we liked. It was a bit of mischief there—

---

* To be clear, the author of this book has no first-hand knowledge of the real-world business dealings or personal affairs of Donald Bren, and saying he was a loose inspiration is certainly not to imply that Mr. Bren has been involved in any of the sorts of shenanigans that were Caleb Nichol's stock in trade.

somebody that Sandy could really spar with in a fun way. And obviously for Kirsten, she loves her father, but she married this guy who is the absolute opposite of her father, which is just no end of infuriating for Caleb. So he was somebody who could come in with a lot of really fun dynamics to play.

Alan Dale: I had done *Star Trek: Nemesis*. I was invited to go to Comic-Con in San Diego. I sat there for the day and never saw one visitor who came to get my autograph because, in fairness, nobody knew that I was in it. About six at night, I'm thinking, *I don't think I'll come back tomorrow.* My phone rang, and it was my manager who said, "Look, there's a new show that Patrick is casting," and I should go in on Monday. I was not expecting much. I was playing a Donald Trump–type character, and I was painted orange like him too, but they seemed to like what I did. So they called me back the next week. And then before we knew it, I was a regular.

Kelly Rowan: I liked working with Alan. Alan is the sweetest man, and he's really funny, but he plays a badass well.

Tragedy in Tijuana

The summer scheduling didn't just influence the ratings, but the creative direction of that batch of episodes.

Stephanie Savage: Because the show was on in summer, we were like, "Let's not even start school in these first six episodes. Let's just keep 'em in the summer."

The early episodes gradually establish the conflicts among the characters: Kirsten's wariness about letting Ryan stay in her home (and Julie's outright paranoia about letting this ruffian anywhere near her daughter), the Ryan-Marissa-Luke triangle, Summer gradually warming to Seth, and more. It was all designed to build to the four main kids getting in trouble on an unsupervised road trip to Tijuana.

Josh Schwartz: That was one thing that I had pitched early on because when I got to USC, all these Southern California kids went to Tijuana.

When it came to the plan to end this summer run, there was unfortunately some déjà vu from the development stage.

Josh Schwartz: [Fox] had this big problem, because our pitch for the cliff-hanger from Tijuana was that Marissa drunk drives off a cliff, basically. We don't know if she lives or dies. And *Skin** was planning on doing the same thing in their bible. I was like, "Really? What does it matter? They're all fake things? We're just making something to show that we have ideas for episodes." Then we had to go back and rework it, and it became an overdose.

The cliff-hanger had a dual purpose: to excite viewers about the show's return a month and a half later, and to give the network executives an escape hatch on a performer they had been wary about.

Josh Schwartz: The reason Marissa may die at the end of the Tijuana episode was because Fox wanted to have the ability to make a casting change. Potentially. And then she broke out immediately—she was how people knew the show. So she was safe.

Stephanie Savage: I don't ever remember having any conversations in the room about, well, "What's the story if Marissa dies?" I don't think we ever broke that story or even really talked about that story.

---

* We would suggest a drinking game every time *Skin* somehow keeps coming up in this story, but we want all of you to live.

Josh Schwartz: We didn't know if the show was coming back from those episodes when we wrote them. So our future was incredibly uncertain going into that episode.

Selling Summer (as in the Character)

If *The O.C.* was being made today, it would have launched with a ten-episode season where Summer remained the shallow mean girl from the pilot, because there would be no room to deviate from the initial plans. In 2003, though, Schwartz and the others had all the time in the world to recognize that Rachel Bilson could offer them so much more than that.

Josh Schwartz: In the beginning, Summer was definitely written as much more of the villain.

Stephanie Savage: Someone that was going to pull Marissa away from Ryan. The idea that Summer would become a part of the posse and it would be a foursome, that's something that grew in series. That wasn't the original idea.

Bilson didn't have to look far to find inspiration for that original take on the character.

Rachel Bilson: The whole thing was modeled after someone I went to high school with. She was one-note, which was fun to play, don't get me wrong. But I'm really happy that they were able to add some layers to her.

As the writers saw what Bilson could do, Summer softened a lot and began hanging out with Seth and the others, and proved that Seth's crush on her ran deeper than just physical attraction.

Gail Berman: Rachel's casting changed everything in many ways. She was so impactful and the character was so good, and that desire from Seth to be with her was just such a good storyline. And the character's named Summer!

Stephanie Savage: In some of our early story notes, Seth and Summer were going to have sex in Tijuana. We had the good sense to slow down that relationship, so that they really connected with each other. I don't know if we ever said it to Rachel, but that episode was like her audition to be a series regular. If she could hold up her corner of the square in the Tijuana episode, that was the future we were going to embrace. And she crushed that episode so hard. She was so funny in every scene that she's in. And then dramatic when she has to be. She blew us away. That was the most we'd ever given her to act.

Rachel Bilson: There was one vulnerable scene in Season One. We're at the lockers in the school hallway, and I remember Josh saying to me, "Dude"—and at the time, this was relevant—"You're like Meg Ryan; you can do it all." And I think from then on, he was like, *I can give her X, Y, and Z and feel confident that she's going to deliver.* That felt very good.

As Seth's romantic pursuit of Summer unfolded, Bilson began to wonder if life was imitating art, especially after the characters shared their first kiss during the Tijuana episode.

Rachel Bilson: It's this weird thing: you have to kiss somebody and then you're like, *Wait a minute, does that mean something?*

The Roads Not Traveled

Allan Heinberg's writers' room from the pilot generated a lot of story ideas while Schwartz was working with Doug Liman. Many of those wound up on the series in some form, while others—like a home invasion episode that would have climaxed with Sandy beating the invader to death with a baseball bat—were soon deemed not right tonally for the show.

Josh Schwartz: I think that [home invasion] story became Ryan and Seth getting locked in the pool house during New Year's Eve.

There were originally plans to do more with Luke's sidekicks, Nordlund and Saunders, and with some of the other popular girls from Marissa and Summer's social sphere. But the writers struggled to find time to feature any of these side characters.

Josh Schwartz: As Bob D would call it, it's the math of the show. You had forty-three or forty-four minutes per episode, and we're servicing X amount of main characters, so it just became trickier to get to these next-tier characters to keep that alive. I think that's something now we would probably be savvier about—we wouldn't have to take a lot of time to keep those guys built up in the story.

Among that abandoned group was Nikki, the girl Luke cheats on Marissa with in the pilot. Heinberg's original series bible fleshed out a whole character arc for Nikki that was later scrapped.

Stephanie Savage: We had the idea that Marissa immediately takes a disliking to this girl, because Luke slept with her. And is maybe going to go mean girl on her, and then finds out that the girl is pregnant. Luke isn't talking to her and Marissa becomes an ally to the girl. Which is a nice story, but it's not reinforcing the Ryan-Marissa story. And Marissa doesn't actually seem like a mean girl or a bully. And then when I was looking in that Tijuana outline, there's crazy things in there. Saunders and Nordlund go to a donkey show where everyone is doing ecstasy. A lot of it's like the *Euphoria* version of episode 7.

"The Model Home" has some funny banter between Seth and Marissa, who have been next-door neighbors for years without ever really speaking, each of them blaming the other for that. As Summer became a more prominent part of the group, direct interactions between her best friend and her boyfriend became few and far between.

Josh Schwartz: We left something on the table with Seth and Marissa. There's a little hint of it in the second season when they're both on the outs and they find each other. And we certainly never went there romantically between them. But there was definitely more to mine even on a friendship level with them.

Adam Brody: Even regardless of Ryan, the Seth-Marissa dynamic was cool. They were next-door neighbors, and yet they were strangers, and there was an awkwardness to it. I thought that was a nice dynamic that I could have seen more of.

Feeling the Fan Love

As the ratings ticked up from week to week, everyone felt confident the show would be around for a while. But it took a promotional event for the cast and crew to realize just how beloved *The O.C.* had already become.

Josh Schwartz: Fox did a viewing party for episode six, which is the one with Caleb and his girlfriend. They rented out a bar in Manhattan Beach. We showed up and there was a ton of fans there, and a lot of paparazzi. It was wild. It was my first experience ever witnessing anything like that. And I think for the cast, it was their first experience going through that. And then we watched the episode and people were cheering and clapping, and seemed to be really invested in the show.

Kelly Rowan: As we were pulling up, there was a sea of people, and we were all, "Wow, I wonder why all these people are here. This is so bizarre." And then we got out of the car and we actually had to go through all those people and of course, they were grabbing at all the boys. It was pretty funny.

Stephanie Savage: I was in the same van with Adam, and when we got there, we told the driver that we must be in the wrong place, because there were so many people here. "Oh, there's some event going on here, keep driving to find our bar." And then we realized that that was where we were, and the people were there to see the cast. Getting out of the van, I just put my arms up around Adam. I'm like, *Holy shit. I'm actually scared for you.* We hadn't brought security. We don't know where to go. We don't know what's happening. We're completely not prepared. We thought we were going to a club with twelve people in it to watch TV, and something different is happening.

Lauren Gussis: I'm a nice Jewish girl from Chicago. The fact that *that* guy is a Beatle made my heart sing. It was the greatest thing ever. He's the cutest, sweetest Jewish boy ever.

Stephanie Savage: It was exciting, but my stomach dropped. I think his stomach probably dropped to where we were both like, *Hey, this is happening and we're doing this.*

Peter Gallagher: For me, the most magical part was making the show before anybody knew what it was. And then it was quite extraordinary when we were down there at that event—when we all realized the show had really touched a nerve. And it's just one of those glorious, glorious things where you think, *Oh, my gosh, if you just stick around long enough, every thousand years, things work in a great way.*

Rachel Bilson: I was like, *Oh, shit, this is successful. People are really into this.* And I remember at that event being like, *Okay, everyone thinks I'm a total bitch because they only know Summer, but I'm the complete opposite in real life.* So I was overly nice to every single person I shook hands with or met that night, like, "No, no, no, I'm a really nice person. I'm not Summer, I swear!" It was my only goal that night, and it was exhausting.

Josh Schwartz: The Tijuana episode aired the following week, and then someone played me Howard Stern talking about the show, and he had a crush on Summer, and they were talking about Jewfro. He was talking up the show. I was like, "What? Howard Stern is seeing the show?" Then it got nominated for Best Guilty Pleasure at the VH1 Awards, which I didn't even know that was a thing. I remember just being whisked from the set to this award show, and we went out on stage to collect this award. And I'm like, *Is this a good award to win? A guilty pleasure, is that a positive?* I don't know. "Guilty pleasure" was always thrown around a lot. And we were a little touchy about it at the time. But now, obviously, it is great.

The summer of Summer had been conquered. Now it was time to make the rest of what would turn out to be a very long and eventful season of television.

CHAPTER 5

The Phenomenon

SIX WEEKS AFTER Ryan carried Marissa out of that alley in Tijuana, *The O.C.* returned on a new night, shifting from Tuesdays to Wednesdays. What followed was one of the wildest, busiest, fastest-paced, most purely entertaining debut seasons a show has ever had, regardless of genre.

Brodymania

The rapturous crowd at the Manhattan Beach viewing party would not prove to be an anomaly, as *The O.C.*'s popularity began to spread in ways both tangible in the ratings, and anecdotal in terms of the unusual audience clusters who were watching.

Bob DeLaurentis (executive producer): My younger daughter, when it came out, was a freshman in college. I remember going to her college campus on the East Coast in Connecticut and walking onto campus and seeing flyers around the entire campus about *O.C.* group screenings.

Josh Schwartz (creator/executive producer): Someone told me they had a friend who worked on the New York Stock Exchange, and stock bros were yelling, "Welcome to the O.C., bitch!" at each other on the floor of the New York Stock Exchange. That line catching on was an indicator that people were watching the show.

Even Schwartz and Savage's TV peers were hooked.

Michael Schur (executive producer, *Parks and Recreation* and *The Good Place*): Everyone was watching it. Not watching it would've eliminated you from next-day conversations in writers' rooms.

Josh Schwartz: [Legendary sitcom producer] Norman Lear called me at the office once because he was recruiting people for one of his Democratic causes. It was very weird that you're on people's radars in a way where they knew what the show was. Howard Stern talked about it. Jay Leno made jokes about it. I went on *Charlie Rose*, which was my dream at the time. I went on Craig Kilborn, and we all went on Ryan Seacrest's show. Ellen came to the set and the cast was all on *Ellen*. The kids were on *Leno* and *Letterman* and *Conan*, and Conan O'Brien talked about the show a lot.

Craig Erwich (programming executive, Fox): It was not just the ratings, but that sense of, *Oh, my God, people are talking about the show. These are the hot kids now.* They went from unknowns to, the next year at the upfront, getting into every club they wanted to.

Lisa Cochran (unit production manager): Once the show aired that summer, Josh changed our location signs, because they were being stolen. We used the codename *The Plank*, which was the name of the newspaper for the high school they attended.*

Rachel Bilson (Summer Roberts): I was offered a Super Bowl Pepsi commercial. Apparently, I passed on it. Now, this doesn't go under "strange." This just goes under stupid. Why the fuck would I ever pass

---

* With the episodes moving into fall, it was time to finally put the kids in an academic setting—sort of. Though many scenes over the next few years took place at the elite private Harbor School, "We had a policy pretty early on," explains Schwartz, "that we weren't going to show kids at desks and lab partners and a lot of that kind of stuff. We didn't want to strain credulity about our actors feeling too mature for some of those scenes." The show would periodically break this policy, especially in Season Two's Ryan and Lindsay arc, but Harbor stories tended to take place in the hallway or various spots where people ate lunch.

on a Pepsi Super Bowl commercial? I'm still perplexed. I'm just going to put that in writing: I don't know what the fuck I was thinking. The strangest thing is, I see these old pictures. There's a group of us at the time who are coming up, like, "Young Hollywood at Knott's Scary Farm," with all these monsters. That was so fun because it was like the first time of "VIP treatment" at an amusement park.

Ben McKenzie (Ryan Atwood): The thing took off like wildfire. Like, you're not going to a mall for the next five, ten years.

Kelly Rowan (Kirsten Cohen): You couldn't go to certain restaurants. Or if you're traveling, you have to travel under an alias, because people look at lists and hotels, and then you don't have any privacy anymore.

Josh Schwartz: The paparazzi were stalking the cast; they were really pursued. Adam and Rachel, any time they walked to Coffee Bean on Sunset, their picture was taken. Mischa was in the teeth of it more than anyone else with some of her romances, being on the front page of some of these magazines.

Melinda Clarke (Julie Cooper-Nichol): I remember once going out with Rachel to the Roosevelt Hotel, and they were chasing her down the street. I was like, *Oh, so that's what that's like.* Because we adults didn't have that problem. I can't imagine being stalked by that whole thing and how to navigate that.

Josh Schwartz: People who didn't know the show knew *of* the show. I got nominated for a Writers Guild Award. I went to the award show, and told someone I wrote for *The O.C.,* and they're like, "Oh, is that the Mischa Barton show?" Mischa took off really fast. She got very famous, extremely quickly, faster than everybody else got out of the gate. She was the first person to get a magazine cover from the show: the cover of *Lucky* magazine. And I framed it and sent it to Peter Roth 'cause I had told him, "One day, she's going to be on magazine covers."

Adam Brody (Seth Cohen): We all hung out so much that I felt in a bubble. I didn't have many Beatles moments.

Or did he?

Rachel Bilson: I don't want to say he's lying because he may not remember. I was at *TRL* once. I left him behind by accident. He was getting swarmed by a mass mob. So he stands corrected. And the Olsen twins rescued me and threw me in their car. I left Brody behind because I was so nervous and didn't know what to do. And they were like, "Don't you need to get your boyfriend?" And I was like, "Oh, yeah, we've got to go get him." He was being mobbed.

In a later conversation, Brody copped to some benefits of early celebrity.

Adam Brody: Very early on, maybe two or three weeks after the show premiered, I remember someone grabbing me and hooking up with me. And right after, she said, "Welcome to Hollywood." We both laughed, but it was an acknowledgment of a stature change. That could seem gross, but I remember it as being very innocent and joyful. And to have never been repeated. That was the only time I've heard that. She was older than me.

Stephanie Savage (executive producer): We went to see Death Cab with Adam and went up to the front of the crowd. I physically put his hoodie over his head because too many people were staring at him—it felt uncomfortable. That was a real "holy shit" moment.

Kelly Rowan: That was a lot to handle. People's lives changed overnight. Everyone got very famous very quickly from that. Peter had had some notoriety and Tate had worked in some big movies and whatnot.

But there was that kind of appointment television fame. There was a hysteria. Let's say you're in New York, you got in a cab and somebody recognized you and they would start screaming. It happened.

Adam Brody: I had this side band with friends I had before the show. We played once a year, and towards the end of the show, on one of the hiatuses, my friends and I went and played some shows that summer. And the fact that a little band with no real album could sell decent-sized places and have screaming fans, it was getting to live a rock star life by virtue of the show.

Josh Schwartz: Peter took me as his guest in Season One to the *Vanity Fair* Oscar party and was introducing me to Tom Hanks. I was meeting all of these people. At one point I was in a circle with [directors] Ed Zwick and John Waters and Paul Mazursky, and I'm like, *What am I doing here?* That all these people knew the show and are congratulating you, it was just surreal.

Adam Brody: At the Emmys, somebody in the crowd asked James Gandolfini to pass this down to have me sign and pass it back, which he obliged. That funny stuff where you're that teen heartthrob.

And how did it feel to be a teen heartthrob?

Adam Brody: Good. Fine. I swear! Right now, it would seem crippling to have that much [celebrity]. But this was essentially pre-social media. I wasn't online, and we're doing the show nine and a half months a year. So even though I'm getting other opportunities—I'm doing a little thing here and there—basically, I'm in Manhattan Beach filming that show. I'm also with the same person, mostly the entirety of that show. So I'm not really out there even socially in that regard, either. I'm just hanging with the same group. It just felt insular.

Lisa Cochran: Could you imagine this show if it had social media? No. Uh-uh. It would have been a much taller order.

Ben McKenzie struggled with his own teen idol status.

Ben McKenzie: It was awesome [at first]. But there was this fear that that would be it. That whenever the show ended its run, you would be relegated to a long, long history of teen idols who had gone on to do absolutely nothing after their brief moment of glory. So I was terrified of that very early on. That fear, maybe it's not the healthiest thing in the world, but if it motivates you to try harder and try other things and to put yourself out there in a way so you can show people you're capable of something else, good. That's what I had to do for *Southland*. I had to audition for it and get it in order to get out of that bunker.

Josh Schwartz: I think Ben was always uncomfortable to a degree with being the lead of a teen drama on Fox. On the "Model Home" episode, he didn't want to wear the tank top. I tried to joke with him and say, "Come on, man, if I looked as good as you in that, I'd want to wear it." And he was like, "See, that's the problem." The way I went about talking to him about it was totally wrong. I was joking and trying to give him a compliment, but I actually was speaking to his fundamental insecurity about it. So that was hard.

Ben McKenzie: Looking back on it, I should have been doing it all the time. That was the time when I was actually in shape.

To the celebrity victor goes the spoils—in this case, lots of swag.

Rachel Bilson: We started getting gifted certain things. We all had Sidekicks—bedazzled ones if you wanted. A Chanel bag or, whatever the Bling Ring can tell you,* I had quite a few. There were definitely these very lavish things being brought to me, which I always was grateful for

---

* Most of Bilson's swag from *The O.C.* days was stolen by a group of teens and young adults who robbed several other celebrities (including Paris Hilton, Orlando Bloom, Lindsay Lohan, and Megan Fox) in 2008 and 2009. They were later the subject of multiple films, most notably Sofia Coppola's 2013 feature *The Bling Ring*, starring Emma Watson.

and never took for granted. It was pretty amazing. And going to the parties and getting to wear the fancy clothes and all of that is alluring. And there's fun, for sure, to be had. But it was also bizarre, especially being followed and having your picture taken eating a bagel.

Chris Carmack (Luke Ward): I was living in a house that probably should have been condemned, and had no business hosting living beings. It was a cash in an envelope deal. Early when I was shooting *The O.C.*, I was told, "*Us* wants to come to your house and take pictures of where you live." I thought, *This is hilarious. Sure! Come show what squalor new actors are living in. This will be great.* And they showed up, were horrified and immediately went to Target and started staging the house. They used a picture in the magazine of a bathroom that was not even my bathroom. And they spun the story as, "He lives by the ocean with ocean breezes in a charming California bungalow." They didn't mention that I had plastic nailed to the ceiling, so that when it rained and the water came in the ceiling, it would shuffle over to the sink and go down the drain. Fortunately, I did not have to stay there long after I was working on the show. But there was a window where I was working on network television and living in a run-down shack.

Ben McKenzie: Well, I got a nicer car. [*laughs*] An Infiniti, which is very 2003. I took a picture of it next to my 1986 Cadillac DeVille and kissed it goodbye. That was satisfying.

Adam Brody: Ben and I joined a celebrity basketball league in L.A., where you have full-on NBA team jerseys. And we were both not that good and not that aggressive. I think we would have been okay if we took it seriously, but we didn't. And just shit like that, where you go, "Okay, I'll do it." So Ben and I had basketball with Mark McGrath and Bill Bellamy and McG on Sundays, and that was fun.

Yvette Urbina (programming executive, Fox): We went to the World Series that year, Josh with his brother. A bunch of us went. Macaulay Culkin was there—he was dating Mila Kunis at the time.

Josh Schwartz: I got flown to the Super Bowl on the Fox jet with Ashton Kutcher and Randy Jackson and [*24* producer] Howard Gordon and [*Simpsons* producer] Al Jean.

Stephanie Savage: Life at Fox when we started was pretty fun. Paris and Nicole had their reality show, *That '70s Show* was very big. I remember at the upfronts before Season Two, we were at some nightclub that was really small. And then Britney Spears came with her entourage and we were all like, "Oh, they're taking up so much room, let's go somewhere else." And I ended up in a cab with Mischa, Lindsay Lohan, and Amanda Bynes all going to Marquee nightclub.

Josh Schwartz: Mark McGrath, Jessica Simpson, the *Scrubs* cast, everybody was in the same orbit.

The once-unknown cast quickly began to receive the VIP treatment around town.

Josh Schwartz: We used to go out in Hollywood before the show came out, and often we would get denied at the door. And very early on, there was a moment where the cast got into some party and I was not allowed into that party. And the woman who was working the door didn't care, because the show hadn't premiered yet. And within three months, if she saw me coming, she was like, "Right this way," let me in, and was extremely nice to me.

In time, the show's notoriety would spread across the globe.

Ben McKenzie: I was on vacation in China with my parents. We were in Tiananmen Square, the site of some fairly heavy stuff. And sure enough, someone taps me on the shoulder and it's Canadian tourists who wanted a picture with me. I'm like, "Tanks rolled over people in this very place, so could we just not do this right now?"

This would not be McKenzie's last overseas misadventure with *O.C.* fandom.

Ben McKenzie: Then I was in Budapest, spending the holidays with my family, in this beautiful little bed-and-breakfast. Every morning, you come down and have breakfast with the owner and her daughter. Then word got out that I was on the show, because Warner Bros. is brilliant with its international distribution. The next day, the daughter was there, and there may have been a marriage proposal involved. There was a language barrier, so I didn't know exactly what was going on, but it was extremely awkward. And my thing with that is, I always feel like I'm somewhat of a letdown. If it's a musician, you can do something that would be cool in that moment, like sing you a song or something. But what am I going to do? Perform a scene for them? So it's usually, "Thanks for being a fan."

Chemistry 103

Actors dating their costars is a tale as old as time, so no one on the show was surprised to realize that Adam Brody and Rachel Bilson had become a couple off-screen, as well as on.

Josh Schwartz: [Brody and Bilson's relationship] never affected work. I always feel like there's that moment when two actors realize they're going to start dating, and there's probably a palpable on-screen chemistry that's happening to you because it hasn't manifested itself. But once they started dating, it didn't dampen the chemistry. It didn't affect anything. There were no storyline requests that were made because of it.* From my memory, they weren't demonstrative about their relationship on set. I think they kept it pretty professional.

Allan Heinberg (writer/producer): It was a blessing. They were in a good place and I was happy for them. It was storybook in a way. That

---

* Well, maybe one or two. But we'll get to that.

was really fun and really easy because [on-screen] they were Lewis and Martin—they were a comedy duo.

Rachel Bilson: It was a very big time of paparazzi. But because I was dating Adam and we were going through it at the same time together, there was some grounding for me personally. So it felt like, *This is really cool. People are liking what we're doing and I can buy my first . . . whatever I wanted to purchase, because I'm making a decent living on my own.* And there were all these perks. Because of having that domesticated grounding relationship, it helped me mentally deal with it all.

Melinda Clarke: They were the couple that everything revolved around outside of the show. They just seemed to fit, and they were adorable together. At the end, there were a few eye rolls here and there in Season Four, but they were really sweet. I think there was a real nice connection with Ben and Mischa in the beginning, and maybe not so much at the end.

Samaire Armstrong (Anna Stern): Rachel and I got to become friends, and Mischa is a little bit younger than us, but we were all very friendly, and Rachel introduced me to all her girlfriends from the Valley, so we all became friends. It was great. Celebrated all our birthdays together and holidays.

Adam Brody: We all hung out a lot as a group and everyone's significant others, when they were seeing people, would be part of it. [Mischa] didn't feel wildly younger than us, but maybe just because we were immature.

Samaire Armstrong: We were really into pranking one another. Adam was the best at it. I remember one birthday, or maybe Christmas, we had a scene where we were dissecting frogs. I made Rachel a gift, and he took the gift out after she had opened it and put the frog in the gift box. It was just so brutal. So then when she got home to show her friend what I got her, she opened it, and there was the frog.

Revenge was soon in the offing.

Samaire Armstrong: We were invited to host an event for New Year's at a club. And Adam was way too cool for that. But we wanted to have a place to go. So I agreed on behalf of him and didn't let him know that he was actually hosting the event. Stuff you probably couldn't get away with now. But we had a blast.

Josh Schwartz: I was inadvertently *Punk'd* in Season One. I was out one night with Ben and Adam at this restaurant in Hollywood, and this guy was trying to start a fight with Brody. It just kept escalating. As a new TV producer, I was like, "Don't hit him in the face!" In one of the only acts of bravery I've ever demonstrated in my life, I put myself between Brody and this guy to preserve Adam Brody's facial bone structure. And then it turned out that we were being filmed for *Punk'd*—Ben had set Adam up but hadn't told me. I almost got beat up! I'm not a guy who normally gets in fights. So I was very unaccustomed to the level of adrenaline spiking. Then they were like, "PUNK'd!!! HAHA-HAHA." And I was like, "It's not funny, motherfuckers, let's fight! We've got to fight, you can't just get me riled up."

Ben McKenzie: Josh was really mad that I didn't tell him. And I was like, "Well, if I had told you, no offense, but you're not a very good actor." It would have been bad.

Rachel Bilson: Samaire, Mischa, and I had a lot of fun. We did the Electric Slide on the stage for one episode, in between setups. We were goofing around, and I remember that feeling, more like hanging out at night with your friends and partying and watching a [music] show, even though we were filming.

Ben McKenzie and Adam Brody got along well, even though they were spiritual opposites in many ways.

Josh Schwartz: Ben went to UVA and got a degree in economics, and Adam always talks about how he figured out he wanted to become an actor by working at a Blockbuster in San Diego. Adam always enjoyed some of the other stuff that came with being a celebrity, or being an actor. He was a big movie buff. He enjoyed going to events and meeting people and just being in the scene for a little while. Then he got over it. Ben, that never really interested him to the same degree.

Ben McKenzie: I have this college degree. I was the oldest young cast member, and I had a little experience outside the entertainment industry. So I knew that whatever this process was, at some point it was going to be over. And I still needed to hold on to myself, because it seemed like it could be quite a ride, and a lot of ups and downs.

Stephanie Savage: Adam loved [indie] music, and Ben liked Journey. Outside of work, we all went to see a lot of music together and did Coachella and all these things. And Ben was not so much a part of that.

Josh Schwartz: I remember even when they were both single, they also had very different taste in women. They would comment on the fact—there was just no overlap. They each had their own lane.

Peter Gallagher (Sandy Cohen): I could sense with Adam sometimes that he's like, God, I hope I'm not compromising my future career by doing this teen soap. And I don't know if he ever called it that, but I could see it, and it had nothing to do with the show. It just had to do with being that age. You could tell Ben was going places, too, because he was very serious—about some things—and really smart. And hard working.

Rachel Bilson: Ben was probably more focused and serious, rather than hanging out and goofing around. He has a great sense of humor and is really funny. But I wouldn't say maybe as engaging while we were working.

The actors who played the adult characters weren't dealing with screaming fans quite as much as Brody or Barton, but they were nonetheless enjoying being on a hit.

Peter Gallagher: We had these young kids, and I'd be walking down the street with my wife. I said, "Honey, you know what? It might never get better than this. I get to sleep at home, and I have a steady job. We're not worried about money. I can be here with the kids; I can take them to stuff on the weekends. Sometimes, we'll be able to have dinner at night during the week. I'll be able to be like a regular dad."

Lisa Cochran: Kelly was a bit of an opposite of Peter. Peter was the showman. Peter would be at video village or cast village trying to perk people up—he would probably sing a few bars of something—where Kelly would just as soon just sit there. Kelly and Peter, I would say, were not the closest—the irony of the two characters. Kelly had a very strict diet. Everything was regimented with Kelly. She was not only vegan, she was everything. She drank stuff on set that was green and brown, and you just went, "I don't want to know what's in it. It doesn't smell good. But this is her health regimen."

Kelly Rowan: People used to laugh at me about my food, because I was not going to eat at Bristol Farms every day. I had this gal make me juices and coconut water and fish and salad and bring it to me, because there was no time to actually even grocery shop.

Melinda Clarke: I was married, but Kelly was single. Everyone was flirting with Kelly—Tate and Ben and Adam. It was weird, but I think they were all flirting with her. Because she's also the giggliest on set. She would giggle the most, and they could break her up.

Kelly Rowan: My daughter has been watching the show, because she's fourteen. I don't necessarily want to watch the whole show again because I lived it, but I popped in, and Adam was doing a scene. He was such a bright light: funny and charming and self-deprecating. I enjoyed acting with him. Sometimes, there were scenes in the kitchen with the Cohens that we just couldn't get through, because we were laughing. Ben and I were particularly bad [about cracking up], but it was a lot of fun.

Lisa Cochran: Melinda was gregarious. She was outgoing. She's the cruise director. She was very, very funny. Very charming. Any guest cast that came on, she made you feel warm. She also understood that the show is about those kids.

Rachel Bilson: Mindy was always so fun, so cool. She was like the fun mom you wanted to hang out with.

If Rowan and Gallagher were less simpatico than the characters they played, the opposite proved true early on for her and Clarke—so much so that it altered the course of their on-screen relationship.

Kelly Rowan: Mindy and I were foodies. So we'd go out and eat. That was our big thing. Then Josh figured out we were becoming friends. Kirsten and Julie hated each other. And then all of a sudden, we were loving each other. And I thought, *How am I going to make this work?* So I'm always curiously looking at Julie with a raised eyebrow, like, *Why am I friends with you?*

Papa Gallagher Sings

Peter Gallagher had helped seal the deal on playing Sandy by belting out a *Guys and Dolls* tune for Gail Berman. This was far from the last time that he would sing around *O.C.* people.

Samaire Armstrong: Peter Gallagher was just amazing. You go to set and he's just singing. He would always sing [*singing, to the tune of "Maria" from* West Side Story] "SAMAIIIIIIIIIRE!"

Amanda Righetti (Hailey Nichol): He would just make up a song and dance, and he'd start to tap-dance. Come on. He's Broadway. He's trained in all that stuff, and it's all about play. Peter was always advising us to appreciate it and be grateful for it and not take it for granted. And that's always stuck in my mind even now.

Peter Gallagher: I cared about them. We didn't really have any difficulties.

Rachel Bilson: One time, I parked in a parking spot that Peter self-proclaimed was his spot, close to his dressing room. And I think he made a comment, like, "Someone's done one too many magazine covers." I thought I could just park wherever I wanted. But it was an innocent mistake. I think he was very cognizant of, *Don't let these kids get too big for their britches.* Which I respect. And he's right. And I think there were times I probably had moments like that, going through the success of the show.

Peter Gallagher: There was tension at various times that I didn't really understand the source of, I never had a problem [with anyone]. Sometimes somebody'd forget the fact that we have to rehearse. [*laughs*] But nothing you wouldn't expect from young, talented people just starting out, none of whom were mean, none of whom were stupid. Just dealing with the awesome surprise of being popular and well-known, all of us, overnight.

You Cannot Make Friends with the Rock Stars

Josh Schwartz was only a few years older than several of the "kids" in the ensemble, which created an unusual showrunner-actor dynamic.

Peter Roth (president, Warner Bros. Television): Josh was a young man with not a lot of experience, and there was enormous pressure. We did twenty-seven episodes in that first season. The combination of it all was overwhelming. By the Chrismukkah episode, he was pretty burnt. He had a relationship with this cast that I believe made his job even harder for him. He was too close to the cast.

Susan Rovner (programming executive, Warner Bros. Television): I think Josh didn't initially have enough of a boundary between him and his stars because of the age—these were his contemporaries. But I think probably he realized it was beneficial to have more boundaries.

Yvette Urbina (programming executive, Fox): He became too close of friends with them. So he had a hard time being the boss.

Lisa Cochran: I think Josh will admit in the beginning, he cared a great deal about the cast and he was friends with them. As a [unit production manager], and now having produced, I recognize that you can be friendly, but you cannot be best friends. Because somewhere along the line, you have to say no.

How did this cause problems?

Peter Roth: By them taking advantage of him, and by his acceding to their demands and wishes more than I felt was appropriate or necessary, both in terms of story and writing and accommodating their exploding egos. These very young kids were finding a lot of fame very, very quickly. And I was feeling increasingly nervous for Josh as I would hear story after story of issues on the set. I was concerned for Josh, because he was more a peer than he was their boss. I remember thinking, *You need to put your foot down. You need to assert yourself. And if you need us to do that, we will do that on your behalf.*

At the same time, there were concerns that Schwartz's youth put him at a disadvantage in dealing with his most senior cast member.

Bob DeLaurentis: I remember taking Josh aside to have the discussion about the nature of the relationship that he wanted to set up with Peter, which was challenging because of the age difference and the experience difference. Josh dealing with Peter one-on-one as the twenty-seven-year-old kid up against an experienced actor, it wasn't necessarily a fair matchup.

Gail Berman (president, Fox): I went to see him because people had said to me, "He's spending a lot of time with the cast outside of the production, socially." And there were some concerns about that. Having produced *Buffy*, I was familiar with things that can happen when you have a young showrunner. You know, "You must be the showrunner. And socializing is tempting, but you've got to knock it off."

Rachel Bilson: I like to torture Schwartz because he's like my brother, and it's fine. And when I asked him what was going to happen to my character, he would always tease me that I was going to get eaten by a shark.*

Late in the season, Bilson learned of plans to do an episode where the guys went to Las Vegas while the women stayed back in Newport. She decided to petition her friend-boss-brother to make a change.

Rachel Bilson: I was like, "Josh, I really want to go to Vegas, too." So Josh literally wrote me into that part of the episode. I don't know if it was part that the Summer in me was like, *My boyfriend's going to Vegas without me. Fuck, no!* Or if it was just, *That sounds really fun. I want to go. It's not fair.* I just wanted to be a part of it. So that was very nice of Schwartz to oblige.

Stephanie Savage: Oh, for sure that happened. That would be a Rachel move to go to Josh and pitch a storyline that was going to be a part of her personal life as well.

---

* "And then in *Hart of Dixie*," Bilson recalls of her second Schwartz-Savage show, "it was an alligator."

When Colin Hanks guested late in the season, he was struck by how well Bilson and Schwartz got along.

Colin Hanks (Grady Bridges): I remember being really impressed by the relationship that she had with Josh. It didn't seem like a boss-type situation. I was really impressed by how comfortable they were talking with Josh and vice versa at that point. Almost jealous, in a way, of the actors, knowing that, *Hey, you actually have someone that you can relate to. And you can actually communicate with clearly.* As opposed to feeling like it's a boss, that there's some sort of disconnect there. I felt, *Oh, wow, that's cool. I wonder what that feels like.*

Rachel Bilson: He was awesome. Every memory I have with Josh was that he was always so comfortable, so nice. He was young, he was cute. It was like, *Okay, this guy's running the show.* And it was always just the best feeling.

Schwartz wasn't the only member of the creative team at this point spending a lot of nonwork time with the cast.

Stephanie Savage: If you'd already gone to the movies on a Tuesday night when everyone finished work at seven, and you'd seen a band on Thursday because Bright Eyes was playing at the Wiltern, it didn't seem that weird that then on Saturday you'd be hanging out at a bar with these same people, because that was just who we knew.

Matt Ramsey (editor): We all went to Coachella. We would go see bands. I remember seeing the Killers at the Troubadour with Josh and Stephanie and most of the cast. It was just a great fun atmosphere.

Rachel Bilson: We went out all the time. Whether it was a club, a party, we had a friend who did a rock and roll seder, which was awesome, which was a lot of fun, a lot of pot. That was our social crew. You're in your twenties. That's what you do.

Josh Schwartz: Everybody was young. It wasn't a creepy "Hanging out at the producer's house who's thirty years older than the actress" kind of thing.

Samaire Armstrong: They were only a few years older than us. They got it. We hung out with them and they understood it. It was really fun.

Stephanie Savage: As the person sitting before you now, looking back, I would caution us on all of it and say, "Maybe don't do that." But at the time, it made sense. It was unusual, but I don't think it made anyone feel uncomfortable. Although maybe if we asked them, they would say something different. But it definitely complicated things as people started to have different feelings about the show, because it felt much more personal. But it felt organic at the time since we were doing a lot of publicity for the show regardless.

Adam Brody: He was up in the writers' room much more than on set, so I mostly saw him socially after we started. It was a tight, tight group. It was a blast, especially that first year where everyone is basking in the success and it's a whirlwind.

House Parties at McG's

McG maintained his role as *O.C.* emcee, inviting the cast and various celebrities to his home in West Hollywood to watch each episode with him when they debuted on Wednesday nights.

Josh Schwartz: You never knew who was going to be there. Might be Gwen Stefani one week, it might be Diana Ross another week. He just made it feel like a party, like a sense of community.

McG: I was with a woman named Robin Antin, and she had put together the Pussycat Dolls. So the Pussycat Dolls were at all the parties. And then because of the rock and roll component, all the guys from

Korn would be there. And then Tommy Lee and Pam Anderson would be there on occasion. It was just a stopping point of the Hollywood party circuit. I think Sam Rockwell and Justin Theroux at some point, so it was fun.

Adam Brody: I remember Justin Timberlake and Cameron Diaz being there once?

Samaire Armstrong: There was one evening I did not hold my liquor in well and I ended up throwing up over the railing of McG's second floor down the side of the house. My boyfriend was like, "Let's go." And then the next day, I had delivered cookies and milk saying, I'm so sorry for that. Like a little gift basket: *I apologize for the puking.* I was invited back, so I think it was okay.

Josh Schwartz: McG had [*Charlie's Angels* TV show producer] Leonard Goldberg and his wife come to one of the viewing parties, and they brought Diana Ross. It was the Season Two premiere. I would get really into it, because it was the show, and I would just stare at the TV. Diana Ross was talking to Leonard at one point next to me on the couch, and without even thinking about what I was doing, I shushed her. And then I was like, *Oh, my God, I just shushed Diana Ross!* I was so intensely into the show that I couldn't help myself. I think she was mildly offended and then moved on.

McG: Josh Schwartz in a great many ways is a mini–Larry David. He certainly understands that vernacular. And that was a *Curb Your Enthusiasm* moment, if I'd ever seen one. It was glorious.

How Many Episodes?!

Successful network television shows circa 2003 made twenty-two episodes a season, leading to a grueling schedule where the cast and crew would generally be zombies by episode eighteen or nineteen. The success of *The O.C.*, plus its early start in the summer, meant that Fox ordered twenty-seven total episodes that first year.

Gail Berman: The pressure that I was under was, "Just keep it going. Keep it going." So while they probably had their own set of pressures, I was probably saying to my staff, "I don't care how, but figure it out."

Bob DeLaurentis: They asked us to do *thirty* episodes. And I went to Josh and I said, "This is where we must absolutely draw the line. We cannot do thirty episodes. It's not a soap in the way they view soaps and daytime television."

Patrick Norris (director): Everybody was really tired. We put in a lot of hours on *The O.C.*, anywhere from sixteen to eighteen hours a day, and the actors were tired. I think it helped them play the emotion actually, because they wanted to cry anyways off camera, because they were so tired and they wanted a break.

Kelly Rowan: It's like running a marathon. You have to really take care of yourself.

J. J. Philbin joined the writing staff midway through the year, not long after the episode order was extended to twenty-seven.

J. J. Philbin (writer/producer): Everyone seemed really, really burnt. They were exhausted and knew that they still had a big chunk of the season left to do.

Some people held up to the extended grind better than others.

Rachel Bilson: I was twenty-one years old, and I had no real responsibilities. So it was fine. You work all year long, essentially. But at that age and my boyfriend was on the show, it was way easier for me, because a lot of my life was there. Looking back at it, it's absolute insanity. I could never do that now.

Alan Dale (Caleb Nichol): We did five half-hour drama episodes of [Australian soap opera] *Neighbours* every week. I'm not saying it was great production values or hugely exciting writing or anything, but we did that every week. Coming across to America and people are [saying], "I'm just so burned out," we're doing an hour every ten days, maybe. So it didn't seem very hard to me, to be honest. I'm not bagging anybody. It's just that they didn't have the experience growing up doing all we had to do in Australia to make a living.

Allan Heinberg: We were living on adrenaline, and we also felt like it was really personal to us. We'd been given this incredible gift, and people were just letting us do our thing. So there was a real free feeling that this is a once-in-a-lifetime opportunity and we can sleep afterward—which turned out not to be true. We felt like kids in a candy store being able to dream this show up and then make it and have it air. The fact that it so instantly struck a chord with its viewers gave us an enormous amount of resilience and a desire to keep going. It felt immediate, even more so than TV usually does.

Funny Business

The first episode after the baseball hiatus introduces a crucial but silent character: Seth's toy horse Captain Oats, who was his best friend before Ryan came along.

Josh Schwartz: It was a Jane Espenson idea. She had written it into one of the scripts early on. I thought it was hilarious.

Jane Espenson (writer/producer): I just wanted to live in the reality/ embarrassment of having someone in your room at that age when you're still kind of a kid, and all your kid stuff is still around.

Josh Schwartz: For a kid who had no friends, the idea of Seth talking to a plastic horse just felt really funny and really fitting. And then

obviously later on, we were able to give Summer the female coun-
terpart, Princess Sparkle, and demonstrate that they were more alike
than they may realize.

Stephanie Savage: The props department brought a bunch of different horses to look at. They were talking about, "Should we make
a horse? What is this horse? It's got to be so special." But then the
generic Breyer horse that just came out of the box was perfect. "Do
nothing to that horse. It doesn't need to be modified in any way."

The twelfth episode opens with a scene that's a personal favorite of several
of the actors and writers:* Ryan and Sandy delight in the travails of Seth
(who is in the midst of a romantic dilemma) and Kirsten (who got overly
drunk at Thanksgiving in the previous episode). You may recall it for Seth
dancing into the kitchen to the Dandy Warhols' "We Used to Be Friends,"†
or for Sandy's frequent use of the word "yogalates."

Allan Heinberg: There's just so much exposition in that scene. So I
thought, *How do you get the audience up to speed in a way that
is charming and disarming and flips?* Once I figured out that for
once, Sandy and Ryan aren't the ones in trouble, then I had the
scene.

Josh Schwartz: That scene was written in a certain way and was very
fun on the page. When we saw the scene cut together, it was a whole
other version where they were just riffing and Adam and Peter were
having so much fun, and Kelly and Ben—it was just this contagious
scene. And then the Dandy Warhols were playing and it was like, "Oh
my God, it's all working." It was just one of those scenes that was the
show at its best, I felt.

---

* Also of this author. Yogalates!

† When the song was praised in one interview, Josh Schwartz quipped, "The producers
of *Veronica Mars* agreed," since the high school detective drama chose it as its theme song
the following year.

Peter Gallagher: I remember going off with the "yogalates," thinking, *I know there's not another "yogalates" in here, but I'm sorry—I'm just desperate for more.* [*speaking quickly in a singsong manner*] "Yoga-lates yogalates yogalates." With that group, you could toss the ball around in a room like that and have fun. And nobody descended from the writers' room with a whip and said, "No more!" That was a moment.

Art Imitating Life

As all savvy showrunners do, Schwartz began to blend fiction with fact, incorporating aspects of his actors' lives into the characters they were playing.

Josh Schwartz: I was doing a lot of eavesdropping. Adam was the one to turn me on to Death Cab for Cutie as one of the bands that he was obsessed with, and that just got written straight into the show. Rachel was obsessed with *The Golden Girls*; that got written straight into the show. Everybody's personalities were written into it. And both Ben and Ryan didn't really seem to have much of an affinity for music, so that's how we ended on Journey.

Stephanie Savage: Ben literally said, "I don't know what you guys are talking about. I like Journey." And then we were like, "Oh my God. We have to use that."

Adam Brody: Josh and myself, we had musical tastes in common. Comic books, which I had had a couple different love affairs with in my life, and was in the middle of one then, were brought to the fore-front of the character too.

Rachel Bilson: [*The Amazing Adventures of*] *Kavalier & Clay* was Brody's favorite book. All the music—there were so many Josh and Brody similarities, too.

Adam Brody: It happened very nicely that Josh and I, our sensibilities lined up so much more than in the pilot as written. That was a really happy accident.

Rachel Bilson: They were really close and Seth was basically a voice for Josh. We hung out so much and Josh got to know us, and he loved taking little things from our lives and putting it on the show. So that happens all the time. There's a lot of me in Summer.

Not everyone's real personality mirrored their character's, however.

Melinda Clarke: Ben is a really funny guy in person. And he definitely had to deal with a lot of the brooding.

Allan Heinberg: With Ben, it was always a bit of a struggle, because I think Josh's initial impulse was to write him as a more laconic, James Dean-esque figure. And I'm sure he was under a lot of stress in the outlines and scripts to give the studio and the network more: *What is he thinking and what is he feeling and what is his arc?* My memory is that we would build speeches for Ben, and then once we heard them, we would cut it back and back and back. It became a dance of trying to find a happy medium, because Ben as a human is incredibly smart, thoughtful, soulful, articulate, verbal, a lot of the things that Ryan isn't. There were times where I felt like, *Maybe we should write more toward Ben and less toward Ryan.* And in some ways, I think the happy medium became giving Ben all that stuff, but not in dialogue form. So giving it in parenthetical or an action line in the script, so that the studio and the network knew what was on Ryan's mind.

David Bartis (executive producer): In the pilot or the second episode, Ben came to us and said, "I think I'm better when you give me less to say." You never hear that from an actor. "Give me *less*"?!?! But Ben got his character really early on.

Ben McKenzie: It was probably fear. I think at the time I was justifying it as, *Oh, it's more powerful if I don't say as much*, which I guess is somewhat true of Ryan. It's such a beautifully written pilot by Josh that, the less you do in terms of your verbal stuff, the more you internalize and play it quietly, the more the audience is on your side in a way. But in retrospect, I probably wouldn't have done that, because what it became was Adam just being hilarious and me just sitting there brooding. Which, to Adam's credit, he's very good at. And to my credit, I was good at brooding.

Alan Heinberg: As verbal as Josh is, as a human and as verbal as his characters are, as a filmmaker, he also intuited the power of silence. Ryan was the archetype of silence on that show.

Lauren Gussis (writers' assistant): [Marissa] was the hardest one [to write for]. I don't want to say she was hard to come up with stories for, because there was so much in that first year.

Allan Heinberg: It couldn't always be "What's going to happen to Ryan?" And I do remember a lot of conversations about, "How does Marissa save Ryan?" We were always looking for ways for Marissa to have agency and independence and depth, and she certainly has more insight a lot of the time than her parents on the show.

Lauren Gussis: There was like a lot of joking about, "What does she want besides him?" When you write for a character, you want to have a clear vision of what they really want. And all she wanted was him. What is she into? Does she want a good relationship with her mom, who's a full shit show? Does she want to get out of there? She wasn't a terribly driven or aspirational character. I think we had this conversation a lot about Ryan's projection on her—that she was this thing he desired. But we would talk about, "We say they're in love, but why?" I think it was escapism for both of them. It was like he represented something for her that she was never going to be able to touch, and vice versa.

Mischa Barton (Marissa Cooper): I think it's pretty typical for young people to fall for their absolute opposites. I thought that common theme of the rich girl falls for the boy from the wrong side of the tracks is very obvious. I think it was important that you felt they just had a magnet towards each other. And that was that. It didn't need to be overthought too much, you know?

Allan Heinberg: Mischa brought so much to the table. There were a lot of specifics about Marissa's story and her place and her family. And I think she was maybe more of a bad girl before Mischa was cast, because Mischa, as everybody now realizes, was incredibly young. We adapted to fit her gifts the way you do with everybody. And then we continued to be surprised by how adult she was on-screen. Off-screen, she's so sweet. I feel like Mischa was able to talk about the things that were important to her, to Josh and Stephanie, and that those made their way into that character through Mischa.

Ben McKenzie: It was perfectly cast, because Mischa was the opposite of me. She came from New York, and she had all this worldliness to her. That was quite funny because, of course, she was far younger than I was, and yet I was supposedly the guy who was wise beyond his years. But in fact, she was the one who really had much more life experience.

Patrick Norris: Mischa was one that you knew was going to get into trouble in her career. She was innocent. I think the actor was everything that the character was, in a way.

If Marissa was the hardest character to write for, who was the easiest?

Lauren Gussis: Oh, come on! It's Seth Cohen. Seth Cohen is everybody's favorite character. At twenty-four, I wish I had dated Seth Cohen.

J. J. Philbin: In trying to think about stories for Seth, you just think of Josh as a starting point. It was a little bit like Liz Meriwether and

Jess in those early days of *New Girl* when you're trying to understand these characters and there's a showrunner right in front of you that is so much like that character, you can't help but confuse them in your brain.

Lauren Gussis: It was the wish fulfillment of the nice guy getting the crazy hot girl.

Or, for a while, *two* crazy hot girls, which brings us to . . .

The Math of Love Triangles: Anna + Seth + Summer

In the season's fourth episode, "The Debut," Seth is the cotillion escort for fellow beautiful nerd Anna Stern. Samaire Armstrong landed what was, at the time, supposed to be a one-shot role.

Samaire Armstrong: Throughout the years from nineteen to twenty-three, I had been going to auditions out there [Manhattan Beach]. I actually said to myself, "I'm never auditioning here anymore. It's such a headache." Then I saw a commercial for *The O.C.*, and I had a vision. It was like time stopped. And then I got a call saying that I had to audition. I'd promised myself I wouldn't audition anymore, but there was something about this that felt right.

Armstrong coincidentally already knew the two actors with whom she would work the most on the show.

Samaire Armstrong: I knew Adam because we had acting class together, and I knew Rachel because Rachel and I had the same commercial agent.

Adam Brody: When I started in that class, she was the cool one, at the top of the class.

Samaire Armstrong: My first audition was with the casting director, and I said, "Oh, yeah, I'm friends with Adam and I know Rachel." But what I mostly did was talk about hamburgers. They wrote it a certain way: the girl had long brown hair and she was on all accounts, very "nerdy." And I was really basing her off of Drew Barrymore in the nineties with the short hair. That's the vibe I was going with. At a Christmas party at McG's office, we were all outside. And I see Drew Barrymore. And she's like, "I love you." I'm like, *You* love *me? I* love *you.*" Like, *I'm you* right now.

Patrick Rush (casting director): She threaded that needle perfectly between who Mischa was and who Rachel was. You've got this tall, sun-kissed, gorgeous supermodel in Mischa and the scrappier Sally Field brunette version in Summer. And then in comes this person who just pops, and you're not supposed to like her, because you want Seth and Summer to be together. And then people liked her.

Though Anna returns to her home in Pittsburgh at the end of the episode, she first delivers a line promising more.

Samaire Armstrong: The line, "Confidence, Cohen," it was in the audition. And when I said it, I felt it. That was frickin' it. It's crazy to have like an "I'll be back" moment like that. People still say that to me.

Josh Schwartz: We really liked Samaire. We really liked the character of Anna. She made a huge impression in a very short amount of time.

Samaire Armstrong: What I brought to it was how I felt when I was in high school, which wasn't that many years prior to me being on the show. I always felt like the newcomer, because I always was moving around, and I was totally different than most people. I was just so grateful for my character to be on television. The only person that I saw when I watched TV that I related to was Kelly Osbourne on *The Osbournes*. It was so refreshing to see someone who wasn't girl-next-door cookie cutter, and I felt liberated. And the responses that I got from people who watched it were like, "I finally feel like I relate to someone on TV."

Anna returns in the season's ninth episode, immediately complicating what had once seemed like an inevitable Seth and Summer coupling—and complicating the real-life relationship between the actors playing all three characters.

Rachel Bilson: I knew Sa before the show. We were always friendly, but I think because of the storyline, it created this weird underlying competitiveness. And I feel like she had a crush on Brody. She had a boyfriend at the time, [but] it did feel like, sometimes life imitates art. We were always friends and friendly, but then there was always this weird undertone.

Samaire Armstrong: There was definitely that. Not necessarily a *romantic* triangle going on, but it was a triangle for sure. Like, *Oh, there's my friend with my other friend. They're dating and what, am I the third wheel? Should I come back later?* It was art imitating life in many ways, and that part was not lost on us, but they were the cutest couple. They were so fricking cute.

After several episodes of waffling between Summer and Anna, Seth opts to date Anna, who has always been upfront about her interest in him, and with whom he has much more in common. It was a choice that divided both *O.C.* fandom and many of the people working on the show.

Stephanie Savage: There were definitely girls that identified with Anna more than they identified with Summer, and wanted Seth to end up with Anna.

Lauren Gussis: I was Team Anna because I identified with Anna more. But as a ten-thousand-foot-view person living in the skin of the show, he has to be with Summer. Even if Anna's the right person for him, even if you hate him for that, she cannot come in and usurp

Summer. There's something that inherently feels wrong about that in the universe of the show. You feel like Seth and Summer belong together.

At this writing, Brody's rewatch hadn't gotten to Anna's appearances later in the season, but even her appearance in "The Debut" had him questioning his alter ego's Summer obsession.

Adam Brody: Having seen just through [episode] five, before Summer really [turns good], it's a no-brainer. Summer's pretty awful and Anna is nothing but great. So run to her! And it's pretty crazy to name your boat after someone that you go to school with for a long time and you've never spoken to, and who's pretty awful outwardly. And I would think that might be a big turnoff for her as well. It's a little scary obsessive. But Anna wants to sail to Tahiti. That's crazy. He should see that through first. I'm like, *I don't know, man. They've got a lot in common.*

Josh Schwartz: Seth and Summer was always the endgame. We were talking about how we don't want to be the show that just keeps them apart for years and years and years. While also knowing that putting them together would potentially be a risk, and that television shows are littered with the stories of these couples that once they got together, that killed the story. But we felt like them as a couple would still have plenty of tension and plenty of things to mine—that it wouldn't just be the end of that tale. I think Valentine's Day was always where we had talked about them sleeping together, but we had the Anna piece we had to play through first.

Stephanie Savage: Anna actually made us feel like it's not just going to be a will-they-or-won't-they story. That triangle was a pretty good story engine, and you could imagine it going in a couple of different ways. It also felt important that this is going to be the *Breakfast Club* model of storytelling that when they're back at school after Tijuana, Summer isn't just going to be now totally aligned with Seth and Ryan and Marissa—that she's not going to be comfortable with the intimacy and the bonds that those guys have formed over that trip. And there's going to be some denial and some pushing away, which is going to be really painful for Seth and feel like a violation of this pact that they all made, going on this journey together. Which then opened up a real possibility for Anna, who didn't have any of those same feelings about not wanting to be seen eating lunch with Seth Cohen, which would create an opportunity for that relationship to have some real ground.

Seth and Anna stay together for a bit, but she eventually breaks up with him because it's impossible to ignore how much Seth continues to like Summer, and vice versa.* A couple of episodes after that, Anna announces that she misses her old life in Pittsburgh and is moving back there, to the dismay of both Seth and the many viewers who had fallen in love with her.

Samaire Armstrong: I wish I could have stayed on the show longer. I felt like I belonged there. But I also understand. It was described to me by Josh at the time, like, "We really don't know where to go with your character anymore." But I have a slogan that gets repeated, and such great memories with Rachel, like singing *The Golden Girls* theme in the bathroom. I can't complain at all.

Well, no. She has one complaint.

Samaire Armstrong: Just for the record, I absolutely hated my hair. I always had my hair short in that period of my life. But how they styled it was just so not cool. If you look at my photos on the red carpet, my hair is so much cooler than [on the show]. We got into a lot of

---

* Summer spends an episode trying to make Seth jealous by dating a character the writers dubbed "Big Funny Guy," played by Adam Brody's friend and bandmate Bret Harrison. The character's sense of humor came out of Brody's hatred of Jay Leno. "The idea that Summer would fall for a guy who had a sense of humor that Seth was so offended by," says Schwartz, "it was very inspired by Brody's point of view on the world."

arguments, the hair guy and I. And then the makeup artist was so sweet. I adored her. I had the worst acne back then,* to the point where the director of photography was literally like, "You need to see the dermatologist. I'm having a really hard time lighting you." And the makeup artist helped. In some episodes, I have a giant beauty mark. It was because I had a pimple that would not go away.

Josh Schwartz: In hindsight, we could have gotten more mileage out of the Anna story, for sure. We thought we were being bold by writing characters off and keeping the show constantly changing and moving and what have you. But then you come to learn that kind of connection between the audience and the character is rare and not easily replicated. Anna had a couple seasons' worth of story in her potentially. I'm not sure if the actress at the time had a couple of seasons in her, just based on some of the personal stuff that she was dealing with. But the character certainly did. And she was charming and she had chemistry with everybody. She had moments with Ryan. We were like, "Oh, there's chemistry there." And we could have put her with Luke. Boggles the mind to even conceive.

Anna and Luke?!?!?

Samaire Armstrong: No. No. God. No. Luke was "Welcome to the O.C., bitch!" I don't think Anna would have been captivated, but it would have been funny, I guess, to watch that. But she liked Seth because he was so cerebral and heavy and complex.

If Anna left earlier than she should have, she at least got a memorable farewell, with Seth rushing through the airport—to Nada Surf's cover of eighties classic "If You Leave"—to express his regret over how things ended, giving Anna a chance to say her catchphrase one more time.

---

* Light a candle for poor Chris Pine, who did not get the same dispensation for his own acne that Armstrong did.

Stephanie Savage: The episode where Anna leaves, we were at the office and Josh had written that scene and said, "I'm going to the bathroom; read it while I'm gone." He came back and I was sobbing at my desk—a gross overreaction to Anna saying, "Confidence, Cohen" with a sock monkey in her backpack as she went through security at the airport. Just feeling the loss of what this character was bringing to the show and the real estate she was holding up as the quirky, cool girl, and just feeling really sad.

Samaire Armstrong: I had so many emotions. I was so grateful. It was such a beautiful scene. I remember on the way to set, I was like, "Josh, that doesn't seem like Anna; she just wouldn't leave like that." And he's like, "You should have called me sooner." I was like, "I didn't arrive to that conclusion until today!"

Patrick Norris: That whole scene was probably one of the most poignant story points in the whole series. Because I thought he should've ended up with her. Her chemistry with him was really interesting to me. Where Summer was the comic relief girlfriend, it seemed like Anna could go a lot deeper. So I was sorry to see her go. It was heartfelt for me.

Samaire Armstrong: It was inner turmoil I was experiencing. You put so much into it and you want to do right by the character for the audience, too. I was like, *I just don't want her to seem like she's running away.* I wanted that to be the emotion—real conflict at the goodbye, like, *I don't really want to go. I don't know if it's the right thing. I have to be brave and do it.* I didn't want it to be because she was lost, or she got beaten down by the O.C. I just thought, *Anna wouldn't be like that.*

Once Seth and Anna break up, he immediately gets together with Summer for real, though their first time in bed is a disaster, soon to be referred to as "the awful fish sex." Fox's standards and practices department had, other than the smoking from the pilot, pretty much allowed Schwartz to show the teen characters engaging in all manner of risqué behavior, including underage drinking, drug use, and sex. But another line was drawn here.

> **Stephanie Savage:** What was not fair game was Summer having an orgasm. That got pushback. Showing female pleasure of any kind was problematic. In an episode that I wrote, Summer had a line where she said that Seth didn't have to do anything; he could just lie there like a buffet and she'd serve herself. I think that line got cut. I was going to write an article for a magazine called "The Year Summer Never Came." There was an episode in the bible called "As Autumn Comes, So Does Summer."

How to Burn Through Story

Most other shows like this would have devoted much or all of a season to Seth dating Anna, before he finally wound up with Summer. On this one, Anna breaks up with Seth within six episodes. That's just one example of many of how Season One of *The O.C.* packed in more incident than most network dramas would feature over the course of three or four years. This was very much to the short-term good, but would be a problem in the long term.

> **Adam Brody:** I recently did Rachel and Melinda's podcast, and for that I watched the episode where we go to Vegas in the first season. And I was like, *Holy shit, the Coopers have already divorced? Wait a second: Melinda is already dating my grandfather?* And I like that storyline. I just think that's a Season Three, Four, Five story. That's early.

There was a lot of debate about pacing among the executives at Warner Bros. and Fox.

Peter Roth: We were very concerned about burning through as much story as we did. And frankly, the network had the opposite point of view.

Gail Berman: At Fox, we like to move stuff along.

Josh Schwartz: Gail was a fan of twists. Like, just keep turning over cards with the audience and shocking the audience.

Craig Erwich: We probably tried to do too much. Characters change, but then you have to start manufacturing new crossroads for these people to be at. There's only so many times you can go to [one] well, especially when there's nothing else to generate story. In the middle of it, Sandy is not going to go argue before the Supreme Court; we're not doing Case of the Week with Sandy. It's a beast that just demands to be fed story and eventually you run out, and I think that's true to a lot of these shows.

At first, the sheer volume of story was applauded by the people who worked on the show.

Josh Schwartz: I remember going to work and the grips being like, "Oh, this is such a good episode. It's so funny when Seth and Summer are eating toast!" And you're like, *Hey, the grips are reading the scripts and coming over to talk about their positive feelings about the storylines and the dialogue,* which is pretty rare.

But there was also discussion in the writers' room about whether they were moving too fast.

Bob DeLaurentis: I was much more concerned and had those conversations with our group, but also with Warner Bros. "You're burning through the show."

Josh Schwartz: There wasn't a lot of long-term planning going on. I think if there had been, we probably would have done it a little differently. But we were just going with it. *If it works for right now, do it.* There was no sense of what tomorrow was going to bring, or what was going to be in Season Two.

Stephanie Savage: And I think we had some naivete and maybe some hubris of, "Well, we'll just think of more story! It's not like there's a finite number of stories that can be told about six people! We'll just keep coming up with them!"

Allan Heinberg: Part of what made the show so special is that we just kept throwing the story at you as fast as we possibly could, and we couldn't risk stopping.

Bob DeLaurentis: It was not a show that was franchised in a specific way—it's not a medical show. So you walk in on Monday morning and say, "What's this episode about?" And you created it out of whole cloth, where is this kid in his larger trajectory of the life. Those are in some ways the most difficult shows. I have been doing *Fargo* for the last several years. You walk in the writers' room on Monday morning and you're talking about a murder. You don't have anything like that in a show like *The O.C.*

Allan Heinberg: We didn't know how long it would last. So every idea we had went into that show in some ways without any sort of, "Okay, let's project that we're going to be a four-season show or five-season show, and maybe not put Julie Cooper through three relationships in one season."

Bob DeLaurentis: So much of what we did in terms of those quick arcs was a function of budget, too. You bring in a character and that character's terrific. And you think, *I could run this through the season.* But then we're going to have to promote that person and give them a bigger deal. And we quite honestly couldn't afford some of those deals we needed. The four episodes in and out? On the face of it, it's a good way to keep the story moving fast. It's also the less expensive way to do it, quite honestly, to make a show where the budget was minuscule by today's standards.

Josh Schwartz: It was reckless in a way that made Season One really fun, but we paid the price down the line. We would not approach it the same way [now].

When a Triangle Is Suddenly a Square

Schwartz had placed the Cooper and Cohen houses next to each other not only to kickstart Ryan and Marissa's relationship, but to set up a romantic entanglement between Kirsten, her husband Sandy, and her ex-boyfriend Jimmy. The latter idea went away almost immediately, since everyone realized how much they loved the idealized Cohen marriage.

Stephanie Savage: *Ice Storm* was a really big reference when we started. The idea of doing a pretty serious adult love triangle, where families might be ripped apart, was definitely a concept of places where the story could go. And then once we got into writing the show, it became very clear that nobody wanted that story. We didn't want that story. Fans didn't want that story, the actors didn't want that story. So we moved away from it.

Gail Berman: I think we were all interested in that triangle at first. But one of the things we found was working really well with the show and with the audience, was that this family was a really positive family. And we really don't want to mess with that. There were some moments when they branched off and thought about it, but the idea of keeping this as a very, very wholesome family was really important to the success of the show.

Tate Donovan (Jimmy Cooper): I think that nobody wanted to see Sandy and Kirsten have marital problems. They were a great couple. They're a great family. They didn't need that.

Without that Jimmy-Kirsten-Sandy conflict, though, and with Julie kicking Jimmy out of the house after discovering he had embezzled money from his clients, the writers almost immediately ran out of ideas for Jimmy.

Tate Donovan: I think that once they realized that you don't want to have a love triangle, they were like, "What are we going to do?"

Stephanie Savage: Jimmy got a condo. At a certain point, Jimmy stopped wearing shoes. He was seen in bare feet a lot, and he gave Marissa a banana when she wouldn't eat breakfast. We wanted Marissa to have a nice connection with her dad, at least, because her relationship with her mom was going to be so troubled. But we really did not have a lot of great ideas of what to do with Jimmy.

Josh Schwartz: In hindsight, we should have done some more Jimmy-Kirsten-Sandy stories. We were so worried about violating that marriage in that moment. That's why Hailey was brought in, as Kirsten's sister. It was the next closest way to do that story that would still maybe make Kirsten jealous, or have feelings.

Enter Amanda Righetti, a young actor with minimal experience.

Amanda Righetti: I was fairly fresh off the boat, I hadn't been in L.A. for even a year yet. I was working as an executive assistant for the CEO of 1-800-DENTISTS, and I was coordinating and producing their independent nonunion commercials.

Righetti had not auditioned for *The O.C.* pilot, but she did for the other two teen dramas that Fox and Warner Bros. were developing that year. She read for Olivia Wilde's role on *Skin* and was cast as the female lead in *No Place Like Home.** Fox didn't pick it up, but the network signed her to a

---

* According to *No Place Like Home* cocreator Amy Lippman, the runner-up to Righetti was none other than Olivia Wilde. (Drink?) And Righetti's younger sister was played by Leighton Meester, who would eventually star in *Gossip Girl* for Schwartz and Savage.

holding deal, which put her on Patrick Rush's radar when it came time to give Kirsten this troublemaking sibling.

> **Amanda Righetti:** She was labeled as Kirsten's fun-loving younger sister. She was the black sheep and a little bit of a homewrecker who liked to have a wild time. To try to stir the pot is what I loved about the character. Hailey was brought in just to make trouble.

While many of the show's actors were significantly older than the characters they were playing, Righetti was the opposite.

> **Amanda Righetti:** I was nineteen playing, I think, twenty-seven or twenty-eight. I was closer in age to Mischa than the rest of the cast. I played one of the older characters, but I was just as rowdy as the rest of them.

Hailey gets one of the more memorable introductions of any character in the series, wandering through the pool house in nothing but her underwear and one of Ryan's tank tops.

> **Amanda Righetti:** The crew really embraced me; it was really sweet. Because I was so young, they took me under their wing a little bit. I remember them all trying to make me feel comfortable, and it's hard enough to try to feel comfortable walking around in your underwear, around a 150-man crew.

Hailey and Jimmy date off and on during the first season. Maintaining that relationship might have given the writers an excuse to keep Jimmy part of the narrative after that first year. But Righetti got an offer for another Fox soap, which she couldn't resist taking.

> **Amanda Righetti:** *North Shore** came up, and it was a matter of which show we wanted to commit to. And this wasn't Hailey's show;

---

* A drama set at a Hawaiian resort, costarring a pre–*Game of Thrones* Jason Momoa.

it's the kids' show. It was always about the drama of high school and coming of age and growing up and the tumultuous world that we live in. I think if I had been cast as something that was as a character that went to school with them, it may have had a different, I might have had more longevity [on *The O.C.*] in that respect.

The Parent Trap

While Jimmy quickly became a narrative fifth wheel, the other adults remained a key part of the show.

Josh Schwartz: We never wanted the show to just be a teen drama where the adults were standing around. We were always conscious about making sure that they had their own stories.

Peter Gallagher: Usually on these shows, the old folks would get kicked to the curb in the first couple of episodes. And we liked each other, and we liked our kids, and also there was humor. That to me was gold, too.

Soon, the writers began treating Sandy as the surrogate father to all the kids.

Josh Schwartz: Peter was having such a good time, and it was contagious on-screen. You could see how much joy he was bringing to the role of Sandy. Summer had an absent dad. Marissa had Jimmy, who was troubled. There was just a lot of room for people who needed a good, stable father in their lives. And who better than Sandy to step in? He's a guy who can't help but, when there's a problem, stick his nose in it and try to fix it.

Patrick Norris: If Peter was late to the set, he was in some conversation with Josh about his scene. So he was very invested. He was probably busting Josh's balls to get to the point he wanted.

Josh Schwartz: Peter would come in with a lot of suggestions for lines. We definitely spent more time going over scripts and Peter's thoughts. Even if he wasn't improvising, he was definitely punching up lines that went into the script.

Josh Schwartz: There was a moment when we were doing episode 108. Gallagher invites me out to his house to talk about the script. I knew I was in trouble when I got there and he sent his family away, and it was just the two of us at this house. He was like, "This right here is just not good writing." It was a scene where Ryan and Julie are meeting in the kitchen and Sandy is brokering the peace between them after Marissa's OD. Ryan has a whole monologue that he gives to Julie Cooper, about her being from Riverside and him from Chino, and Sandy was a referee in that scene, but he wasn't super active. So Peter was like, "This is just not good." And he said, "I did a little pass on the scene." And it was basically the monologue that Ryan has, except it said "Sandy" instead of "Ryan" [over the monologue], and it said, "Julie, you and I aren't that different, I'm from the Bronx. You're from Riverside." I was thrown by it, and I rewrote the scene to split the difference. It can't fully be Sandy having this scene, but he had taken Ryan's monologue and made it Sandy's monologue. And I was like, *I don't know what to do here.* And then Peter, to his credit, reached out to me afterwards after he read the new version and said, "You know what? I think it worked better the original way." So I don't know if he was testing me or he legitimately had the concern and then when he read it, it didn't work.

Schwartz and Savage had no children, even as they were writing parenting stories. The same was true for Kelly Rowan and Tate Donovan at the time as they played parents.

Peter Gallagher: There were a couple of little bumps in the parenting where it's like, "If I were to say that, social services should really just come and take me away because there's no fucking father there." So Josh said, "Well, what do you think?" And then it evolved to, my wife and I would read the script on a Sunday just for the parenting bits and talk about it. And then I'd talk to Josh.

Stephanie Savage: Tate has sisters and he was a bachelor in Season One, so he had really no clue about a good dad paradigm. Josh had his own dad who was our Sandy Cohen. And other than that, I think we were all pretty clueless about it. Tate's sisters were like, "Dude, you're a terrible father. Sit those people down who are writing these stories and get them to read some books about child-rearing!" And Josh and I were just, "What are you talking about? Jimmy's amazing! He cockblocks Luke! He knows how to make French toast! The guy's a ten out of ten, what are you talking about?"

Allan Heinberg: Josh had a really unique take on that particular world, and on parent-child relationships, as well as romantic relationships. And I think that resonated. No matter what Josh's age at the time, I think Josh had a lot of emotional wisdom and a great deal of humor.

Was Kirsten a good mom?

Kelly Rowan: I think she did the best she could with what you know at the time. What was interesting about all these characters is that they were flawed, but they kept trying to be a family, Sandy and Kirsten being the moral center of that universe. So even when things go slightly awry, they always come back. What I've been told is, parents could watch the show with their kids. Because you had all these kitchen scenes with people trying to be a family. And Kirsten and Sandy did show up for their kids. They would talk to them. They tried to have dinner with them. There were lots of things going on that were untoward, too. But they loved their kids.

Though Peter Gallagher and Kelly Rowan's names appeared first in the opening credits every week, they and their peers quickly saw that the show was much more about the high schoolers.

Bob DeLaurentis: I think there was a general sense from the adult members, if you will, that they were—and I may be overstating this—the second-class citizens of the show. The show was about the kids and the phenomenon of the show was teen-centric. I think that wasn't always the most pleasant emotional environment in which to work. *I'm having my one scene today with Ryan because Ryan is having a crisis. What about my story?* Because of the huge success of the kids, it was only natural for them to feel a little unloved. So I always tried to go down to the set and give them a little extra love to reframe their perspective. I was pushing a rock up a steep hill, but it was all very collegial.

Josh Schwartz: Tate would never complain about anything; he'd make the most of the screen time he had.

Peter Gallagher: I didn't have any illusions. I was number one on the call sheet, but the engine of the show was the kids.

Sandy starts the series as a public defender, but soon transitions into a corporate law job, where he represents the plaintiffs in a lawsuit against Caleb and the Newport Group.

Josh Schwartz: I think that's another example of us moving pretty quickly to deconstruct the show we'd set up. But it was an interesting story to us. Sandy was always the moral center, and we had the idea of this guy who was not in it for the money suddenly being offered money. It's not an uncommon occurrence for people who get into it full of ideals and then they can get compromised by money. We talked about other Sandy public defender stories. But that was a hard world to service.

Stephanie Savage: What, are we going to do another "Sandy saves a troubled kid" story every week? The idea of giving him a job where he could go toe to toe with the Newport Group and be put in conflict with Kirsten and Caleb, that felt like a story we could actually service.

The writers did not naturally gravitate to the business side of this world.

Allan Heinberg: We did our best to try to give that stuff texture and background. And that when you're doing a business story between Caleb and Kirsten, or Caleb and Sandy, you're really telling a father-daughter or father-son story. But it felt cumbersome to have to get into the mechanics of the family business. And so we were forever struggling with, like, "Is Sandy going to open a restaurant?"*

Peter Gallagher: I was sad. I loved being a public defender. And I started changing so many jobs: public defender, hospital administrator, restaurateur, fishmonger. I didn't know what was broke that needed fixing. But nobody asked me.

Luke, Come Away from the Dark Side

Luke rescues Ryan when the model home catches on fire, but otherwise spends all of the summer episodes and many of the early fall ones as a villain. In the twelfth episode, "The Secret," Luke—whose taunting of Ryan and Seth often came with an added layer of homophobia—discovers that his father is gay and has been having a secret affair. Rejected by the other popular kids for this scandal, he soon joins Ryan's little band of outcasts, and turns out to have a much softer side than the guy who once called Ryan a bitch.

Josh Schwartz: It was definitely a reflection of Chris's talents and that he's naturally this warm and friendly open guy—the opposite of Luke as a dick. He had some quirkier things to his personality. He was always strumming a guitar under a tree, singing a song. We wanted to work that in. And this goes towards the general impatience of Season One, that we dismantled Luke as an adversary and

---

* Sandy and Jimmy do, indeed, briefly run their own restaurant, then sell it to Caleb. After which we never hear about the place again.

then made him even nerdier and goofier as part of the group, and another outcast.

Stephanie Savage: He reframed Seth as cool.

Adam Brody: That switch, where Luke's a dumb puppy dog and Seth is the wise owner, is very funny.

Luke soon became part of an unexpected new love triangle with Julie Cooper and Caleb Nichol. First, with Jimmy out of the house and Julie's finances in a shambles, she decides to turn Kirsten's father into her own sugar daddy.

Josh Schwartz: We wondered, how do we take the two antagonists in the story and put them together and then make them potentially family for the Cohens? And then obviously, that would really complicate Ryan and Marissa's relationship.

Stephanie Savage: Julie's got to stay in the O.C. at any cost. So I think she starts out pretty cynically pursuing Caleb.

Melinda Clarke: One of my favorite scenes is when Caleb shows up with carnations and Julie says, "Is this a booty call?" And Alan Dale really didn't know. He says, "What's a boo-ty call?"

Alan Dale: When you're offered a babe like Melinda—my God, what a gorgeous-looking person—I didn't have any doubts at all. She was an absolute pleasure and wonderful. She played that role so well.

And then Luke and Julie massively complicate things by realizing they are attracted to each other.

Allan Heinberg: Once Luke became one of the boys we did Julie Cooper, in order to keep Luke around and create new conflict. I remember saying to Josh, "Yes, there's an age difference, but emotionally, they're exactly the same." I'm rooting for them, and I think there was part of the audience rooting for them, because Luke brought out such an innocent part of Julie. I was very proud of the way we handled that, and it was delightful to write. It took these two characters so far from where they started.

Melinda Clarke: I was like, *Damn, I officially love this show!* We were actually closer in age [in real life]. I was only maybe ten years older. We're adults—he definitely wasn't [really in] high school. So we were like, "Look what we get to do!"

Chris Carmack: I thought it was great. I thought it was so much fun. I love Melinda. I loved working with her. What's funny is, it's scandalous on the show, Luke sleeping with his girlfriend's mom. But in reality she was three years older than my girlfriend, so it was not a shocking thing for me as a human being.

Stephanie Savage: It was like a classic eighties teen movie story that we felt must be told.

Josh Schwartz: If you stop and think about it for a minute, it's his ex-girlfriend's mother. How that would land on Marissa had a lot of complications that were interesting. But they also just had really good on-screen chemistry and were both really game.

Chris Carmack: There was the night where Luke and Julie were going to kiss. I was over at the crafty area, looking for something to eat. And they were like, "We have these chili dogs, you want one?" I was like, "No, I have to go through this scene right now where I kiss Melinda." And I turn around and there's Melinda with half a chili dog sticking out of her mouth, with onions hanging off of it, the whole nine yards, and I die laughing. And she looks at me like, "Yeah, this is what we're doing." And I got myself a chili dog.

Once again, though, Fox standards and practices interfered in an unexpected way.

Chris Carmack: Josh came up to me, with great fanfare and excitement. He said, "Chris, first I gave you 'Welcome to the O.C., bitch.'" And I said, "Yeah?" And he goes, "You're about to have your next iconic line." I said, "Really? Okay. What is it?" He goes, "'Julie, you're such a MILF.'"* And I was like, "Oh, awesome, this'll be great." And it never cleared!

Matt Ramsey: I think a couple of days before air, Fox must have finally figured out what "MILF" stood for.

Chris Carmack: Josh was so devastated. He said they asked him, "What do you think this means?" And he said, "Mother I like to be fond of . . . ? Mother I'd like to have fun with . . . ?" And they said, "Our research tells us it's 'Mother I'd like to eff.'" And he was like "Really? No! I don't think so." But they didn't buy it.

Luke and Julie's affair proved a double-edged sword, giving Carmack his best material of the season, but also writing the character into a corner—how can Marissa stay friends with the ex-boyfriend who cheated on her and then slept with her mom?—from which the writers didn't think they could get him out. So they decided that, after Marissa found out about Luke and Julie, he would follow his father north to Portland for a fresh start.

Bob DeLaurentis: We all liked him but we all thought this particular relationship would not carry another season.

Chris Carmack: Luke started out as a guest star, and they brought me on as a series regular. Then in the middle of the season, they demoted me to guest star again. Then it was pilot season again, and I was already auditioning for stuff because I was a guest star. I was on a hit show, so chances were good I was going to get something. And

---

* Would *that* really have become the show's next iconic line? Schwartz: "No one's right 100 percent of the time."

that's when they invited me to be a series regular again. I was invited into Josh's office to talk about this, and really, they should have been calling my agent. It never should have been a twenty-two-year-old kid talking with the executive producer. And I was like, "How do I know you're not going to just drop me at the end? If I'm a series regular, I can't go out on these auditions. Can you guarantee that I'll be a series regular next season?" Which apparently is not something you ask for. [laughs] And he was like, "No, we can't do that." And I was like, "Well, then I can't come back." My agents would have handled it differently, and I think we might have had a different outcome. I wasn't getting paid a whole lot to be on *The O.C.*, and if my agent had been called, maybe they would have been able to figure something out.

Josh Schwartz: I don't specifically recall that,* but that seems like the kind of conversation we would have had. I think we all really loved Chris. He was so good, and he did literally everything we asked him to do with that character, which was a broad spectrum of things, including singing. But ultimately we felt like we had defanged him as the villain, and therefore it was hard to keep him in the show, and didn't want to prevent him from being able to have other opportunities.

Norman Buckley (editor/director): I also think that was one of the big mistakes that everybody realized is that he should have never been written out of the show.

Josh Schwartz: Obviously, we got a lot of mileage out of that story in Season One. But we could have introduced some other quirks to his character, or some more of the story with his dad, or find new ways to reignite his conflict with Ryan, put Marissa between them a bit more, let him have more time when there is more drama to be had there. He's still remembered as the guy who kicks sand in

---

* Nor does he specifically recall Carmack being demoted back to guest star status prior to being written out. "I think he was made a series regular for the whole season."

Ryan's face and says, "Welcome to the O.C., bitch!" I think he could have served that role in the show longer. Even with us knowing more about him and making him more multidimensional. But we sent him packing.

Chris Carmack: I feel like Luke went from antagonist to silly real fast. Knowing what I know now, I would have slowed that down. I was happy to do it, but I get the sense, rewatching it, that it feels a little chaotic.

Merry Chrismukkah to All!

Among the show's most enduring concepts was popularizing the idea of interfaith families combining Christmas and Chanukah into the super-holiday known as Chrismukkah.

Josh Schwartz: We all love holidays in real life! Always loved holiday episodes of television shows growing up, like *Family Ties* or Festivus on *Seinfeld*. We couldn't get enough.

Stephanie Savage: We didn't have a franchise. So we realized that holidays could be a franchise if we did them all. That would give us five or six episodes a year that we knew what those were going to be.

Allan Heinberg: They were very assimilated, the Cohens. My family always celebrated both, but I don't think we called it Chrismukkah. We may have called it Chronickuh. It was something Lauren Gussis's family celebrated.

Lauren Gussis: Josh came into the room so excited: "I want an episode where Ryan has a candy cane and Seth has a menorah, and it's like a fight: menorah, candy cane, menorah, candy cane, menorah, candy cane." And I'm like, "Oh, it's Chrismukkah." The whole room stopped and looked at me. I was like, "I grew up in a neighborhood where we were one of four Jewish families. A little boy across the street told me that I killed Jesus when I was four years old, which is why we moved when I was nine. But all of our friends were Gentile. So I grew up celebrating Chrismukkah and also Eastover, but we're not there yet. That's a different part of the season." And Josh looked at the room and said, "Write me an episode about Chrismukkah." That was it. And then it became a cottage industry.

Stephanie Savage: Little did we know.

Josh Schwartz: Gotta trademark that shit.

Rachel Bilson: I thought it was a genius thing to call the holiday Chrismukkah. Even though my dad's Jewish, he loves Christmas. So we grew up with the tree on Christmas, because he loves it. But we'd still go to my grandpa's and have a Chanukah party. So I did both, but I always had a tree. So similar to the Cohens.

Adam Brody: I loved it. I loved getting to host it. I loved the blasphemy of it. I don't have much of a reverence for religion, and was so happy to mold it into any fashion that will create joy and harmony. I grew up in a Jewish household, and was bar mitzvah'd and went to Hebrew school, 100 percent against my will. But I also knew very few Jews growing up. So I thought it was very nice to be able to celebrate both Hanukkah and then also the fun of Christmas. For Jewish kids, I don't think it had the same impact as, say, Adam Sandler's "Chanukah Song," but it did the same popularizing in a fun way, that custom and culture.

Among the episode's memorable bits of business: Seth boasts that he has gotten everyone a "Seth Cohen Starter Pack," containing Michael Chabon's novel *The Amazing Adventures of Kavalier & Clay*, a *Goonies* DVD, and CDs by Bright Eyes, the Shins, and Death Cab for Cutie.

Josh Schwartz: The Seth Cohen Starter Packs, we spent a lot of time discussing what would go in those.

Stephanie Savage: Josh was definitely the arbiter of the stuff. He curated the Starter Pack.

Josh Schwartz: A little bit of all of us is in that bag, I would say.

"The Best Chrismukkah Ever" would be Stephanie Savage's first produced script of any kind.

Stephanie Savage: One of the critiques that Josh had of the script was, "You made Seth too smart, and too literate and articulate." And I was like, "What are you talking about? Seth's, like, supersmart?" And he's like, "No, he's not a *smart* nerd. He's just likes comics and indie music, and that's different." It helped me understand Seth in a different way, that he was just a man of particular passions, versus someone who was up in his head.

This is also the episode where the Summer-Seth-Anna triangle really heats up, as Anna draws Seth a comic book to impress him, while Summer dresses up like Wonder Woman.

Stephanie Savage: We told Rachel after Tijuana that she wouldn't have to wear bikinis anymore. Wonder Woman was a lot of clothing compared to some of the other outfits she had to wear, like when she was in a bikini flipping burgers on the grill.

Rachel Bilson: My reaction is, *I'm five foot two. How the hell am I going to pull this off?* And I still feel that way to this day. They put me in a real Wonder Woman costume. To my recollection, Warner Bros. had a real Wonder Woman costume from the Lynda Carter show. I put it on, and I put on a ton of hair. There was, like, ten pounds of hair on my head. I didn't feel like, *Oh, I look good.* I felt like, *I look ridiculous.*

Everybody Hates Oliver

The Chrismukkah episode's final scene introduced another Season One villain: Oliver Trask (played by Taylor Handley), a wealthy, mentally unstable pathological liar who becomes fixated on Marissa and begins plotting to steal her away from Ryan. He would prove to be the most divisive element of a season that otherwise seemed to be universally loved by its audience.

Stephanie Savage: The biggest problem with Oliver was he was in too many episodes, and we introduced his character too soon. The idea was, Marissa is healing herself and taking some onus off of Ryan. And as she's healing herself, she's also finding this kid who in her mind is also healing himself and has lots of insight into self-help and psychology. In fact, he's already probably a sociopath that no therapist can help, but she has no idea what's going on with him. He's like Emily Valentine from *90210*.*

Yvette Urbina: I remember thinking, *People are going to be mad.* I don't think we were all in agreement about that character.

Stephanie Savage: He's someone who comes in from the outside and is on a different wavelength than the kids in the show and creates trouble by being reckless, putting them into dangerous situations, fucking with their relationships with each other. And that's what he gets off on. And introducing this character, I think, *That's a good character.* I don't think, *That character doesn't belong on* The O.C.

Patrick Rush: You were supposed to hate him. So the fact that people hated him so strongly, he did exactly what he was supposed to do.

---

* The first serious girlfriend of Jason Priestley's character, whose initial arc ended in a high school *Fatal Attraction*, closely followed by in-patient mental health treatment.

Stephanie Savage: I think that when our episode order got extended, we were like, "Well, we'll just burn these off in Oliver episodes." It was too many episodes.

A big problem, the producers only realized after the fact, was that the audience learned that Oliver was not to be trusted well before Marissa and the others did.

Stephanie Savage: Nobody knew that Oliver was bad, then Ryan knew Oliver was bad, but no one will believe him. But it took too long for the truth about Oliver to land on our characters. And I think that was a very frustrating story for the audience.

Josh Schwartz: But I will say, as much as people complained or hate it or shook their fists at Oliver, that's when the ratings for the show really started to go up.

Yvette Urbina: To this day, I remember the vitriol I was feeling from [television reporter] Michael Ausiello. He came up to me at a TCA* party, and it was like I had personally attacked him. Michael was so upset, and I don't even know him, really. I was like, *What's happening right now?*†

Josh Schwartz: People were watching those episodes. They were talking about those episodes. They were screaming about those episodes. There was a lot of controversy and conversation around those episodes. I know it was frustrating. I think a lot of people just wanted Ryan and Marissa to be happy. And now there was this guy, and it

---

* The Television Critics Association press tour is a twice-annual event where TV critics and reporters spend a few weeks interviewing and mingling with stars and creators of TV shows.

† Reached for comment, Ausiello not only did not recall the conversation, but said he had to Google "Oliver from *The O.C.*" to remind himself what that subplot was about.

was so obvious to the audience that Ryan was right. So it's really frustrating for the audience that no one would believe him. It even started to hurt his relationship with Seth, because Seth didn't believe him for a little bit. That's just a tricky way to tell that story. But it did juice the show in a very successful way, from a ratings standpoint.

Stephanie Savage: And it did give us those marketable moments that were still character-driven, like Oliver saying, "Stupid! Stupid! Stupid!" and breaking plates. That can be in a trailer where you can be like, "I wonder what's going on in that story?" in a way that Seth playing with a plastic horse is maybe not going to drive viewership to the next episode.

When You Realize You Want to Spend the Rest of Your Life with Somebody, You Want the Rest of Your Life to Start as Soon as Possible.

The first full Oliver episode ("The Countdown") does, however, feature one of the grander moments of Ryan and Marissa's entire relationship. Earlier in the hour, Marissa says "I love you" to Ryan for the first time; a stunned Ryan can only stammer out, "Thank you?"

Josh Schwartz: I guess [that same exchange] was in an episode of *Friends*, but I was not aware that that same thing happened. After it aired, Allan was like, "Oh yeah, I thought you knew that." And I was like, "No, I didn't know that! If I'd known that, I would have been like, 'Why are we doing the thing from *Friends*?'"

Ryan's fumbling of this crucial boyfriend moment is made worse by Marissa's newfound closeness with Oliver, who invites them both to a New Year's Eve party in his hotel suite. Ryan and Seth instead wind up locked inside the pool house so they can't shut down the rager Hailey is throwing at the McMansion, making it out with barely enough time to get to Marissa before the clock turns twelve and she has the opportunity to kiss someone else. As Finley Quaye & William Orbit's "Dice" blasts on the soundtrack, Ryan has to run up the hotel staircase to get to her before midnight, arriving with seconds to spare so he can return those three big words and kiss her.

Josh Schwartz: That was very much inspired by all the great rom-coms ending with someone running. Like, in *When Harry Met Sally*, he's literally running to get to her on New Year's Eve. That was a big inspiration, and *Jerry Maguire*, just lots of great movies where people are running in slow motion to get to someone. Not always at midnight, but nonetheless.

Norman Buckley: That was something that Josh wrote into the script, and we built the whole episode to that crescendo.

Stephanie Savage: I think that was a pretty unusual thing to do in a network television show—to build a sequence like that. We were already doing some things with music and montages that were unique, but we were like, "We're really not fucking around. It seriously needs to be in slow motion. We need to have lots to cut together. We need Ryan going around the corner, going up the stairs, door push, hand on door, door opening, all of it." To really get all those pieces and build it. A sequence where like you just see Ryan running, that wasn't going to cut it.

Josh Schwartz: Maximum romantic angst.

Though Ben McKenzie was in great shape, the magic of TV production made the task easier on him than it was on Ryan.

Josh Schwartz: He was running up the same four stairs, over and over again, in the writers' room stairwell.

You Know Who Sings This Song? Rooney!

Oliver is also responsible for the series' first big music-driven episode, when he invites the gang to come watch a show by the up-and-coming band Rooney.

Stephanie Savage: It was going to be a camping trip. And the script didn't really come in in great shape. And when we read it, we're like, "It's too early for a camping trip. They're in tents? And they're like making s'mores? Where are we going to shoot this? And it's going to be all nighttime exteriors?"

Josh Schwartz: So concerts. We like concerts!

Stephanie Savage: We called [music supervisor] Alex Patsavas. We were shooting it in ten days, and we asked, "Who can we get who's in town who would like to be on our television show?"

Alexandra Patsavas (music supervisor): I had a very panicked week on an actual telephone that was sitting on my desk. We didn't have a budget to fly bands in, so we focused on who was either in L.A. or touring through L.A. But Rooney's label was excited to fly them.

Josh Schwartz: They toured with the Strokes. They were a band with a lot of heat.*

While Rooney's performance of their hit "I'm Shakin'" felt very much of a piece with the show's soundtrack to that point, it was hard not to notice the frequency with which the band kept getting name-checked throughout the episode.

---

* Rooney was also an "all in the family" situation: their front man, Robert Schwartzman, was the brother of former Phantom Planet drummer Jason Schwartzman, who had co-written "California."

Josh Schwartz: Maybe because we had written the script so quickly, we didn't realize how many times people were saying "Rooney."

Stephanie Savage: If you have to write your script the day before production, you just make every eighth word "Rooney," and the script fills up with words, and you just shoot it [laughs].

Luke in particular takes quite the personal journey over the course of the episode, from being completely ignorant of the band ("Which one's Rooney?" he asks an amused Seth) to screaming their name over and over as they slay Newport Beach.

Chris Carmack: I am a music person, but in all truth, no, I had not heard of them. McG, if you've spoken to him is a very, very enthusiastic guy. So when you have somebody like McG excited about something, it's like, "GUYS! You won't BELIEVE what's happened: ROONEY IS GONNA BE HERE!" He's playing all the songs for you. The enthusiasm with which they were presented to us was unmatched.

The success of filming a fake Rooney concert emboldened the show to feature more live music going forward, and made the management of every indie rock act in the country eager to get their bands a similar spotlight.

Alexandra Patsavas: What a love letter to that band! So of course after that, every label and publisher was like, "We'd like to have a Rooney episode." But there was only one Rooney episode.

Welcome to *The Valley*?

Josh Schwartz's sense of humor became even more palpable after the summer episodes, particularly his love of comedy in which the characters comment on the nature of being characters on a prime-time soap opera.

Adam Brody: In many ways I think of the show so much more—my character in particular—as a comedy than a drama.

Allan Heinberg: It was 100 percent Josh to go meta and have the characters on the show be self-aware enough to comment on what was going on. I remember being the guy who was saying, "Are you sure?" And it became one of the most charming aspects of the show. That was an organic process where I got to watch and enjoy Josh becoming himself on the page and putting all of it right there in the show. Which gave the rest of us permission to do that, too.

Matt Ramsey: Somebody wrote an article about *The O.C.* and they mentioned the sarcasm and the irony in the editing. And I was like, *Oh, my God, they're getting it.*

Josh Schwartz: The meanest review was Tom Shales in the *Washington Post*. It just eviscerated me personally—talking about my age and how apparently, I couldn't sell out fast enough. It was rough. So then when Summer was working as a candy striper at the hospital, Tom Shales is one of her patients, and he's incontinent.

Stephanie Savage: By the way, a lot of the things that hard-core fans and people on message boards were not liking, such as Oliver, were the breakout stories that were making the show pop out in the [Nielsen] Top 20, which is very, very hard to do. For a Season One show on Fox to burst through into that is very tough, and that happened in a period where fan discontent was percolating, but those were the stories that were making the show pop and go bigger.

Josh Schwartz: So there is a moment where we sync up. There are places where we start writing some of the stuff into the show. The show starts to get more self-aware or deconstruct itself based on what people are saying about the show, I start to make the awful discovery of Television Without Pity and reading recaps and comments on the show.*

Stephanie Savage: It escalated pretty fast. Then we started pushing it with pop culture references to Lindsay Lohan or things that Summer was reading in *Us*, and they all got through. That emboldened us to keep doing that, because it was so fun and people weren't really doing that at the time.† And one of the fun things about TV and how fast it moves is something can be in the zeitgeist, and you can write it into a script, you can shoot the script, and it can be on TV in three weeks.

As a running gag, we find out that Summer's favorite TV show is a teen drama called *The Valley*, which sounds an awful lot like the one in which she herself appears. Eventually, it went from background humor to the subject of an entire episode, "The L.A.," where the gang heads to Los Angeles to go clubbing with actors from *The Valley*. There was an obvious choice to play *Valley* star Grady Bridges, that show's equivalent of Adam Brody.

Josh Schwartz: Colin Hanks was in *Orange County*, and was Brody-esque. It was, "Okay, we have this young actor, who's like a Brody on *The Valley*," because they each had their own counterparts. And it was *Orange County* coming onto our show. It was so meta, your head was gonna explode—like a hat on a hat on a hat. We knew Colin, and he was very game.

Colin Hanks: Josh reached out to me and said, "We're poking fun at ourselves here." I had already been on The WB [in *Roswell*], so I

---

* Put a pin in this particular Schwartz obsession until we get to Season Two.

† Sometimes, the writers realized they were taking things too far, like a Sandy rant against the People's Choice Awards, inspired by the cast being ordered to attend the awards that year, only to lose to *Joan of Arcadia*, which, like so many of that night's winners, aired on People's Choice network CBS. It was cut when everybody realized this would not be a topic Sandy Cohen cared about.

was not wanting to really be in that world. But definitely I would love to poke fun.

Hanks had not really watched the show to this point, and as a result received a startling introduction to it.

Colin Hanks: The first day I report to set and the set PA is getting me settled in, he just said, "Welcome to *The O.C.*, bitch." And I did not know that reference. I instantly was like, "What was that?" And he was like, "Oh, it's a line from the show." I remember wanting to say, "Hey, don't do that. That's not a good look on you. Not everyone's going to know that." Like, what the fuck?

Hanks was not the episode's only prominent guest star.

Josh Schwartz: We landed Paris Hilton, and then the joke was, "What if Paris Hilton was really into magical realism?" She was writing her dissertation on Pynchon.

Stephanie Savage: Allan Heinberg pitched that, because that's what David Duchovny wrote his dissertation on.

Josh Schwartz: Paris was very nice and very game, but instead of "magical realism," she kept saying "magnetic reality."

Colin Hanks: I actually know her. Our paths crossed many times before, when we were young kids. And then it was very scene-y. The marker when I knew that I was really out of place is when I saw that we were at the same place, where it's like, *I don't know if this is me punching above my weight class.*

Though Grady Bridges would occasionally be heard on Summer's television in later episodes, this was the character's only on camera appearance. But not for Colin Hanks's lack of trying.

Colin Hanks: I talked with Adam about this, and I think I pitched Josh as well. I said, "What you should do is what *South Park* did their first year: have an episode be on April Fools' and come up with a trailer for it. And then not have an episode of *The O.C.* and just broadcast an episode of *The Valley*." There's no way on earth that would ever happen, but I thought it would be so hilarious if they did something like that.

Having done his own time on a teen soap, Hanks came away impressed by this one's atmosphere.

Colin Hanks: I remember going in and thinking, *So do they all hate each other yet?* That can come off in such a bad way, but I don't really mean it that way. The reality of being on any show is very, very different from what you assume them to be. The grind of doing an episodic show is enough to drive anyone insane. Then you add into the fact that it's a hit and you need twenty-seven episodes for a first season? You spend more time with your castmates than you do with your family. But I remember everyone being great. My job was to try and play to the vibe of the room. And luckily, the vibe was great. Everybody was just happy to be there.

Viva Las Vegas

The season's later episodes included a visit from Seth's grandmother, played by Linda Lavin and referred to by all (like Schwartz's grandmother) as "the nana,"* along with a guys' trip to Las Vegas for Caleb's bachelor party. The latter was filmed on location.

Josh Schwartz: We went out in advance and we did a scout at the

---

* "The Nana" also gave Schwartz a chance to do another holiday episode: "I loved the idea that we had the two hottest pinup teen icons on television in that moment wearing yarmulkes and celebrating Passover. I felt very good about that."

Hard Rock to figure out where we could set up and where we could shoot stuff. And they were going to let us have access to the penthouse with the bowling alley. That was a win. When we were shooting in Vegas, somebody had a *USA Today* lying around, open to the ratings, and that was the first time we had made it into the Top 20. And growing up, if you're in *USA Today*, forget it—you've made it.

Taking production on the road for the first time provided another way to gauge how deeply the show had penetrated the public consciousness.

Yvette Urbina: When you go to another city, you can see it—just people stopping and staring wherever you go. I was overwhelmed by it—the chaos of it all. People were really going nuts, and you started to feel that everywhere we were.

Lisa Cochran: We shot at the registration desk. I couldn't believe it. In a working casino! At working tables! We stayed there, we ate there. And then we were on the Strip as well. Everyone thought it was going to be a piece of cake, but for production, it was hard to nail when we could navigate and move from the registration desk to the gaming floor. Or when we could be out front when the limousine pulls up, with a crane so that we could see the guitar and the name of the hotel. And then as a UPM, you hope that your crew behaves: *They're in Vegas, for God's sake.* There was one person who didn't [behave], and probably had an incredibly extensive hangover for days, but did not get in trouble.

Josh Schwartz: I had a companion ticket, and I brought Bret [Harrison, Adam Brody's friend and bandmate, and once and future *O.C.* guest star*] as my companion. I don't believe he had ever been to Vegas, and he had definitely never gambled or played blackjack before. I remember leaving him at one point to go to the set, and finding him two days later having *not* gotten up from the blackjack table. I

---

* Harrison returns in a new role, as spring break emcee Swerve, in Season Two's Miami episode.

don't know how much money he lost over the course of that forty-eight hours, but he got very into blackjack very quickly.

Schwartz would end up personally rewarded for indulging Rachel Bilson's desire to be written into the Vegas half of the episode.

Josh Schwartz: I had met Rachel's friend from high school named Jill over Christmas break one night at, I think, a Pussycat Dolls show at the Viper Room. And then she went back to college. We're shooting the Vegas episode, and I overheard Rachel telling Ben that she had a friend that she wanted to set Ben up with when she got back from college. And I said, "Wait a minute, is this Jill, the one that I met? Why are you setting up *the actor*? He's the lead of a television show! What about the writer?" And I did not know that at the time, Rachel had been talking to Jill about that, and Jill was like, "Ben, is that the actor? What about the writer guy?" So that's what I'll tell my kids: "That's how I met your mother."

The Chino Undertow

Ryan's late season arc involved Theresa Diaz, his former flame from Chino, who had been introduced in the Thanksgiving episode.

Patrick Rush: It was a time in which we were like, "We need to introduce some sort of diversity on the show." At the time, twenty years ago, when that wasn't [considered] as important.

Though the original *Newport Beach* pitch involved an interracial romance, the final product had turned out to be extremely beige.

Samaire Armstrong: How blatantly white was [Ryan]? Like, nobody's ever addressed that. The down and out, totally cookie-cutter white kid. What?

Patrick Rush: I think the goal was to possibly find someone Latin.

The character remained Latin, but the role went to Navi Rawat, whose background is Indian on her father's side and German on her mother's, and who was treated as variably ethnic by casting directors at that stage of her career.

> **Navi Rawat (Theresa Diaz):** At the time, it was like a lot of the parts that I auditioned for. It was me and all sorts of actresses. I think for this part, they just wanted somebody who maybe even resembled [being Latin]. It wasn't like how it is today.

> **Patrick Rush:** I think Navi brought an interesting, different diversity to it. Less stereotype-y to me.

> **Navi Rawat:** Today, I went in to read for something for a casting director who's actually cast me before. That [character] was Native American, and I'm Indian, and he just screamed at me. But back then, it wasn't something I thought of. I was just grateful to have a job, to be honest with you. *The O.C.* is one of the only shows that I was on that I started watching. I was having fun watching it.

Rawat would wind up appearing in thirteen episodes across the first three seasons.

> **Navi Rawat:** People always want to hear horror stories from *The O.C.*, because it was a dramatic, soap opera show. And I just don't have negative things to say about the show. I really loved working with Ben. There were a couple of times where there was some sexual stuff we had to do, and he would always be at ease and make me feel comfortable and just really protected me and had my back. I actually met Mischa on another show right before; she was finishing guest-starring on *Fastlane*. I was coming to a table read, and I remember seeing her and her mom and being awestruck by what a beautiful young girl she was. And then when I came to work with her, I got to know her and her mother quite well, because her mother was a constant presence. I really loved her. I felt like a

protective big sister over her. And that was our dynamic through-out our relationship. We used to go for dinners together sometimes and shopping and stuff, and she was just a sweet, young, beautiful, beautiful girl.

Theresa temporarily moves in with the Cohens to escape an abusive relationship with her boyfriend Eddie, played by guest star Eric Balfour. She and Ryan briefly become an item again, and he later finds out that she's pregnant.

Josh Schwartz: The end of Season One was not going to be a pregnancy story. It was going to be an Eddie story: Eddie was abusive to Theresa, and Ryan was going to go and take matters into his own hands, and end up in a lot of legal jeopardy, which was going to pull Sandy back into that story. It was like a precursor to the Trey story that we ended up doing in Season Two, but not involving Marissa.

There was just one problem with the initial pitch: Eric Balfour didn't want to do it.

Josh Schwartz: I think Eric had issues with the character. He wasn't comfortable doing some of the things that that character was going to do. That had upset him too much. He didn't want to play someone who was abusive in that way.

Patrick Rush: We needed him to come back for a couple more episodes and he was in Hawaii, and he [didn't want to] come back.

The Grand Finale

The Season One finale, "The Ties That Bind," does not lack for major incident. Julie and Caleb get married, and Caleb blackmails Marissa into living with them instead of Jimmy. Ryan decides to move back to Chino to take responsibility for Theresa and what he thinks is his child. And Seth, horrified at the thought of a life in Newport without Ryan by his side, hops on *The Summer Breeze* to finally make that trip to Tahiti. It all concludes with a tearful montage set to Jeff Buckley's cover of Leonard Cohen's "Hallelujah," back in the days before it became one of Hollywood's most overused soundtrack cuts.

Josh Schwartz: Marissa was this princess trapped in the palace tower, all alone and drinking again. Summer's love was not enough to offset for Seth what life was going to be like without Ryan. Everybody is pulled apart at the end of the episode. For a show that was pulling itself apart multiple times, how else could we end but simply deconstructing the show? "Hallelujah" was the song that my uncle played to give him solace when he was really sick. And so that felt like a natural way to bring it back.*

Rachel Bilson: I felt like [Seth] was a little bitch on the boat! That's how I felt. Who does that? He leaves because Ryan leaves, but he has a girl. It's very bizarre. Honestly, it's bringing back things. I remember watching it and I'm like, *Really??* . . . There's a little Summer in me.

Josh Schwartz: We were shooting the finale down in Malibu. I was staring at the water, and I had this real sense of, *This will never happen again. When this season ends and everybody goes away, it's going to close the chapter on this particular experience.* Even though there were more years to come, it felt like the end of something when we got through Season One. And the show was never the same after that, in terms of how everybody approached it. It was a rocket ship, and then it was a job.

---

* Buckley's version had already been featured near the end of "The Model Home."

CHAPTER 6

The Sequel Season

THE CONCEPT OF the sophomore slump is one of those clichés born out of truth. Novelists and musicians often pour a lifetime of thoughts into their first books or albums, then struggle to come up with new material in a much shorter time frame the second time around. *The O.C.* producers had just hurled every idea they had into the initial twenty-seven episodes. Now they were being asked to do it again, all while trying to incorporate new characters, dealing with a less enthusiastic vibe on set, and being placed under much heavier pressure to deliver ratings for Fox. The season features a lot of ideas that tried and failed, particularly in its first half. But it also features some of the most memorable *O.C.* images and scenes ever, climaxing in perhaps the definitive moment for the whole series.

The Storm Before the Storm

The Season Two drama began before Season One had even finished airing, as Fox and Warner Bros. became eager to strike again while the franchise was hot.

Josh Schwartz (creator/executive producer): Everybody wanted me to write a spin-off of the show. I didn't want to write a spin-off. And everybody's all about, "Anna goes to Pittsburgh, do that show."

Stephanie Savage (executive producer): There was pressure on Josh to write a spin-off. We were in the Endeavor conference room and Ari Emmanuel was acting out throwing suitcases of money out a window, because we were throwing money away. What Fox really wanted was to peel off a character from *The O.C.*, whether it was Summer moves to Los Angeles and goes to fashion design school, or Anna's in Pittsburgh. Even Anna in Pittsburgh, I think would have been a bit of a compromise for them. And we didn't want to tear the show apart.

Josh Schwartz: We were doing that well enough on our own.

Gail Berman (president, Fox): I'm sure Josh was overwhelmed by it and wanted to please, because he was wonderful in that way.

Schwartz attempted to appease his network bosses in another way.

Josh Schwartz: I had this other idea for a show, and it never fully came together. It was a very different show, but it would be a spiritual companion to *The O.C.*

Stephanie Savage: Fox says, "Oh, by the way, can you also write something else that's going to be a new show that we are going to announce at upfronts?"

Josh Schwartz: They had me record a video for the upfronts in 2004 pitching this new show. It was on the schedule!

Usually, the networks' upfront presentations involve screening sizzle reels of their upcoming series. Not so much in this case.

Stephanie Savage: They didn't have anything to show. It was Josh describing the show in an interview that was on a giant screen.

Josh Schwartz: It was called *Athens*. It was set at a college in New England, and it was the story of this fuckup young professor, and his relationship with this troubled kid, and about the kids that kid falls in with. It definitely had a lot of *O.C.* elements to it. I grew up near Brown and I took Stephanie on a tour of Providence and the town around Brown on Thayer

Street. This is such a cool world. There's indie record stores and thrift shops and art house movie theaters. And everybody at the network was, like, "Could it be a mall?" It was a bit too indie for its own good, I guess.

Craig Erwich (programming executive, Fox): There was also a whole behind-the-scenes fight with Warner Bros. the night before the upfront over the license fee on *The O.C.* and whether we were going to actually announce *Athens* or not. And we had a show called *Point Pleasant* that we probably should have announced, because that was actually a show.* In those days at upfronts, you had to have news, and you had to have some heat. So we announced that, and then it just never really came together.

Bob DeLaurentis (executive producer): There was a lot of enthusiasm from Peter Roth about doing this. And look, Peter has his job to do. I don't want to make him the bad guy, or McG. Their organic sympathy was for, "Yeah, let's do another show." And I pointed out that, to my knowledge, no one has ever developed a spin-off after a Season One. I just wanted to bring it back to reality. This would be an enormous and potentially disastrous undertaking for the show we're doing. And pilots are hard to write even under the best of circumstances.

Coming off the endurance marathon of Season One, these were not the best of circumstances.

Yvette Urbina (programming executive, Fox): They really wanted another show from him. They were taking a lot of his time, and it was stressful for everybody.

Josh Schwartz: The idea that I was going to do twenty-seven episodes of a first-year show, have a three-week hiatus before embarking on another season of the show, and use that time to write and potentially launch another show—I feel like someone should have

---

* *Point Pleasant*—in which the Antichrist, in the form of a teenage girl, washes up on the beach of a Jersey Shore town—was canceled after eight episodes aired on Fox.

intervened and been like, "We cannot do that to this person." But I was a people pleaser and I was ambitious and I wanted to do it. I stumbled into Season Two with my head still in this other script that I never fully figured out, and I was trying to work on that and get that to work while the Season Two ship was sailing.

Schwartz wasn't the only producer whose focus was being split.

Josh Schwartz: The other thing that was tricky was The WB had a pilot that was in trouble called *The Mountain*. They brought McG and Stephanie on to do that. Stephanie rewrote the pilot, got the show ordered, went to the upfronts that year, and it was like, "From the producers of *The O.C.* comes *The Mountain!*" And then they made Steph the co-showrunner of that show. So she was gone. We're coming off this incredibly insane first season. I'm trying to get another show off the ground in the three-week window I have. Stephanie's gone, and Allan was eventually going to depart, and that was a big stress test to put on the show. And I think I was resentful, feeling like we should all be rowing together.

Stephanie Savage: I barely survived. I would say physically, there were lots of nights where I didn't sleep at all. I had all my Wonderland responsibilities, I had my *Mountain* responsibilities, I had my *O.C.* responsibilities, I had my *O.C.* companion piece responsibilities. I would just work through the night, have a shower, and then go to my office. I drank so much coffee, it couldn't be measured, and knew that at some point I might have a nervous breakdown.

Allan Heinberg (writer/producer): I probably should have just been hospitalized at the end of Season One.* And if I should have, then you can only imagine Josh's state.

---

* Heinberg would depart the series partway through Season Two. "I was burnt out," he says. "I think I hadn't had a day off in three years. I just decided at a certain point for my own health to be a consultant for the rest of the season. And not be the guy in the writers' room, continuing to try to pull the show in a new and different direction."

Josh Schwartz: Finally, I had to go to everybody at Fox and at Warner Bros. and just say, "I can't do this. I can't figure out this script. It's not working, and I'm not invested in [The O.C.] in the way that I need to be, because I'm so worried about getting this other show off the ground."

Craig Erwich: We dropped it because it was a show whose purpose was to fulfill the needs of an upfront announcement, not some creative vision that Josh wanted to fulfill for himself or his fans.

The Big Move

The second half of Season One had aired after the *American Idol* results show, at a moment when *Idol* was the Death Star, obliterating the rest of prime time.

Preston Beckman (head of scheduling, Fox): I did not want to put it on after *American Idol*. I had wanted to put it on Thursday at eight immediately. There was a lot of "Wow, it's going to be a big hit now. We'll put it on after *Idol*," and I made a lot of arguments against it. The number one argument was it was too white. If we looked at the audience makeup of *American Idol*, part of its success was a larger than average Black viewership. So I wanted to keep *The Bernie Mac Show* there.

It was an incredibly safe and lucrative timeslot, and one that went away quickly when Fox decided to launch Season Two on Thursdays at eight to compete with NBC, which was trying to keep its Must See TV bloc going without *Friends*.

Gail Berman: We had nothing going on Thursday. We needed to do something. There's research that tells you this is a good move and . . . [*long pause*] I regret it.

Preston Beckman: NBC owned Thursday, eight o'clock. *Friends* was going away. I wasn't afraid of [*Friends* spin-off] *Joey*. It's like, "This is not the Must See TV lineup anymore. Let's just establish a young appeal show at eight on Thursday that's hot at the moment. And let's see what we can do. From an advertiser point of view, it's a good night to put your punch up."

Gail Berman: [Warner Bros. was] furious. *Furious.* I was at a hotel. I was supposed to join my family for dinner. I never left the hotel room. I was being reamed by those guys. It was a tough evening.

Stephanie Savage: They were promoting the show at the start of Season Two when they moved us to Thursday night as *Friends* had just ended—basically, "These are your new friends." I forget what the exact tagline was.

Josh Schwartz: When we were behind *American Idol*, we got a nice boost and cracked the Top 20. But I don't think we had any illusions that we were *Friends*.

Stephanie Savage: My sense was terror and a pit in my stomach thinking, *The show is not built to be* Friends.

Preston Beckman had run NBC's scheduling at the peak of the Must See TV era, before moving on to Fox.

Josh Schwartz: It really hurt our ratings. The response was basically, "Yeah, but we really killed NBC." So Preston may have been operating out of a vengeance fight.

Preston Beckman: I think they were already running out of steam. It came up with a couple of cultural icons, like Chrismukkah. But at the end of the day, it wasn't a mystery and there was nothing really going on—kids getting high and fucking each other.

Josh Schwartz: We're moving the show to Thursdays, so there's more pressure on the show than ever before. The fact that we survived, and that Season Two had some real highlights, is a minor miracle.

Vibe Shift?

Despite the grueling schedule—or perhaps because of it—the cast and crew were incredibly tight throughout the first season. All oars were rowing in the same direction. Nobody turned into a diva when everyone reported for work in Season Two, but there was a palpable change, starting with a decrease in group activities away from set.

Ben McKenzie (Ryan Atwood): Initially, we were all a part of this clique. We were all hanging out together and we'd go out together and Josh would go out with us. It was really fun and we were able to have a sense of a shared experience. But eventually, reality sets in and it becomes more of a job, albeit a wonderful job. And people get different interests and different relationships. So it was pretty tight, and then over time, it became more differentiated and individualized.

Gail Berman: There's a camaraderie. Everyone is experiencing something for the first time during the first season, and the show takes off and this one gets a publicist, and this one's agent decides to change, and they go to this agency. The desire to keep that team spirit is invaded by a lot of external forces: who's on the cover of what magazine and other things. Partying, things that weren't necessarily available to unknown young people—who are now known young people. I've had it happen in many things I've been involved in.

Josh Schwartz: I think it was a slower roll over the course of the season. Because there are still a lot of those episodes in Season Two where I feel like everyone's really invested, performance-wise. But there were definitely some bumps as we got near the end of Season Two—some grumbling about some storylines, or feeling like we're moving too quickly through some storylines.

Peter Gallagher (Sandy Cohen): I remember it generally as a period of change and conflict. And I think in the back of my mind, I was half waiting to read the episode where some criminal from Sandy's past puts three quick ones in the back of his head. You never know what's going to happen. "The ratings are dipping. We've got to kill Cohen!"

Melinda Clarke (Julie Cooper-Nichol): It will happen to so many people. Look at David Caruso. But when you're being told by your representatives that you're getting offered this movie and this movie and that movie and you're not available because of that show, you're missing out. So it's easy at a young age to become resentful of the thing that's actually helping you get there.

Bob DeLaurentis: Everybody changed in Season Two. All the kids changed, the adults changed. When you're on a bona fide hit and you've been anointed, you come back with a new attitude, about money, how much you're being paid. With the possible exceptions of Rachel and Melinda, who were rock solid.*

New recurring players Shannon Lucio and Michael Cassidy hadn't been there for the one-for-all, all-for-one atmosphere of Season One, but they could feel the tension bubbling up.

Shannon Lucio (Lindsay Gardner): I do recall that there was some grumbling. There were moments of discontent about the storylines, and also how certain characters weren't in the show as much anymore, while these newer characters that people didn't love—and weren't there to watch—were getting more of the focus at that time. To be honest, as a person who now watches certain shows and loves them for the characters, I understand when audiences complain about that, and also being the actor who's like, "Wait a minute, it was us and the dynamic that we created that made this popular."

---

* It is important to note that, whenever the topic of behind-the-scenes drama from the later seasons came up, virtually everyone interviewed, other than Rachel Bilson and Melinda Clarke themselves, reflexively added some version of, "Well, except for Rachel," and/or "Except for Melinda." So whenever you read a quote in this book describing general ennui from veteran cast members, please mentally add, "Except for Rachel and Melinda. They were great."

Michael Cassidy (Zach Stevens): I'll never forget shooting a scene in a car with Adam and Ben. They're changing a shot, and they both pulled paper scripts out from under the seats. I was like, "Adam, are you reading?" And he's like, "*Ice Age 2*" or something. And Ben's like, "I'm reading this cop thing."

Bob DeLaurentis: Adam probably had the most difficult time in some ways with the ongoing nature of the show. I think he felt the most restricted in terms of his desire to be doing a certain kind of creative project.

Adam Brody (Seth Cohen): That bit of frustration happens almost instantly, especially in these old network shows that are filming nine and a half months a year. You want to capitalize on it. And it was tricky. Not that I can point to a lot of heartbreak or things necessarily. But there were some, and I'm sure there would have been perhaps more opportunity I'm not even aware of, because it never got that far, because it was an impossibility so early on.

Bob DeLaurentis: You could see it beginning in Season Two. He and I used to have a lot of conversations about movies, and that was clearly what his passion was. And you couldn't divorce that from the fact that he's not doing any movies because he's stuck in a television show that goes on longer than any television show in individual season. It's like you get your sentence at the beginning: "Here's your order! You're in it for the year, buddy." If you got a few weeks off at the end, maybe you can make something.

Michael Cassidy: At the time that I was on the show, and maybe into the third season, those guys were turning down stuff every day. They had to do ten months of the year on the show. And I think that that was very difficult for them, because they had all the opportunities, but it was all vapor. They could do one thing outside of the show per calendar year. But between the [two] of them, they probably turned down every huge movie over the course of those middle couple of years.

Adam Brody: But who knows? At the same time, I wasn't punching the wall, frustrated at all. I'm sure I was disappointed occasionally, but in hindsight, I don't care. It was not all that long. And [it was] enjoyable. And I don't know what I would have done with any of those opportunities anyway.

The cast was also being featured in the press more and more, in ways both positive and very, very negative.

Melinda Clarke: They put you in big headlines and break you down at the same time for being too thin or you put on some pounds, and they pick you apart and they follow you with paparazzi. I didn't experience any of that. So I would only imagine that the mental health conversation was a very real valid one based on what those girls were going through in the early 2000s.

Lisa Cochran (unit production manager): Season Two was a lot harder in a production scheduling manner, because now you have people who are being invited to go to New York to be in an interview, go here, go there. Now, the cast had invitations to be places.

Melinda Clarke: There's no Instagram. We didn't have any control over publicity. So you could choose to hire a publicist. And there's a Motorola party on Monday. There's the Kia party on Tuesday. And then there's a Warner Bros. thing at the Academy of Television Arts and Sciences that you have to go to. And all of these things happen Monday through Thursday, never on the weekends. And you have to know your lines. You have to be at work. You have to be a smart person and remember that it's a working thing. You're not going to be drinking. Well, maybe you drink too much and then you have to go to work at 6:00 a.m. Those are the lessons that you have to learn. I saw some pretty bedroom eyes sometimes first thing in the morning. I was like, "Wait a second, I left early. How late did you stay?" I learned that when I was younger, but it's really important to remember that those things are still work.

Josh Schwartz: The cast collectively turned down a "Got Milk?" ad that would have been the first cast to do a "Got Milk?" ad since . . . the first cast ever? They turned down the opportunity to do a Letterman Top Ten list. They would've been the first cast since *The Sopranos* to do a Letterman Top Ten List. I realize that to an audience today, a "Got Milk?" ad and a Letterman Top Ten list are lost to time. But they were big deals then. In Season One, everyone's doing what's in the best interest of the show, because what's best for the show is ultimately in the best interest of each individual person. And there's a mutually beneficial quality to it. When we got to Season Two, it was definitely much more about, "What's good for me?" There was a lot less shared publicity. There's a lot less doing covers together.

Reset the Board

Even if the actors had all been happy campers, there was still the matter of how many plot ideas the writers had already used up over the course of Season One, leaving them scrambling for new material for what would be a twenty-five-episode season.

Yvette Urbina: My God, we had burned so much story.

Gail Berman: You're producing so many episodes. This is not like it is now where it's eight episodes [in a season]. By the time we're finished with Season One, you've got four seasons of a Netflix show.

Allan Heinberg: There was a bit of a hangover going into Season Two, where it's like, "Okay, *now* how do we do that? And have a sustainable model that can take us through any number of seasons moving forward, so we're not burning through story quite as quickly? But we keep the audience as addicted as they were in Season One?"

Josh Schwartz: I think our approach with Season Two, wisely or unwisely, was to take a lot of the things that had worked in Season One and challenge them or invert them. *Can I turn things on their head? Have Ryan date someone who's closer in this position to him?*

Allan Heinberg: I think most of what we were up against was the audience's desire to have what they had in the first season.

J. J. Philbin (writer/producer): I think there was a feeling of, *We can't do what we did last year. We'll never be able to do it.* So we have to reapproach the way we tell stories. We were going to slow down stories and incorporate a little bit more of a *My So-Called Life* style attitude of just getting into what it's like to be kids this age—their struggles within their families and in their relationships and things like that. It was like trying to learn a little bit of a new language, but also give the audience what they had become accustomed to, which was big, splashy stories week after week. We were always trying to figure out that balance, and sometimes we would overcorrect in one direction or another.

The Season One finale had also dramatically rung several bells that the writers now had to clumsily un-ring, starting with Ryan's self-exile in Chino, which had already been a source of disagreement between Schwartz and Heinberg at the end of Season One.

Josh Schwartz: Allan was very passionate about the fact that Ryan's going to come back to Newport. He was like, "Why are we doing this?" He just had more experience breaking television than we did at the time, knowing that the Season Two hangover was coming. And we were like, "What are you talking about? Who cares, Mr. Doomsday? Why are you being so negative?" And then we were back in the room being like, "Oh yeah, I see what Allan was talking about now. How are we going to do this?"

Ultimately, the writers had Theresa, feeling guilty about Ryan's responsible but miserable new existence, fake a miscarriage so he would be willing to move back to Newport.

Josh Schwartz: We weren't going to do an abortion story. It just wasn't really something that the show had the language for—it wasn't the tone of the show.* It was not that we were antiabortion by any means. How to have it feel like Ryan wasn't abandoning Theresa? So we had this idea that she lost the baby. Or did she really lose the baby? Did she lie to Ryan? That was the trickiest story to navigate.

Stephanie Savage: And in the end, a weird story. But it served the purpose of getting Ryan back. How to get everybody back in the world was a huge thing.

Seth also had to return home—and from a different destination than the writers had intended when they had him set sail for Tahiti. Instead, he sells his boat and takes a bus to Portland to stay with Luke and his dad, until Ryan convinces him to go back to Newport with him.

Josh Schwartz: We were informed by many viewers that Seth would not survive making it to Tahiti on his own. And so figuring out where he could stop along the way and have that be Luke, that was a fun story.

Marissa, meanwhile, remains a princess trapped in Caleb and Julie's castle,† leading to the much talked-about—if polarizing—moment in the season premiere where Julie asks how she feels. Marissa flips over her pool chair and lets out a primal scream.

Josh Schwartz: I will take responsibility for that. I definitely wrote that. People remember it.

---

* The abandoned story from early in Season One about Nikki, the girl Luke slept with in the pilot, involved Nikki becoming pregnant, Luke ghosting her when it came time for an abortion, and Marissa taking her instead. At the time, Savage felt it would have been strange to give a relatively minor character "a bigger story than anybody else on the show had."

† "Caleb's house was [ex–football star] Brian Bosworth's house in Malibu," says Savage.

Stephanie Savage: It made it to being a meme.

Josh Schwartz: In the moment, I think some people may have found it not as dramatically effective as what we were going for—but maybe it was more the critics of the world. I think the younger audience really identified with it and remember it—just that feeling of frustration and alienation as a teenager, where there's really nothing you can say or do to express that rage except just let it out. And how shocking that would be for Julie, to see her daughter becoming almost animalistic. I have a vague memory of McG or somebody raising their eyebrows and being like, "Really? You want to do that?" But it was effective and it definitely told you where Marissa's headspace was. And Mischa was committed to it; she really went for it.

Stephanie Savage: It was like that moment in the Chrismukkah episode, when she and Ryan are fighting by the side of the road. In those more dark, weird indie moments, she was always just excellent.

Mischa Barton (Marissa Cooper): It was just easier for me to play. I didn't really like the more ditzy banter. I just had more fun with something I could sink my teeth into.

Josh Schwartz: She was always able to access that pain and that emotion. Her ability to cry on cue and do it over and over again was like staggering. It was her secret superpower.

Mischa Barton: There was a lot of real frustration in that scream, not really knowing how to play the bratty teenager. There was so much going on with the character, all of these different turns, which led to larger frustrations. So I felt I could just throw it into that scene.

Melinda Clarke: She did that in one take. When the camera cut to my face, I was thinking, *Oh, that was real*, because I thought she did a fabulous job.

Goodbye, Jimmy Cooper

Tate Donovan returned for the season's first seven episodes, but only to set up Jimmy's departure from Newport Beach.

Josh Schwartz: We had played through the Hailey storyline with Amanda Righetti, and I think we just got to a place where we weren't really sure what else we could do with Jimmy. Tate was a veteran actor and he was expensive and, as successful as the show was, it wasn't like we had unlimited money. We were still a network show. We still had a limited budget. $2.7 million per episode for the budget in 2003, which is about $4.5 million today.* It was a decision that was really heart-breaking. We didn't want to lose Tate; he was such a lovely performer and part of the ensemble and a friend to everyone. But we couldn't figure out enough storylines to justify making the financials work. It was a tough conversation. He took it as well as you could. But it sucked.

Melinda Clarke: I remember sitting watching a Season One episode with Josh once and it was a scene with Jimmy and Hailey. Josh shook his head and was like, "I don't know what to do anymore."

Peter Gallagher: I was sorry to see Tate go. My feeling was *God, the first season was so great. Why? If it ain't broke, don't fix it.* But I wasn't driving the bus. And I couldn't write a word.

Tate Donovan (Jimmy Cooper): I was looking to buy an apartment in New York. That was always my dream, and I was making good money, so this was the time. I was in Tompkins Square Park, and I got a phone call from Bob DeLaurentis, and he's like, "You're only going to be in the first seven episodes of the next season," and, "Now you're

---

* The biggest cable and streaming blockbusters of today can cost $20 million per episode or more, but even the broadcast network dramas of 2023 tend to cost at least $5 million per episode.

transitioning to being a director. I think it would be really good for you." And you try to spin it like it was like my idea. Anyway, I gave up my apartment search.

The New Kids on the Block

Donovan's exit was story-driven, but it had a financial advantage when it came to replacing some other characters who had been written out—and to deal with the fact that Season Two begins with the two main teen couples broken up.

Stephanie Savage: Anna left, Luke left, and Jimmy—honestly, with Jimmy Cooper no longer being a series regular, we had some money to hire some actors to repopulate our young world.

The new characters, all brought in as love interests for the returning cast, brought fresh blood into the show, but received mixed response from viewers.

Stephanie Savage: The actors came with a lot of enthusiasm and that made people excited to be there.

Allan Heinberg: The audience, they want the Core Four characters to be together. So the obstacles you have to invent to keep them from getting together have to be incredibly compelling. They have to be cast perfectly. Everything has to work as well, if not better than the Four Core characters. I feel like people loved Anna the most, and they were able to love Anna because [at the time], I don't know that they ever believed that Seth and Summer were going to get together. And then Seth and Summer get together. It became harder for every other character you invent to separate that.

Norman Buckley (editor/director): I feel like there was a nice balance in the first season between drama and comedy. And I feel like one of the mistakes they made was to try to bring in these subsidiary characters and introduce these other relationships that nobody gave a shit about. You have people wandering off with alternative partners. What everybody wanted to see was that Core Four together. And when they were together, the show worked, and when they weren't together, it did not work as well.

My So-Called New Girlfriend

Once Ryan returns to Newport, he begins to click with Lindsay, a fellow new kid from more modest means, and a brainy girl who just wants to focus on school.

Josh Schwartz: We were looking for our Claire Danes, *My So-Called Life* kind of character. And we thought, *Okay, we found this really nice actress, and she and Ryan have this sweet chemistry.* And she was a different girl than Marissa intentionally. No drama, bookish. She plays the oboe.

Shannon Lucio was hired to play Lindsay.

Patrick Rush (casting director): I got fired off *Everwood* for casting her on *The O.C.* There was some talk of me giving them all the good kids. I said, "You guys saw her and said she looked too much like Emily [VanCamp]!" And they fired me.

Shannon Lucio: I didn't really know anything about the show, other than it was very wildly successful. I wasn't really watching a lot of TV, so it wasn't a knock on the show. Then I was like, *Okay, well, I need to know what this world is about. Let me watch it.* And I got so addicted so fast. I took two episodes, and I was like, *What's going to happen with Marissa and Ryan?*

Josh Schwartz: One of the other challenges of Season Two was, how much can we continue to make the show primarily the story of Ryan as an outsider who is new to this world and who doesn't quite fit in? At a certain point, he is a part of the Cohen family. That outsider story is hard to keep alive. That was a struggle, because that was the primary archetype of Ryan's character, and the conflict of the show. With the introduction of Lindsay, we're telling a very different Ryan story.

Stephanie Savage: One of the premises of the show is that Ryan is really smart. And being in Newport and going to the Harbor School is an opportunity for him to have a future that he wouldn't have had without Sandy's intervention. Ryan being smart in school, those aren't really stories that we told in Season One. We wanted to touch that base and get into that world, and Lindsay was a good person to do that with him.

Josh Schwartz: The idea with Lindsay was Ryan had obviously been so tethered to Marissa's story and Theresa's story, and those were characters who brought a lot of melodrama into the show. So what if Ryan was with someone who came from a different show? Like, more from the *My So-Called Life* or the *Freaks and Geeks* or *Gilmore Girls* world. What if Ryan was just dating a sweet, smart girl who didn't have any of that drama?

At first, Shannon Lucio got a little too into character as Lindsay the stand-offish outsider, and didn't get to know her new costars.

Shannon Lucio: Ben really was the person who reached out and tried to get to know me and was really sweet and curious about me. He broke down whatever wall I was putting up. I felt more comfortable and like I belonged. I really enjoyed working with Ben. We had a good time off- and on-screen, and he was very committed to his work and being in the moment. He wasn't phoning it in or anything like that. So you really got to play when you were working with him.

Though the creative team liked Lucio's work, the character wasn't leaving a strong impression.

Allan Heinberg: Because we had burned through so many episodes, that's where we ended up coming up with . . . you know, I can't remember the character's name. I'm so sorry—Ryan's new girlfriend?

Norman Buckley: It felt like that whole storyline was just forgettable, because we had no investment in that character. And I feel like that's so often the problem. Having worked on a lot of these kinds of teen dramas, you can't deviate too far from the initial paradigm. It's fine to bring in the girl from Chino. That's a good storyline to tell, because it's directly related to where he comes from, and she gave a completely different vibe to the show. That was a successful storyline that had some emotional resonance, as opposed to putting Ryan with some random girl in class who's an egghead. That story just didn't go anywhere.

Struggling for Lindsay-specific stories, the writers hit on the idea of making her Caleb's illegitimate daughter, a secret even to Lindsay herself.

Josh Schwartz: It became, "How do we turn this into an *O.C.* story?" Gail Berman looked at me and Bob once and said, "It's not a complicated genre, guys." And she was right in a lot of ways. We made it extra complicated on ourselves. I think she would've been the first one to say "Just put everybody with everybody else." And then we would try to steer away from that, and outsmart ourselves into a corner.

After a few episodes of trying to bond with Caleb—and Caleb using her as another excuse to hate Ryan—Lindsay leaves town with her mom, becoming one of several recurring characters to exit roughly midway through that season.

Josh Schwartz: You would make a deal with actors for a certain number of episodes, maybe six, maybe thirteen. So we were at the end of those runs and feeling as if we wanted to get back to the core dynamics, and also had enough feedback from the audience to know they were pining to see the kids get back together again as well.

Shannon Lucio: No one told me this, but I thought it was because Josh and Stephanie were maybe reading that a lot of people didn't like the character, and didn't like Ryan being with her. There was a lot of Lindsay hate and [maybe] they felt like, *Okay, this is not working. We need to move on from this.* That was my egotistical fear about it all. I don't know what they would say about it. Maybe they always had those intentions, but considering they set her up to be the illegitimate daughter of Caleb, it seemed a little strange to me. But also it's like, where are you going to go? Is she just going to be a new fixture of the family, and Ryan's girlfriend, and then what? Where's the tension for him? Or they're going to break up and then it's going to be awkward because she's around all the time. So maybe there was no real graceful way for her to leave other than the way she did, which was like, "This is too much. I'm getting the hell out of here. I'm taking my oboe with me. Bye-bye!"

Seth, but Better?

Summer, meanwhile, begins dating Zach, star water polo player, handsome, friendly, and popular—but also a big lover of comic books.

Stephanie Savage: We talked about the idea of "the Prince of Newport Beach," who's like the JFK Jr. The guy who has it all, is athletic but smart, is going to go to USC or an Ivy League school, has great parents that are married to each other and not dysfunctional. And even Seth was like, "Damn, I can't hate this guy because he likes comics."

Michael Cassidy got the part.

Josh Schwartz: Michael Cassidy is an unbelievable force of life—one of the most positive people of all time.

Rachel Bilson: Michael Cassidy is one of my favorite humans on the planet. So much energy, such an awesome person. I was thrilled that he was who I was working with, because we were always laughing and having fun.

Michael Cassidy: I wasn't familiar with the show. I didn't know anybody who watched the show. We filmed for four months and then, two weeks before the season premiere aired, I remember Adam or Ben was like, "Are you ready for what's going to happen when this thing airs?" And I was like, "No, what do you mean?" "People are going to interact with you differently." And I was like, "Who? Like you?" And he was like, "No, strangers are going to know who you are, and they're still going to be a stranger to you."

The instant celebrity did not quite come, though, for Cassidy or any of the other newbies.

Michael Cassidy: When I was with those guys hanging out, I would see it happening to them. And in almost every case, even though I was standing there, it was still happening to them, but not me. We were satellites to that operation.

Zach was more easily integrated into the main group than the other additions.

Allan Heinberg: The audience is very savvy: "We know what you're doing. You're just inventing someone to separate Seth and Summer. So we're not going to invest, because we know Seth and Summer are going to get back together eventually." But Zach wasn't just conceived as a romantic foil for Seth. We wanted to invest in Seth and Zach's friendship, and that friendship was going to be at stake if Seth and Summer got back together. So it was very strategic that we not just bring in a handsome guy to fuck things up, but that had become emotionally complicated for Seth, who is essentially fucking Zach over by going after Summer.

This storyline is also where the writers begin to acknowledge that Seth Cohen is a massive narcissist who avoids being insufferable largely because he is played by the superhumanly charming Adam Brody.

Rachel Bilson (Summer Roberts): I've come to learn in life there are two versions of narcissists. There's the narcissist and then there's the nice narcissist. Seth falls under the nice narcissist, where you still love him. He's a good guy. He's just very self-involved. Let's give Brody credit where credit is due. Absolutely attribute that to some Brody-isms.

Michael Cassidy: By the time I was working with them, they had already had twenty-seven episodes to absorb the material and then get it into the camera. So they were looser in their different ways. Adam's loosey-goosey is that he can discuss the cosmos and then they say "Action," and he can improvise/say the hyper-specific voice of Seth in a way that's perfectly timed, perfectly metered and perfectly spontaneous. He could just flip that switch by the time I got there.

Though everyone loved Cassidy, Zach was written out midway through the year because the writers were done postponing the inevitable.

Josh Schwartz: It was just a sense of, *Okay, we've got to get Seth and Summer back together at some point.*

Meet the Yard Guy

Marissa, meanwhile, hooks up with D.J., a character named in tribute to D.J. Cotrona, who went far down the line in the auditions to play Ryan, before ending up as the star of *Skin.** Played by Mexican American actor Nicholas Gonzalez, this D.J. was the frequently shirtless landscaper—or, as Marissa and Summer called him, "yard guy"—at Caleb's mansion.

Patrick Rush: We needed a hot guy to be competition for Ryan. The other thing is, neither Ben McKenzie nor Nicholas are tall gentlemen.

* Drink?

And Mischa was a tall woman. So there was always some tricky photography. And, of course, adding in some diversity.

Yvette Urbina: I'm Mexican, just to put that out there. It's really hard for me to reconcile that path for myself and doing my job. But I know Josh and Stephanie know that it was challenging.

Shannon Lucio: I knew Nick Gonzalez. When I first started acting, I tested with him on a show that Olivia Wilde ended up getting, called *Skin.**

Josh Schwartz: D.J., the idea was Marissa finding somebody who was going to make Julie Cooper mad. Like, "You thought me dating Ryan was an affront to your sense of who I should be with? How about somebody like D.J.?" The original impetus behind it was, "Let's put someone who is working class, not white, and someone who might start as an act of rebellion or as a physical thing and then uncover some deeper layers and levels with him along the way."

Whatever the intentions, D.J. had by far the shortest tenure of the newbies, appearing in only six episodes, and rarely interacted with anyone other than Marissa.

Josh Schwartz: We didn't feel like that story had the same amount of pop as the other ones; it just felt like it wasn't working in the same regard.

Stephanie Savage: Lindsay got folded into the school story, and then she got folded into the Cohen stories, so that had some longevity to it. It was a lot harder for Marissa to date a character that really only existed at her house, or if she brought him to an event. But there are some really nice moments, like when Ryan calls out Marissa and

---

* Okay, maybe don't drink? We're starting to worry about your health.

Summer for referring to D.J. as the yard guy, and he gives D.J. his tie so that he can get into some event where you're supposed to have a tie. Ryan's a sweet ambassador of the O.C. to D.J., which also shows how Ryan is now master of this world more.

Some of the people who worked on that season wonder if there couldn't have been other ways to integrate D.J. into the show.*

Michael Cassidy: Look, nobody wants this in the book, but I want to say that I have never not been aware of the benefit of looking the way that I look—this raised-white sensibility. To be in this handsome part of that subgroup, through no fucking effort of my own, is all upside that I benefit from. It's a good deal for me. But this show reflects that we value handsome whiteness and youth. So it was very easy for me to be part of a triangle and have it be good, because it was good before I ever touched it. And I don't feel that way about Nick's story.

There was another factor the producers were worried about: earlier that fall, a new ABC show called *Desperate Housewives* instantly became more popular than *The O.C.* had ever been. One of its stories also involved a romance between a wealthy woman and her hot, shirtless yard guy.†

Josh Schwartz: I was obviously highly attuned to any external criticism that was going on at the time. *Desperate Housewives* premiered before us in Season Two and took the zeitgeist as soon as it hit the ground running. And they had a gardener story. I was driving, and there was a radio DJ doing the morning news, breaking down the two gardener stories, and how much more they liked the one on *Desperate Housewives*. *USA Today* or somebody did a side-by-side comparison of the two stories. The *Desperate Housewives* one was the main

* Maybe he could have gotten a scholarship to Harbor? That's not more implausible than Ryan inadvertently dating his foster mother's secret half sister.

† In that case, though, the ethnicities were switched: the woman was played by Mexican American Eva Longoria, the guy by white actor Jesse Metcalfe.

love story, and the story that was really exploding out of that show. And we looked like we were copying them, even though obviously we had come up with the storyline in a vacuum; we didn't know what *Desperate Housewives* was when we were writing this. Suddenly it felt like we were a step behind and we were copying some other show, which was not a position for us to be in, because we had been the fresh-faced innovator just a year before. So that may have influenced my own personal feelings about wanting to wrap it up.

It was also easier for the show to say goodbye to D.J. because the writers had already lined up a new love interest for Marissa—even if said love interest was first going to date a different member of the ensemble.

Wilde at Last

The last of the four new kids was Alex, the manager of the Bait Shop, a local music club that would become a major setting for the show, as well as an opportunity to feature more live music. Though Olivia Wilde had not gotten the role of Marissa, she remained friendly with the producers and cast—she even went with them to Coachella one year—and with *Skin**
now canceled, she was available again.

Josh Schwartz: Olivia was somebody who was on our radar, and we wanted to create a character for her, to bring her onto the show. We liked the idea of having the story start as a love interest for Seth, with someone who is almost more of a young adult person working in the world, who was not going to take his shit in the same way. A boss for Seth.

Rachel Bilson: Olivia Wilde has been and always will be, whenever I encounter her, one of the coolest people. Kindest, coolest, smartest. I absolutely love her, respect her, adore her. She could not be cooler

---

* Yeah, put the bottle away. Safer for everyone.

and she's a wonderful actress. And an awesome director. But I think she's so rad.

Adam Brody: She was very luminous. Everyone really liked her; she was instantly popular. She jumped right in the fold.

Mischa Barton: I love Olivia. I think she's wonderful and easy to work with. Just a down-to-earth, easy person. The casting in that could have gone many different ways. Thank God it was Olivia.

Alex begins the season dating Seth, leading to the only time in the run of the series where Rachel Bilson felt a pang of jealousy about Adam Brody playing romantic scenes with another woman.

Rachel Bilson: Only when it was Olivia Wilde because I would have dated her. [*laughs*] It was like, *Well, you have Olivia Wilde—come on!* But I think we both handled it pretty well. Olivia Wilde was the only one when you're like, *Aw, man.*

Alex and Seth drift apart, and she eventually winds up in a relationship with Marissa, as one of the first prominent bisexual characters on American television.

Josh Schwartz: The idea that that story would hand off to Marissa eventually felt like an interesting dynamic for us. We're building out the Bait Shop, and we wanted to anchor that world with a character who brought us in there, give Seth a job, some responsibility. And this was a very different vibe for the show. Somebody who came in with a mohawk and more of a Gwen Stefani vibe, who was confident in her bisexuality, and someone who reframed our kids as kids a little bit, while not being that much older than them herself.

Stephanie Savage: I think there was enthusiasm for [portraying Alex as bi]. I don't recall people particularly being passionate about representation, or understanding that had a prosocial function. It was just that it was a juicy twist on a new character, and it would create lots of story.

Allan Heinberg: I wasn't the only gay writer in that room that year. My sexuality is out there in the room. And I think I'm always craving representation. But a lot of that was also trying to subvert audience expectations for Alex, and an attempt to grow Marissa. We didn't want to be trapped in terms of always having Ryan and Marissa gravitationally connected. We could open up this whole other world for this character, and that was really interesting to us. So I think a lot of what we did was about really wanting to surprise and delight people, and not be put in a box, we just wouldn't be able to sustain it if we didn't open these characters up in the ways that we did.

Mischa Barton was surprised by this development, not because she objected to a queer romance, but because it was yet another wild shift for a character who kept dancing out of her grasp as a performer.

Mischa Barton: I was pretty taken aback. It just felt like it was going all over the place.

What Does Janet Jackson Have to Do with This?

Again, bisexuality was still relatively taboo and misunderstood on television in 2003, let alone when it involved characters on a teen drama. Only a few years earlier, the supposedly progressive Carrie Bradshaw from *Sex and the City* had dismissed the whole concept of bisexuality as "a layover on the way to Gaytown."

Maria San Filippo (author, *The B Word: Bisexuality in Contemporary Film and Television*): It was quite novel to have a prominent, recurring TV character—on a network series, especially—be bi.

Bringing in a character like Alex, and then having her date Marissa, was not something many viewers were prepared for.

Craig Erwich: Fox made its bones on being the subject of those controversies. If you read the history of the network, Fox wouldn't exist without Terry Rakolta, who did that *Married . . . With Children* boycott.* She should own part of an equity stake in the network. It's in the network's DNA.

Allan Heinberg: I remember having to sweet-talk the studio and the network into letting us do this. I don't think it would have been their first choice, but I think we also were working with people who understood the box that we had put ourselves in. They, too, wanted a long life for the show, and we were given permission to pursue it. Looking back, I was surprised at how open-minded they were in terms of allowing Marissa to have that experience without any judgment. And letting Julie Cooper speak for the viewers who might have those concerns.

For the most part, the subject is treated with surprising sensitivity for an era when the concept of two beautiful women kissing was mostly presented in the media as a male fantasy. There is, however, a moment where Seth walks in on Marissa and Alex and does a prolonged, cartoonish double take that includes him rubbing his eyes while making a squeaking sound, as if he can't believe what he is seeing.

Josh Schwartz: Brody was definitely like, "Really?" I'm like, "Just do it once. It'll be funny." And then he went for it. It was in good fun, [but] there are moments in that episode that would probably be adjusted for today.

---

* Michigan suburbanite Rakolta was so offended by an early *Married* episode that she began writing to advertisers, asking them to stop sponsoring the series. She was successful in getting several of them to agree to her request, but on the whole, the boycott backfired, bringing more attention to both the series and Fox than either had had before.

Allan Heinberg: I remember I felt a little queasy about Seth's fantasizing about Alex and Marissa. But even that was like, "Okay, well, Seth is going to learn something about how bisexuality works."

Stephanie Savage: We would have kept her with Marissa for a longer time. That was a story that could've had more and more complications and more twists and turns and ups and downs than it had the chance to do.

Instead, outside pressures, including tensions between Fox executives at the network level and the people running various Fox affiliate stations across the country, got in the way.

Josh Schwartz: I'll never forget when we were forced to cut their first kiss way back before it aired. And then we saw the promo that they ran for the kiss episode and they hyped the kiss up so much in the promo. I'm like, "What are we doing? Why are they doing that? They just made us cut this thing down to like a tiny little smooch. Now they're really overhyping this." It was very confusing.

Stephanie Savage: The marketing people wanted a story that they considered promotable—this titillating, sexy kiss. But then the affiliates were getting complaints that [their viewers] didn't like this story. And then the affiliates were getting back to the network saying, "If this doesn't go away, we're not going to air your show anymore." So Fox was really at war with itself. And it landed on us in a way that was just really confusing. *Do you like kisses on the beach or do you not like kisses on the beach?* It was definitely a mixed message from our perspective. We cut the kiss down, but we didn't cut it out. And we knew we could still tell our story, even if we had some parameters on, like the visuals that went along with the storytelling. You could also push back and go, "Fuck those guys if there's some affiliate in some small town somewhere that doesn't want to show *The O.C.* They don't have to show it." That was a little bit of a feather-ruffling conversation. But it was a fight we were going to lose, because the rules had changed.

This goes back to the Super Bowl halftime show from early 2004, where Janet Jackson and Justin Timberlake's duet included the infamous "wardrobe malfunction" where Timberlake accidentally ripped off part of Jackson's top and exposed her nipple to an audience of millions. The moment proved so controversial that there were government hearings about it, which roped in Gail Berman, even though the game had been broadcast on CBS, not Fox.

Gail Berman: I get called to Congress, and it's very frightening. When we come back, there's a target everywhere on every broadcast network. It's definitely a change. And we have to be mindful of that. And so changes that we made were not so much in direct reference to it, but we were thinking more cautiously. That's how I would put it.

Josh Schwartz: I don't remember where the edict came down from, or what the conversations were, but it was made clear to us that that storyline needed to wrap up, that it was just not the right time for telling that kind of story based on what was happening in the culture. That wasn't even necessarily what the executives wanted or agreed with, but they were facing enough external pressure both from affiliates, and from the FCC.

Gail Berman: I can't remember that there was a specific order, like, "Let's get rid of this lesbian storyline." I remember it being more across the board at the network.

Yvette Urbina: I can say pretty definitively we never gave that directive. I can say that we gave the directive that they could kiss, but I don't believe we ever gave that directive. I know that we were pretty specific about it just being kissing.

Allan Heinberg: I am grateful to Josh and Stephanie that they weren't afraid of any of that. I felt utterly supported internally. And whatever network or studio feedback we got was about not wanting to turn off the audience that we had who might not be as open and accepting and loving as we are in our Manhattan Beach enclave. That they were allowing us to do it and to take it as far as we did is a tribute to them, because they could have said, "Please don't." So I credit them and I credit Josh with the fact that it exists and was so nonjudgmental and positive in its portrayal.

Mischa Barton: That was one of those storylines that never got seen through. And I think that's a shame, because there could have been a lot more to it. It felt like there was yet another thing that she was just experimenting with. But I suppose that works. Because at that place in your life when you're young, those things can be short-lived. But it did feel like that maybe needed going into more depth. That was one of the things that I felt was not fully fleshed out about her.*

Though Olivia Wilde had been the best received of the new recurring cast members, the premature end of Alex and Marissa's relationship also led to the end of her time on the show.

Josh Schwartz: I think we had gotten to the end of her initial deal. It wasn't like we told her, "You're being removed." I think we were all feeling like she was such an exciting presence on-screen. She might have been a love interest for Ryan, given that they had some edgier qualities in common. But we had not figured that out. And when she was in a relationship with Marissa and that ended, it would be hard to then flip her back to dating Ryan without undercutting a lot of the integrity of her relationship with Marissa.

---

* Unsurprisingly, the queer community was also disappointed by the abrupt ending. "It wasn't full-on 'bury the gays,' but it was hardly satisfying," says Maria San Filippo, especially because Marissa "appeared unchanged and even oblivious thereafter—as if the [bisexuality] arc had all been a dream."

The Meta-Morphosis, or: Never Read the Comments

In Season Two's Chrismukkah episode, Seth worries about a backlash to his invented holiday. In the next episode, he asks Ryan, "Would you punch someone, please, for old time's sake?" Eventually, Ryan tells Seth that maybe he remembers last year as being better because it was all new.

Josh Schwartz: Well, gee, that's transparent. Talk about wearing your neuroses on your sleeve.

Seth also develops a new pop culture addiction that season—*Sherman Oaks: The Real Valley*—inspired by another competitor to the show: a new MTV reality show called *Laguna Beach: The Real Orange County*.

Stephanie Savage: Now *The Valley* has a reality show.

Josh Schwartz: In between Season One and Season Two, *Laguna Beach* had premiered. I was very freaked out about *Laguna Beach* because they were able to shoot in Orange County, so it just looked more real. And they were actual teenagers, so I was convinced that they were also going to eat our lunch. We were getting it from the *Desperate Housewives* side and the *Laguna Beach* side. Seth is talking about watching *Sherman Oaks* and says, "Why watch the angst of fictional characters when you can watch real people in contrived situations?" It was me voicing my deep despair about the popularity of *Laguna Beach* at the time.

Schwartz had already dwelled too much on Internet reaction even during the acclaimed first season.

Tate Donovan: [At one of McG's viewing parties], I remember Josh leaving and wanting to check the chat rooms. He'd come down and we'd be like "That was an awesome episode," and he'd be like, "I don't know. People in these chat rooms are ripping it to shreds." That is ridiculous. Why would you go online? Just watch the show with us!

Josh Schwartz: I once had dinner with Chuck Klosterman, and he said something to me that I'll never forget: "Why do we always think the mean critics are the smart ones?" If one person was complaining online about something, that's what I was locking in to. And if there was a thread that was just for people saying this season isn't as good as the first, that's something that I would lean into and read about.

When online sentiment became much more mixed in Season Two, it only fed into Schwartz's innate self-doubt, creating such a feedback loop that it's amazing he was able to write episodes of the show at all, in between his time doom-scrolling through reactions to D.J., Lindsay, the potential breakup of the Cohen marriage, and more.

Josh Schwartz: We were trying to keep the show fresh and new. But we were also aware of the need to deliver on at least some of the same conflict that had gotten people excited about the show in the first place. We had to figure out how to evolve the show enough so that it doesn't feel stale, but not so much so that the audience who tuned in doesn't understand why the things that they tune in for are no longer happening. We definitely walked it with different levels of success at different points in the season. And then I think the show got its way back to the right balance of familiar conflict, but in a way that felt fresh and new. And that really is the challenge of any television series. Whether you've just done eight episodes in your first season or twenty-seven.

The Internet could prove just as dangerous to the show's actors, if not more.

Samaire Armstrong (Anna Stern): I had a manager at the time who was like, "Promise me you'll never Google yourself." And I did it a few times, and I was like, *Oh, my God, I'm never doing this again*. At the beginning, you're in the Christina Aguilera era with torn-up dresses and it was anything goes with what you wear. And there was a transition point where all of a sudden you needed a stylist, and if not, you're ending up in the Worst Dressed thing. I loved fashion, and I'd be in the Worst Dressed list. I'd be mortified. That just broke my heart.

Shannon Lucio: I went online. And I quickly learned after my first couple of episodes came out to stop, because people are horrible. For as many that love you, there's maybe double that hate you. If you're going to pay attention to the ones that praise you and think you're so great and great for Ryan, blah, blah, blah, you have to pay attention to the other ones, too. After a while, you realize, *I'm getting really picked on for things that are just totally outside of my control. And they're not even really about me. They're about the character.* But you feel responsible for them, because you're the character. It was hard on my ego.

Josh Schwartz: The idea that there was all these people that would gather to talk about a TV show, this was still a new concept to me, but also relatively new for the Internet. There were forums. They were really watching the show closely, which was both gratifying and terrifying. They were reading things into the show that you maybe didn't intend. It was just too much information and more feedback than honestly any human brain could process.

Television Without Pity—It's Right There in the Name, Josh

The crux of Schwartz's Internet obsession was a website called Television Without Pity.* Founded in the late nineties by Tara Ariano, Sarah D.

---

* Originally, it was called Dawson's Wrap, and then Mighty Big TV.

Bunting, and David T. Cole, TWoP (as it was referred to by its writers and readers) was a trailblazer in the TV recapping space, featuring exhaustive commentary on everything ranging from *The Sopranos* to *America's Next Top Model*. Recaps tended to come in at ten thousand words or more, and usually lived up to the site's tagline: "Spare the snark, spoil the networks." Each show TWoP covered had its own subsection of message boards, where the commenters could be even more cutting than the recappers.

Josh Schwartz: Yeah, that was terrible. That's something like when you hear people talk about a drug they wish somebody had never given them. It appealed to both whatever level of narcissism that I had, because all the writing was about me, and a level of masochism I had, because they're writing mean things about me. It felt like a humbling way of being able to read about your show.

Stephanie Savage: *Fastlane* obviously was not a Television Without Pity kind of show. We'd get crucified every week, and we just laughed at it. Our writers were like, "These guys are hilarious." And no one's feelings were hurt.

Josh Schwartz: It started as me genuinely being excited for it. Allan Heinberg turned me on to this. He had no malice when he did it, but he didn't realize what he was unleashing.

TWoP in those days was occasionally visited by the people making the shows they were recapping. Sometimes, it went well when one of them announced themselves to the community. (Bradley Cooper was so excited to find that TWoP loved his *Alias* character, Will Tippin, that he agreed to a lengthy interview with the show's regular recapper.) Sometimes, it went very, very poorly. (Aaron Sorkin was so peeved with how he felt he was treated, he wrote a petty *West Wing* subplot where Josh Lyman gets upset about a barely disguised version of the site.)

Tara Ariano (cofounder, Television Without Pity): I think we thought it was cool, because if people were reading the site, we

figured it meant they got it, and they didn't take themselves too seriously. Generally, when people would reach out directly to us, it would
be in a friendly way. It wasn't "How dare you?"

Schwartz did not make his presence known, and some of the Season Two
recappers were both surprised and somewhat alarmed to recently learn
about his addiction.

Heather Cocks (Television Without Pity recapper): At the time, I
definitely had no inkling he was reading. We knew TWoP had gotten
on producers' radars in the past, and yet every time it was confirmed,
it felt like a real "holy shit" surprise. But the longer I've been online,
and the more I've written, the more I'm like, *OF COURSE they were
Googling what people thought of the show.* The instant feedback of
the Internet was really just starting to explode, and it makes sense that
it'd be irresistible. Personally, I'd rather read the one-star reviews of
something I wrote than a two- or three-star review, because the former
is more likely to be a case of "Well, then we just aren't simpatico,"
whereas the latter will probably have logic and reason behind them,
and that can really stick in your craw and make you crazy.

Jessica Morgan (Television Without Pity recapper): STEP AWAY
FROM THE BOARDS, JOSH. TV showrunners and writers should never,
ever, *ever* be reading TWoP, in my opinion. Although I'm sure they enjoyed reading it in the first season when everyone was obsessed with
it. I'm sure I was critical of creative choices they made in a way that
I would not be so unvarnished or unmeasured about now. The early
Internet was, in many ways, unhinged—and in that, I do include myself.

Stephanie Savage: Allan Heinberg had a very different point of
view about the message boards. Early on, using them as a gauge for
whether things were working or not working was instituted in the show.
We were trying to hit those targets and deliver the version of the show
that they would like, which was not the version of the show that Fox
would like, because they wanted something bigger, bolder. Soapier,

less with the small, blink-and-miss moments that the message board people liked.

Daniel Blau Rogge (Television Without Pity recapper): I feel like the boards were pretty fun on this show, with the exception of some pretty negative discourse around Mischa Barton. There was lots of grousing at every development and every new character, but it felt pretty good-natured overall. People were there far more for the Ryan and Seth relationship than they were for Ryan and Marissa.

The Parent Trap II: The Cohen Marriage on the Rocks

For the most part, the writers were able to give the adult characters credible and interesting stories of their own throughout the first season. In Season Two, this became a real battle.

John Stephens (writer/producer): One of the reasons you write shows about kids is that people go through these dramatic life changes, and they go through them all in five months. They wake up in the morning and they're like, "Oh, this is my best friend." And they come home from school like, "I hate that person." From the course of one year to the next year, you have a totally different person. And I don't know about you, but I'm fundamentally the same person I was fifteen years ago. The gradations that you go through as an adult, they're so much smaller. The stories are different to tell and you have to be much more fine-edge.

Sandy departs the corporate law firm where he spent much of Season One to open his own office,* and is recruited by his old college professor Max to

---

* "Sandy had to quit his job because we needed the actual real estate, not the story real estate," explains Savage. "We needed the physical footprint to build the Bait Shop, so we couldn't have an office anymore. Partridge, Savage and Khan was gone."

help Max's fugitive daughter Rebecca Bloom (played by Kim Delaney)—aka the woman who was once the love of Sandy's life. Meanwhile, Kirsten and Julie launch a magazine called *Newport Living*, and recruit jaded, hard-drinking, but terribly handsome journalist Carter Buckley (Billy Campbell). Inevitably, both Cohens find themselves tempted by these new additions to the recurring ensemble.

Josh Schwartz: [We were saying], "Hey, everybody loves this. If they're really invested in Sandy and Kirsten, and really believe in this couple, then how outraged, how glued to their televisions, will they be if they're tempted?" Billy Campbell was somebody who had a really good following coming off of *Once and Again*. And felt like he could potentially bring potentially new adult female viewers to the show.*

Allan Heinberg: I remember there being a, "They're not going to cheat. We're not going to do that" decision very early on—that this wasn't going to be one of those shows where that happens. But it didn't mean that we weren't going to explore what it means to be in a loving marriage. It doesn't mean that you're not going to be attracted to someone else, and it doesn't mean that you're not going to have ghosts in your past that show up, like the Rebecca character in Season Two, and exert a pull.

Josh Schwartz: Campbell's story, I think, works well. It was a little bit more about testing Kirsten, or just presenting Kirsten with an option, and he was a fun rogue. The Rebecca story, we went much deeper with. I think it was deeply upsetting to the audience, and not in the way that we intended. Rather than people being like, "Oh my God, what's Sandy going to do?" they were more like, "What the fuck is this show

---

* Campbell had been on an early list of names to consider for Sandy Cohen, but casting director Patrick Rush says he didn't stay on there very long, because, "When you talk about Billy Campbell, you don't think he's, like, a New York Jewish guy."

doing? Why are they messing with Sandy?" You need to have a moral center. I think, had everything else in this show been static and the one couple we were going to challenge was Sandy and Kirsten, maybe audiences would have ridden with it. But in a sea of a lot of change and a lot of new characters and a lot of new dynamics, I think not having the Sandy-Kirsten anchor in that moment was just too much for the audience.

Peter Gallagher: I was sad about that, too. It didn't necessarily feel like the same marriage that we started with.

Kelly Rowan (Kirsten Cohen): My concern was how far they would take it, because I thought, *Well, if they break the marriage, how will that work for the show ultimately?* It wasn't my show, but you can have concerns in the back of your mind going, *Oh, I don't know if this is such a good idea.* Thank God they didn't, because I don't think testing the marriage worked really well.

Season Two does have one extremely romantic Cohen marital moment, when the boys help Sandy stage a last-minute twentieth wedding anniversary celebration at the Bait Shop, which includes Sandy serenading Kirsten as lead singer of the makeshift band Sandy Cohen and the News.

Josh Schwartz: Peter was always singing. [Doing it on the show, as Sandy] was something that he had pitched us that we had kicked around; it seemed like a fun, albeit maybe somewhat out of character for the character thing for him to do. My original pitch was I wanted him to sing "Glory of Love" from *Karate Kid Part II*. He was polite about it, but I don't think he was really into it. So then we had the idea of "Don't Give Up on Me" by Solomon Burke, which had played over a Sandy-Kirsten scene in Season One.

Peter Gallagher: I was nervous driving to the studio to record. This girl pulls up next to me and she says "I'm a lesbian, but I think you're awesome." And I thought, *God, that's a sign. It's going to go okay today.**

Does Whatever a Spider Can

Speaking of big romantic gestures, one of the season's most memorable sequences comes in the fourteenth episode, "The Rainy Day Women." Even though Summer is coming to realize that Zach's not quite the guy for her, she has spurned Seth's advances. A complicated series of events ends with Seth hanging upside down from the roof of the McMansion, in the pouring rain, wearing a Spider-Man mask. Summer shows up, finally forgives Seth for all his immature stupidity, and recreates the upside-down kiss scene between Tobey Maguire and Kirsten Dunst from the first *Spider-Man*.

Josh Schwartz: I had two ideas that I presented that were completely half-baked, as many of my ideas were. I wanted it to rain in Newport Beach. As an East Coast jerk coming to L.A., I remember being shocked at how people could not drive or function if there was like half an inch of rain in Los Angeles. And I had this idea that Seth was going to somehow end up on his roof with the Spider-Man mask on— that he didn't own a hat or umbrella or any waterproof clothing. The only thing he owned was this Spider-Man mask. And he was going to fall off his roof and hang upside down and he and Summer were going to kiss.

Stephanie Savage: It was almost like a *Seinfeld* episode where you start with the end and ask, "How does this happen?"

---

* This feeling proved correct: the day after the episode aired, Gallagher says Solomon Burke himself reached out and said, "You, sir, have soul." The two would later perform together at a blues festival in Melinda Clarke's native Dana Point, and the episode earned Gallagher a deal to record a record of soul covers called *7 Days in Memphis*.

Filmmaking isn't all glamour, as the actors involved in this romantic moment discovered.

Adam Brody: I really liked that director [Michael Fresco]; we were friends. But hanging upside down, the blood rushes to your head. It's not pleasant, actually, at all. And I'm beyond vulnerable and helpless to get myself down, and just being fucking pissed because I want to get down and [Fresco] was, "Just go again and again." It was discomfort mixed with a little bit of a flash of anger. Even though I did love that director.

Rachel Bilson: It was wet and it was soggy, and I can still taste his makeup that was running into his mouth. None of it was romantic. It was very soggy. It was miserable.

Josh Schwartz: I got a call the next day from Avi Arad, who was running Marvel Films at the time. His kids had watched it and he had heard about it, and no one was like, "You stole this and we're suing you." Everyone felt like it was a really nice celebration. People went with it.

Let's Go to "The Mallpisode"

With D.J., Lindsay, and Zach gone at midseason, and Alex on her way out, the writers were looking for an excuse to have the Core Four spend a concentrated period of time together. This led to the Savage-penned "The Mallpisode," where the kids are accidentally locked inside a Newport shopping mall after hours.

Stephanie Savage: We had a really, really tiny amount of story for that episode. This was when we found out that we had to bring the Alex story to an end. So Marissa and Alex needed to be physically separated, and Marissa needed to realize that she missed Ryan and wanted to get back together. That was literally the only story point that happened in that episode. So somehow we had to fill forty-two minutes with something.

Josh Schwartz: Stall.

Stephanie Savage: It's called stalling. So I went to [music supervisor Alex Patsavas] and I was like, "Alex, we have no story material in this episode. Please help us elevate it. How can we make it special?" And she was like, "Well, let me see who I can come back to you with, who would give us a full album of music, or has a big song that we could break."

Beck had a new album, *Guero*, due to come out a few weeks after "The Mallpisode" would air. Patsavas arranged to feature five songs from the album, along with Beck's cover of Daniel Johnston's "True Love Will Find You in the End." As a result, Patsavas and some other members of the creative team refer to this as "The Beckisode."

Josh Schwartz: We had one Beck song, and we asked, "What about if we could do five?" That had never really been done. When we were working on *Athens*, there was a concept that I had: "What if every episode is an album?" *Guero* was such a great album and the perfect one for us to do with all the songs. There was a lot of variation too. I felt like it would work.

Adam Brody: When we got trapped in a mall in the middle of the second season, I thought, *I remember the same story on* Saved by the Bell. Not that they were lifting it from there, but I just thought that there should be no overlap, and it's not a good sign that there's overlap. And thinking, *Oh, this is silly.* Of course a lot of the show's silly, but I just remember thinking a bit like, *Uh-oh.*

Stephanie Savage: It was definitely not a message board—or cast—favorite at the time, but it's an okay rewatch. Roller hockey to "E-Pro"!

Welcome to Miami/Bienvenidos a Miami

The guys' Season One trip to Las Vegas for Caleb's bachelor party had been so successful and fun to make that Schwartz decided to do another destination episode for Season Two. This time, Sandy, Seth, and Ryan head to Miami, where Sandy becomes concerned that the Nana* has gotten engaged to a gold digger, Seth takes surprisingly well to life in a retirement community, and the boys get mixed up in spring break shenanigans.

> **Josh Schwartz:** There was some article that was bemoaning something about Season Two of the show. I was immediately sent into a spiral. All of my good feelings evaporated. But we're in Miami.

> **Lisa Cochran:** We went to South Beach basically during [the real] spring break.

> **Josh Schwartz:** Much like the rain episode was basically designed to get Seth Cohen upside down in a Spider-Man mask, going to Miami for me was primarily about Seth playing shuffleboard.

While the Vegas trip had mostly gone down without incident, the mixture of the actors' rising celebrity and the chaos of spring break made "The Return of the Nana" a much harder episode to produce.

> **Josh Schwartz:** The cast was definitely at the peak of their fame.

> **Lisa Cochran:** They wanted to do a walk-and-talk down the main street in South Beach. If you look at the footage, you see the crowds in the background that are just staring at us. There were police. The local location team said, "Okay, here's the budget." And I said, "Why would we need twenty-five or thirty cops?" They said, "Oh, you don't understand." And we needed 125. They lined up so that the guys

---

* Schwartz: "This had to be the only time in television history where both Linda Lavin and T.I. appear in the same episode."

could walk down that greenbelt area. Everything was fine during what I would call the dinner hours. We had some green rooms in one of these hotels that was right across the street. But we literally had to put almost a tunnel up on either side to get the cast inside unharmed—and I mean "unharmed." They were just drunk, crazed fans. When we're done, the van takes off at the curb. The crowd is all around. And I look and see Adam's still standing next to me, and I thought to myself, *Oh my God*. We hailed a cab. Cab came up. I said, "When I cue you, we are *running* into that cab." And I literally throw Adam in, close the door and say, "Just get to the hotel." That night was insane.

Josh Schwartz: I have a distinct memory of Brody having to walk through Collins Avenue covered in whipped cream, which I found amusing.

Rachel Bilson had pleaded with Schwartz to write her into the Vegas episode so she could keep an eye on her boyfriend. This time around, she found an extracurricular excuse to be near Brody while he was filming on location.

Rachel Bilson: I was like, "I have to go to Miami." Josh is like, "I can't bring you to the Nana's condo. There's no way for me to fit you in." I got offered to promote a nightclub in Miami at the time. So I was flown to Miami, and Josh said while they were filming, they had to stop for noise, and the plane overhead had a banner that was like "Bilson at the nightclub tomorrow night." I was interrupting production, which is pretty good.

Josh Schwartz: That's how she made her way down there to once again keep Brody under close watch. We all went to dinner before at some ridiculous sushi restaurant where everything was comped and it was insane. Then we went to a club. When Ben, Adam, and Rachel walked into that club, it created a frenzy that they had not really expected or anticipated. And it was pretty crazy, pretty hectic. At the time, all people are doing is telling us our ratings aren't good enough, and you have to do mallpisodes and get Beck to get attention. And then we walk into this venue and you're reminded that the show was still resonating with young people.

This Is How It's Done in *Atomic County*!

Michael Cassidy returned late in the season to wrap up an earlier subplot where Zach and Seth collaborated on making their own comic book, *Atomic County*, featuring superpowered versions of the Core Four: Ryan was Kid Chino, with atomic-powered fists. Marissa was Cosmo Girl, whose powers came from drinking out of a magic flask. Summer was Little Miss Vixen, who hurled razor-sharp credit cards as if they were throwing stars. And Seth himself was the Ironist, a gadgeteer who mostly disarmed bad guys with his quick wit.*

Seth's love of comics had been a core part of his character ever since lifelong superhero fan Allan Heinberg joined the writing staff back in the development stage. Heinberg had worked comic book references into his earlier work, most memorably a *Sex and the City* episode where Carrie dates a hot young comic shop clerk. Initially, Seth's fandom was just there to give the character another thing to be passionate about, but also because it was a subject Heinberg knew so well.

Allan Heinberg: Josh is passionate about the bands he loves, and I am about the books I read. When you're generating that much material that quickly, you don't have time to go out and have life experiences and make shit up. You're writing exactly what's going on in your life right now, because there's a deadline. Early on, I would put comics in the scenes that I would write, just as texture. The scenes were never

---

* Seth's drawings were actually the work of comics artist Eric Wight, who would later team with *O.C.* writer John Stephens to create a series of *Atomic County* "mobisodes" for Verizon Wireless customers. The full season is on iTunes these days, and includes a parody of Marissa's Tijuana overdose where Cosmo Girl drinks too much and vomits all over her car. "What a great message we were putting out there!" Stephens recalls with a laugh. "It's a little bit like Jackie Chan's *Drunken Master*."

really about the comic book stuff. Or I would pitch that Seth talks too seriously and too passionately about comics to Summer.

Rachel Bilson did not need to search for motivation in those scenes.

Rachel Bilson: My dad loves comic books. Brody loves comic books. If someone starts to talk to me about it, I instantly tune out. I'm like, "I can't do this anymore."

In time, though, Heinberg discovered that Seth's comics advocacy was putting a new face on fandom, when for decades comic book nerds had been looked down upon by pop culture.

Tom Brevoort (editor, Marvel Comics): Going back to the fifties, that was a code for the stupid character, who reads comics because he's not sophisticated enough to read books with real words in them.

Seth Cohen, on the other hand, was so quick-witted, so funny, and, yes, so handsome, that he immediately shattered the stigma that non-nerds generally associated with comics.

Allan Heinberg: I remember being touched and surprised that that was an aspect of the show that people were latching on to, because it suggested to me that there were more of us out there than I knew. They weren't just talking about the fact that Seth was obsessed with indie bands. It was indie bands and comics. So it immediately elevated comics to the level of cool that these indie bands were, which I loved.

Paul Scheer (actor/comedian/podcaster/writer/*O.C.* fan): I saw myself in Seth. I loved seeing that on television, because it legitimized those interests. If he liked it, it was cool to like it.

The *Atomic County* story began as an easy way to complicate the new Seth-Summer-Zach love triangle: Seth wants to hate the guy who's dating his ex, but said guy turns out to be a fanboy like himself.

Allan Heinberg: Okay, here we are in Season Two, thinking, *Summer is going to reject him. Let's try to keep them as far apart as we can for as long as we can. So what else is he passionate about?* Sailing was not going to be high on the list in terms of what to write scenes about; it was expensive. Much easier to talk about comics, because they can go with you anywhere—you just carry them into a scene. It was surprising to me on a rewatch to see that we got away with it—that comics were so center stage for that bromance between the two of them.

Michael Cassidy: The scene where I join the [comic book] club is such a great example of the conversation that now, literally the most powerful people in Hollywood are having: "Why would Superman be cool? We need to figure this out." There are people who are making $10 million a year having that conversation. And we had that conversation in the second episode of the second season. Seth is like, "What? Superman? That's a terrible superhero to pick!" And I defended him in this geeky way that blows his mind. And it's not lost on me that literally, the fate of Warner Bros. Discovery is now tied up in these kind of conversations.*

Heinberg got to be on the inside of that transformation, first invited by Brevoort and other Marvel editors to write a new title called *Young Avengers*, and later getting the chance to cowrite the first Wonder Woman movie and to run Netflix's adaptation of the iconic fantasy-horror comic *The Sandman*. And now the normies have become nerds, to the point where the average moviegoer has seen enough MCU films to be able to tell the difference between the six Infinity Stones. It is Seth Cohen's dream world made into our reality.

Adam Brody: They were well on their way there anyway. But it helped mainstream them and make them a little cooler.

---

* Cassidy had, in fact, auditioned for McG's attempt to make a Superman movie; he didn't get the part, but McG recommended him to *O.C.* casting director Patrick Rush.

Michael Cassidy: I wasn't a comic book guy, but *The O.C.* was way ahead of the curve on comic books being fucking cool and interesting.

Paul Scheer: When I was watching *The O.C.*, it helped to get me back into comics. What the show did was allow me to let that freak flag fly, because I thought it was a freak flag. And then I'm like, *Oh, actually, it's okay to be a comic book fan. It's okay for me to embrace this.* And that was a big thing for me.

Tom Brevoort: You'll still get the outlier of the comic-reading guys who are geeky. But these days, more often than not, when it's depicted, it's depicted with a certain seriousness and with a certain respect, even if the material itself is a little loony. It's hard to make fun of the guy reading *Avengers* when everybody was in the movie theaters watching four *Avengers* films. Twenty years ago? Not a chance.

A Galaxy of Filmmaker Far, Far Away

The *Atomic County* storyline climaxed with the guys having to choose which of them will take Summer to prom, and which will take a meeting with George Lucas about turning their comic into a movie. The original pitch for the story, though, featured Schwartz's old *Punk'd* nemesis Ashton Kutcher instead of the creator of *Star Wars*.

Josh Schwartz: We had some relationship with Ashton in those days, and we were trying to get him on the show. I think Ashton was going to star in the comic book [movie]; he wanted to option it to star as Brody's character. And then Summer would have a thing for him. That didn't work out. So we're like, "Well, who else could option Seth's comic book that would blow his mind?" George Lucas quickly came to mind, and the third movie of the prequels was launching.

As luck had it, Lucas's teenage daughter Katie was a big *O.C.* fan, so George agreed to do the show, and there were plans to run a commercial during the episode, where Adam Brody would promote *Revenge of the Sith*.

> **Josh Schwartz:** Which he didn't want to do. He is not a fan of the prequels. Everyone on set was so starstruck and so psyched to have like George Lucas there. And Brody, 100 percent was not. Brody was not into the prequels and therefore was not excited about acting opposite George Lucas. I was like, "Classic Brody." He required a little arm-twisting to ask him to shoot this commercial where he's sitting on the bed with a *Star Wars* helmet and a lightsaber.*

Lucas had played himself a few years earlier on an episode of *Just Shoot Me!*, but being in front of the camera was still an alien experience for him.

> **Josh Schwartz:** I remember that one time, he called "cut" because he wasn't used to not being the director.

The Long, Wondrous Life of Julie Cooper-Nichol (and the Death of Caleb Nichol)

The one adult character the writers rarely had trouble coming up with story ideas for was Julie. In addition to becoming a Newport Group executive and helping Kirsten to launch the magazine, she was blackmailed by porn producer Lance Baldwin (played by Johnny Messner), who had put her in some of his films (including one called *The Porn Identity*) years before.

> **Josh Schwartz:** That was super fun, and something we were really excited do. We knew Melinda would be excited to do it, and Johnny

---

* In fact, Brody is holding Obi-Wan Kenobi and Anakin Skywalker action figures—which he announces he intends to keep—and making them fight, and later dons a Darth Vader helmet. He also refers to *Revenge of the Sith* as "the final *Star Wars* movie ever."

Messner was someone that Marcia Shulman, who ran casting for Fox, was a big fan of. I think he had multiple shows he was almost the lead of on Fox around that time.

Melinda Clarke: The actual shooting of the porn, I was very uncomfortable with. Because I guess as an actor, I've done it. I did a few nude scenes in the early nineties, and at one point I said, "This is so awful, I'm going to quit acting," because of how people acted. Like, everybody shows up on set to get a glimpse of you naked, and then they make fun of you because you asked for a closed set.

Josh Schwartz: The characters that were the most successful in terms of longevity were the characters that were able to touch a bunch of different worlds or fold into a bunch of different stories. So Caleb could be in a Julie story and a Marissa story, which then became a Ryan story and a Lindsay story, while also combating with Sandy and being with Kirsten. He was just an extremely fun and effective foil for so many of our characters.

Despite Caleb's versatility, the creative team decided to kill him off at the end of the season. Caleb gets fed up with Julie's various extracurricular activities and plans to divorce her, which would leave her poor again thanks to their prenup. She contemplates poisoning him, but is spared the decision when he has a fatal heart attack that night and falls into his swimming pool.*

Josh Schwartz: There were ideas of who else Julie Cooper could be with. And we'd exhausted the Newport Group stories. But Alan Dale was fantastic. We obviously worked with him for multiple seasons on *Dynasty*. It was great. We were ramping up the Julie Cooper storyline,

---

* Schwartz says, "I have a big regret—among many—that at the top of Season Three, I didn't think of it in time to have the police show up, and Julie Cooper thinks that they're there to arrest her for killing Caleb, and then Marissa steps out from behind her and puts herself in handcuffs. And that would be the first time Julie learned about the Trey shooting. It was a fun missed opportunity."

and it was just too good of an opportunity, and one that was a shocking twist that really worked for the audience.

Alan Dale (Caleb Nichol): I was just disappointed, mainly because I was having a blast and it was so convenient. It was close to home. Life was wonderful. The show was great. The kids and all the people were just wonderful to be with.

Kelly Rowan: I was really disappointed when he was no longer going to be on the show, because I thought he provided a really important character for everybody to bounce off of, because he was so awful.

Besides losing one of her main scene partners, Melinda Clarke had a more pressing concern about the manner of Caleb's death.

Melinda Clarke: I read the scripts and it says, "Julie Cooper runs in a bikini into the pool." And of course, the ego in me says, "What? No, no, no. I'm a thirty-three-year-old who's had a baby!" So it was the first time I did a cleanse, for a week, and dropped five pounds. I had two tickets to the U2 concert, and I was drinking a protein shake. I saw Josh Schwartz there, and he was like, "What are you doing?" I was like, "I'm on a cleanse, because I have to run in a bikini on Friday."

Alan Dale: I think they had in mind that I would be beside Melinda as she was [in a bathing suit and nothing else], but there was no way that I was going to do that. I had to be fully clothed, I'm sorry. "I'm going to be next to *that*?" So that was a slight change in the script, and I fell in the pool fully clothed.

Hi, My Name Is Kirsten, and I'm an Alcoholic

Season One often went for comic relief by showing Kirsten reaching for a tall glass of wine whenever an event turned chaotic. In Season Two, the writers decided to turn this running gag into fodder for drama, with the family (including Hailey, in Amanda Righetti's first appearance since the season's second episode) staging an intervention when they realize Kirsten has a genuine drinking problem.

Stephanie Savage: When we started it, it was more like making margaritas in the blender and drinking chardonnay at Thanksgiving. That she was a wine mom seemed funny. We did a bunch of stories where we were making light of something, and then we're like, "Is that funny or is that actually problematic?" You can have storylines with teenagers having sex, and then at a certain point, you're like, "Should someone get pregnant? This isn't just a comic storyline." But those stories are really hard to do, because they don't actually fit in the tone of the show.

Josh Schwartz: I remember Brody having a real issue with the Kirsten intervention, feeling like, "Okay, if we're going to do that, does it have to happen as quickly? It feels like it really escalated." Which was fair. I think it was part of his mounting concern about some of the direction of the show. I was putting off having a conversation with him. We finally did have a conversation on the night we went to see Muse in concert at the Greek. He was honest about it and it made a lot of sense. It made me wish I'd had a conversation with him earlier, because he had actual motivated, considered feelings, reasons for why he was behaving that way. It wasn't just "actor behaving badly." He was feeling like some stuff that had been played for laughs was becoming more dramatic. And I think our creative working relationship had drifted apart, as well.

Kelly Rowan: Playing drunk is not easy, but it gave her this other dimension. And it was an interesting storyline to do. We had some discussion around the big confrontation, because I think at first it was going to be Ben's character that was going to say, "You have to go to rehab." And we discussed it and then it was decided that it was really when Adam comes into the room. With the whole family being there, it's so sad. You look at what the stakes are in terms of what she's going to throw away if she doesn't get herself together.

Trey II: Trey Harder

The O.C. begins with Ryan's older brother Trey stealing a car and bringing a wary Ryan along for the joyride. The character, played by Bradley Stryker, returned briefly in Season One's Thanksgiving episode, and he continued to lurk in the back of Schwartz's mind as Season Two was being plotted out. This led to a climactic arc where Trey moves to Newport after being released from prison, gets a job at the Bait Shop, and struggles to stay on the straight and narrow, and to resist an attraction to Marissa.

> **Josh Schwartz:** We didn't get to do the Eddie story we thought we were going to do with Theresa at the end of Season One. That had become a different story. It wasn't about something more potentially violent and abusive. But the idea for that story was a good one, and Trey was a really compelling character. Ryan's mother had already come back. Theresa already came back. The only other figure in his life who could be up to no good, that he would be conflicted about what to do about it, would be Trey. Trey going for Marissa, and Ryan wanting to believe the best was the opposite of the Oliver story as well, where he's the one who wants to believe in him the most. And ultimately, that gets betrayed in the most primal way and led to, I think, our best finale.

Though Bradley Stryker received some consideration to reprise the role, the producers and Patrick Rush decided a new face would be better.

> **Patrick Rush:** I was like, "I think we have to have a conversation with the original guy." Which was, if he wants to come in and fight for this—because there wasn't much to do for the character originally—he's

welcome to do that. And he came in and he fought for it, and ultimately didn't get the part.

Josh Schwartz: It wasn't a knock on Bradley Stryker, who was a nice actor and did what we wanted him to do. But when we first cast that role, it was a two-line part. And even in that Thanksgiving episode, it wasn't much more expanded. It felt like we needed an actor with more potential experience. We had a better sense of what we were going to be asking that actor to do.

Instead, the part went to Logan Marshall-Green, an actor on the rise who had done summer stock with Ben McKenzie in Williamstown, Massachusetts, two years before *The O.C.* debuted.

Patrick Rush: People were talking about this kid. I didn't even think we'd get him. He has that Ben McKenzie intensity, where you don't know if he's going to kill you, or hug you like Peter Roth. He's a serious actor.

Ben McKenzie: Bob D said, "Hey, we got this guy who says he knows you and did theater with you." And I was like, "Oh my God, this guy is really a good actor." The buzz at Williamstown and elsewhere was that he was going to go on to great things. So I was surprised that he was there, but also really excited by the possibility. And he came in and crushed it.

John Stephens: It's interesting that he and Ben are friends outside [the show], because you understand it. They both are similar. They both bring a lot of toughness and vulnerability to their parts. And Logan absolutely had that. What was powerful about it was they delivered on the brotherhood story.

Stephanie Savage: When Logan showed up, I think that also reinvigorated people. He seemed like he was a really good actor and it was exciting when he was on set. And that storyline felt like a really good storyline for us, because it had melodrama, but it also felt like it was in the right tone of the show.

Where viewers rebelled against other antagonists before and after this storyline, Trey seamlessly fit into the show.

Josh Schwartz: It fits because it's Trey, it fits because it's in the DNA of the show from the pilot. I think that's the difference. It doesn't feel ginned up. It doesn't feel manufactured. It's in the first episode, that dynamic.

While Ryan is in Miami with Seth and Sandy, Trey tries to rape Marissa. The scene required special handling.

Stephanie Savage: We were operating in the time before intimacy coordinators. Anything that involved intimacy or violence was making sure one of us was on set, talking about how the actors were in charge—specifically, the female actor was in charge of the scene, and she could call cut at any time. No one was supposed to do anything to anybody without talking about it first. Logan was really well trained and came from the theater world, so we thought the scene would be safe in his hands. Mischa, my memory was that she was excited about this storyline. I think she felt more comfortable in the more dramatic storylines versus the more comedic storylines, just as an actor. So I think she was excited to do something that felt like a more important story and something that played to her strengths as an actor.

Mischa Barton: I don't want to get too much into all of that. But there were varying degrees of how comfortable that stuff made me or didn't make me. A lot of the beach stuff wasn't comfortable for really obvious reasons. And, yeah, that was a bit of a heavier scene. So I don't know how to answer that.

Marissa refuses to tell Ryan about the sexual assault to avoid hurting him, but he finds out anyway, leading the brothers to begin brawling in Trey's apartment.*

Stephanie Savage: I remember coming to the rehearsal and watching Logan and Ben go at it in a way that had an aggression and realism and commitment from the actors, that felt like it was another level for the show. It wasn't like Luke kicking sand in his face at the beach. You really had to feel like Trey was going to kill Ryan.

Josh Schwartz: The actors just threw themselves into it. They really committed. They didn't actually beat the shit out of each other, but they came as close as you're legally allowed to.

Ben McKenzie: Back then, I loved that part of the job. And so did he. I think we were both also ready for some release because the season is a long slog. So yeah, we just let it all hang out. That was the fun of acting for me—just being able to do shit you would never be able to do in real life, because they'd probably arrest you.

Mischa Barton: I think the boys had a lot of fun with it.

Michael Cassidy: Ben, I remember the face he makes before he fuckin' lunges at somebody. I was always like, *Goddamn it, that feels like what I would do if I was in this situation.* It felt very real to me, and I was always impressed by that.

Mischa Barton: It was a long day. It's funny that Rachel and Adam just show up at the very end of the scene, after we've been filming for probably twenty hours. I think me sinking down that wall was really the feeling I had at that time of night.

* Trey was living in Alex's old apartment, a way for production to save money by reusing a preexisting set.

As Trey is on the verge of beating Ryan to death, Marissa grabs Trey's gun and shoots him in the back, accompanied by the haunting strains of British singer-songwriter Imogen Heap's "Hide and Seek."

> **Josh Schwartz:** When I heard that song for the first time, I was like, *I don't know where this song is going in the show, but it's got to go on the show.* I begged Alex to ask Imogen to not license it to anyone else so we can have it for ourselves. I felt like Caleb's funeral would be a great place for that song to play. And then Norman had the idea* of reprising it when Marissa pulled the trigger. That really helped make it so iconic, as well as that look that Logan Marshall-Green gives back to the camera, and back to Marissa, after he's been shot. Just disbelief.†

The final sequence is arguably the most famous moment of the whole series, and easily among its creative high points—the final upswing on what had been a roller coaster of a season. It also left many questions in its aftermath: Was Trey dead? What would happen to Marissa after shooting a man, even if it was in defense of someone else? And what could *The O.C.* possibly do for an encore? Everyone was worried that this would be hard to top. But no one imagined just how bad things were about to get.

To get your spirits up before that, a musical interlude!

---

* Norman Buckley declines the credit on this one. "That wasn't me. As I remember it, he wrote the script with that in mind—that it was going to be used over the funeral, and then it would come in again at the end."

† This moment would later take on a second life through an *SNL* Digital Short called "Dear Sister." More on that in Chapter 11.

CHAPTER 7

The Soundtrack

IT IS THE creakiest of clichés when a showrunner declares that a location, a stylistic choice, or any other nonhuman aspect of a series is "like another character for us." When it comes to the songs of *The O.C.*, though, it is hard to dispute. Not only is the indie rock–laden soundtrack absolutely another character on the show, a reasonable argument can be made that it is the most important character. With every plaintive melody, soaring harmony, and beseeching lyric, these anthems enhanced the experience of every scene in which they appeared, amplifying and commenting on the characters' emotions.

DJ Josh Schwartz Sets the Tone

The musical language of *The O.C.* originated with Josh Schwartz, even if it wasn't the kind of music he listened to at first. He grew up in Providence with the same middlebrow tastes as every other MTV kid from Generation X.

Josh Schwartz (creator/executive producer): The most impactful musical moment I saw on-screen was when my musical hero Huey Lewis and my acting hero, Michael J. Fox, converged in one movie. By the time I was in high school, I was still pretty basic, but I was definitely music-curious. That was the explosion of the alternative music moment—the more *Spin* magazine–approved music. WBRU, the Brown radio station, had a great alternative music thing going on.

When he arrived at USC, Schwartz discovered the vibrant L.A. music club scene, and bounced around venues like the Troubadour and the Greek, eventually discovering the kinds of bands that would appear regularly in his work.

> **Josh Schwartz:** I was going to a ton of shows and listening to a lot of music, and spending a lot of my weekends over at Amoeba Records going to buy CDs, and then having to completely reshuffle my Case Logic CD cases to make room for new entries in the order that I methodically kept them in. This was around the time of *High Fidelity* the novel, which made an impression.

When *The O.C.* began, Schwartz functioned as the de facto music supervisor. The pilot and the remaining summer episodes largely featured songs straight off his iPod, as he instinctively recognized which tunes would fit.

> **Allan Heinberg (writer/producer):** Josh would often say that he couldn't properly write a scene until he'd found the right song for it. Even if that song didn't make it into the script or on the air. The idea for the scene would lead him to the right song, and then he'd write the scene to that song on a loop. So music—even if unheard by the audience—was woven into every scene Josh wrote. And if a song did appear in the script, and I didn't already know it, it would usually become my new favorite song.

Schwartz was excited to curate the soundtrack and introduce his favorites to a mass audience, and to his colleagues—like the time he, Heinberg, and Stephanie Savage listened to "Rain City" by Turin Brakes in Heinberg's car. They would use it in the third episode, over a sequence where Ryan's mother Dawn sneaks out of the Cohen house without telling Ryan.

> **Allan Heinberg:** I was as moved by Josh's instincts then as I am now. I love everything about those scenes, with that song, because it was clear that Josh was feeling everyone's pain in that moment. He wasn't

judging Dawn, just as he hadn't judged Kirsten for having reservations about taking Ryan in. That song was perfectly, gorgeously communicating Dawn's sacrifice, Ryan's loss, and the bittersweetness of his becoming a Cohen because of her sacrifice. It was heartbreaking and gorgeous and uplifting all at the same time. All guided by Josh's instincts and heart.

As that initial batch of summer episodes was coming to a close, though, Schwartz realized he couldn't do it all himself.

Josh Schwartz: I got to a point where I was like, "I think I'm running out of music. I don't really know what else to write into scripts. I'm in trouble here, guys." As the machine of the show had taken over my life, there was a lot less opportunity to hear new music and go to shows.

Birth of a Superstar Music Supervisor

Alexandra Patsavas was a music supervisor who had worked at Colin Hanks's old stomping grounds at *Roswell*, and, more importantly in this case, *Fastlane*, where she had collaborated with Savage and Norman Buckley.

Norman Buckley (editor/director): I also worked with Alex on a couple of independent features, and I knew that her music sensibility was very similar to Josh's, just by a lot of the songs he'd written into the pilot script. I thought, *Okay, this is the type of music he likes, and who do I know who really has that musical aesthetic?* Alex was always introducing me, even before *The O.C.*, to various bands that she thought I should listen to.

Alexandra Patsavas (music supervisor): I viewed it as the opportunity of a lifetime.

Josh Schwartz: We hit it off right away. She totally got what we were going for, and she had the added benefit of not only having great taste, but also having a lot of intel about when records were being put out, and what would be a good time for certain bands' music to appear on the show.

Alexandra Patsavas: Josh was a huge, huge music fan. I felt like I was having a conversation with friends about great art. And also we had those teenage characters that this all fit in so naturally with. It never felt like we were plopping music over strange events. It felt like it was all natural to them.

Patsavas signed on and quickly began assembling "comps"—mix CDs containing songs she thought would work for the show. It was not a fast or easy process.

Alexandra Patsavas: Twenty years ago, music wasn't as immediate. You didn't get digital tracks in three seconds. You couldn't go to Spotify. iTunes was just in its infancy. So I sat in a tiny office on Sunset and Cahuenga with a great team that were really instrumental in helping me gather music. Andy Gowan, Andrea von Foerster, there was a ton of great people over the years, and there were just stacks of CDs everywhere in this office. Everybody had headphones on—this was pre-headphone culture—so that many people could be going through music at the same time.

The first comp she gave Schwartz featured two songs that would be among the most memorably used of the series. One was "Paint the Silence" by South, which plays as Ryan and Marissa kiss on a carnival Ferris wheel.

Josh Schwartz: It just gave you all the feels. As soon as you hear that song again, it feels like it's the show. As soon as you said the words "Paint the Silence," I had this full-body rush of emotion and nostalgia. The song is just epic. You're looking for those anthemic songs.

The other was "Dice" by Finley Quaye & William Orbit, which plays as Ryan runs up the hotel steps to say "I love you" to Marissa on New Year's Eve.

Alexandra Patsavas: That's a magic song. Right? That's in my top ten magic songs. It's beautiful and anticipatory. When you watch those two get together, and hear that, it's [John] Hughes-ian.

The show's early success, and the way that it brought songs like "California" into the mainstream, quickly turned Patsavas into the belle of the music publicity ball.

Alexandra Patsavas: Once the labels and publishers knew I was on *The O.C.*, I would get a mail pail of submissions every day, and we put everything on a CD player.

Lori Feldman (Warner Records executive): The music supervisor is the gatekeeper. And the gatekeepers really only have so much time in their lives, so they can usually only talk to the labels they know, etc. So for her and her team to make time to really go through all of these baby bands, and their commitment to new music in this indie, precious lane, I always thought was really remarkable. I always wondered how she and her team could possibly get through what I envisioned was this mountain of music that she got. And I myself discovered a ton of music through my experience working with them.

For Patsavas, it was a chance to practice music evangelism at a very high level, curating a sound that could impress a serious indie rock nerd like Schwartz or a music executive like Feldman, as well as *O.C.* viewers who had never listened to anything outside the Top 40.

Alexandra Patsavas: It was so exciting to be able to think about all the music that wasn't known outside of pretty fervent fan bases.

Josh Schwartz: We knew there was going to be a big part of the audience that was desperate for this kind of music and had no access to it. I was really excited about the opportunity to be a bridge for people. And I think that actually helped bring in a different audience for the show as well, or made it feel safer for maybe a more NPR-affiliated audience—people who might look down their nose at a teen drama on Fox.

Alexandra Patsavas: I was giddy for four years. It was such an incredible experience to be part of this team. It was a once-in-a-lifetime sort of show and music that we loved—music made by our friends. It was pretty heady stuff. I remember always being frantic to deliver—like, *Could I clear it on time? Could I make it work? Were we going to be able to get the money to work?* Everything was really important to get right.

Making Magic with the Music

Alexandra Patsavas: There's something about music that you hear when you're first really discovering music when you're a teen—or a teenager of any age—that you hang on to forever. I try to think about programming the music in *The O.C.* to evoke that. Like, if you connect, you feel wonder. I play some *O.C.* stuff at home, quite a bit.

Lori Feldman: When you're making an appointment to see characters every week that you love and whose stories move you, and you put the right song in at the right moment, that song will stay with you forever.

It sometimes felt like it took forever to find the right song for the right moment.

Alexandra Patsavas: In the editorial process, there were a billion pitches to get to the right thing. And we would try many songs. You would pick something off of a comp to put in, or [editors] Norman or Matt Ramsey or Tim Good would. I remember them arguing over songs sometimes. That was very flattering for me.

Josh Schwartz: Matt would be in his editing room, and you could hear a song coming out of Norman's room, and he'd be like, "No, I had that in my episode!" And they would get into a fight, and we'd have to come in and settle it.

Norman Buckley: We would get instrumental tracks and build them into the score.* We would repeat songs over and over again, so that there were repeating motifs through the episode. The Dandy Warhols' "We Used to Be Friends," I have that repeat several times in the episode. They were really open to trying things. There was one episode where I had two different versions of the old standard "Caravan," and I had one version that was more instrumental and one that was lounge, and I play one for Anna, and a different one for Summer.

Some songs made such a mark that they would appear on the show in multiple episodes.

Josh Schwartz: If something worked so well musically, and was such a part of the scene, it felt like reprising it was both okay and actually helpful. Because the music was so evocative, and we were trying to evoke the same kind of moment—like Ryan carrying Marissa up the driveway, and then Ryan carrying Marissa out of the alley. [Both scored to "Into Dust" by Mazzy Star.] The scenes evoked themselves. Therefore, it felt like the music could also match.

The show could also go old-school when it wanted.

---

* Though needle drops comprised much of the show's sound, there was also an instrumental score, composed at first by Christopher Tyng, and then by Richard Marvin. When Marvin arrived midway through the run, he understood the hierarchy right away. "You're getting X dollars per episode, and they're spending maybe six or seven times that amount on songs," he says. "It was a very diplomatic exercise to be in sessions and figure out if it's a song or if it's score. I don't remember having any problems with Alex. It was a very collaborative experience—always a friendly discourse. And I couldn't argue with any of the songs on The O.C. It was known for the songs."

Alexandra Patsavas: There's no fighting the Journey when it's scripted. You just plow ahead and clear.

Matt Ramsey (editor): There's an episode in Season Three where Seth smokes weed. [Postproduction supervisor] Rick Hubert was like, "He's got to listen to Black Flag's 'Wasted' while he's smoking weed. That's legit." Bob DeLaurentis was like, "I'm an old punk fan," and he loved it. I think Alex had to fax with the guy to get it cleared, because he would only communicate via fax. That's what's great about *The O.C.* We were breaking new bands, but you could have this great old band like Black Flag.

"It Was Good to Be Popular"

Josh Schwartz: We were fortuitous at the beginning that the music that was on the show that I was listening to at the time was cheaper, because it was truly indie. And all we could afford.* So that worked to our advantage. Our disadvantage was some of these bands being a little skeptical of their music appearing on a Fox teen drama, especially when the show was unproven. But a lot of them I think were happy with the checks.

Alexandra Patsavas: We charted a course where bands were excited about being on the show, because they knew they were going to be used respectfully, and with enthusiasm. Josh and I talked in interviews over and over at the time about how we were fans, and I think artists could tell that we meant it.

It also quickly became apparent to the music industry that being featured on *The O.C.* was a promotional godsend to any act not mainstream enough

---

* The music budget did not increase substantially as the show grew more popular. Still, Patsavas grew annoyed when people would suggest that money was the primary driver of which groups they featured. "Everyone was like, 'You must have leaned into indie artists because you got them cheaply.' We leaned into indie artists because it worked [creatively] for the show."

to make it onto Top 40 radio, at a moment where it was hard to find music in other places.

Ben Gibbard (Death Cab for Cutie): There was no YouTube. File sharing was sort of a thing, but it certainly wasn't what it became. So you would have to ask yourself, *How would anybody hear a band like ours in 2003, and what are your options? Is MTV not really playing videos anymore?* We're in the hangover of rap-rock and super-aggressive, rape-y, bullshit music. The radio is not playing music like ours. So where would you possibly hear a band like us? I don't think it can be understated that [on *The O.C.*], this music would be beamed into the households of millions of people. That was our viral moment. That was our YouTube. That was our radio. That was a huge springboard for the band.

Josh Schwartz: There's a lot of Gen X energy in *The O.C.*, and the Gen X ethos is really about fear of selling out. I think a lot of the cast members' discomfort with the success of the show was that feeling of selling out and wanting to be indie and wanting to have credibility. And that was something the bands had too. That now seems like the most antiquated and adorable concern, because you cannot "sell out" anymore. The whole goal is to sell out.

Lisa Cochran (unit production manager): These groups became huge. It started when Phantom Planet did the theme. You could drive to work, and it was on FM radio at the time. So the theme song for the show, I think, set the tone that music was going to be an important part and it was going to be very up-and-coming.

Josh Schwartz: Somebody showed us the stat sheet on Rooney, of what their album sales were prior to their episode and after their episode, and it was pretty significant. It moved the needle.

Alexandra Patsavas: There was a moment where marketing departments started to call me from labels and publishing companies and I was like, *What's a marketing team? Why are they calling me? I'm trying to* *fax for an approval!* I felt the seismic shift in what this opportunity meant for bands, how meaningful it was. I heard later that getting a sync* on *The O.C.* became an agenda item in a marketing meeting at a label.

Soon, it wasn't just the indie bands eager to place their music on the show.

Josh Schwartz: I remember getting calls from Alex, like, "Hey, the Beastie Boys want to premiere their new song in the Vegas episode. How do you feel about that?"† And just being like, "Are you kidding? That's one of my favorite bands of all time!" Then in Season Two, Alex is like, "Hey, post-Beastie Boys, U2 would like to premiere their new song on the show."‡ And you're like, *What is happening here? This is insane.*§

Alexandra Patsavas: It was good to be popular, wasn't it?

Josh Schwartz: It was such a unique moment where a TV show could have that impact. Everything is so fragmented now—even *Euphoria*, for all of its cachet—that it's hard for things to really land. But that was an amazing moment.

In the Mix

Lori Feldman: Within three or four episodes after it launched, we were taking meetings with Josh and Stephanie about doing soundtracks. We had all kinds of crazy ideas.

---

* i.e., having your music featured in a TV show a movie, or a commercial.

† "Ch-Check It Out" plays as Ryan, Seth, and Summer walk down the Strip after Ryan has won a lot of money in a poker game.

‡ "Sometimes You Can't Make It on Your Own" plays over an early montage of the Core Four with their new romantic partners.

§ Many of these deals with more famous artists came as a result of Patsavas's strong working relationship with legendary music manager John Silva, who helped place the Beastie Boys and Beck, among others, on the show.

Josh Schwartz: That was the dream. Are you kidding? We were so excited. Nothing was more fun than trying to figure out what songs were going to go on that soundtrack. It was such a mix culture at the time—you were always making mixes and burning them on CDs for people—and Alex was making a version of that as well. The idea was to make the ultimate mix of the show. Alex and I went back and forth about sequencing, so that we didn't have too many downtempo songs, and how do we mix it up and finish strong? It's got to have a narrative to it. You didn't just hit Spotify shuffle and then hear whatever came on from the algorithm. You were trying to tell a story through the music and remind people of the experience of watching the show. But it was hard to whittle it down.

The first soundtrack album, *Music from The O.C.: Mix 1*, was released late in Season One, opening with "Paint the Silence" and closing with "California." Just as Schwartz and Patsavas needed time to figure out what songs to include, Warner went through some trial and error with some of the technology of the day.

Lori Feldman: On *Mix 1*, because we were ahead of our time and nobody realized that they should probably stop us, we were able to use the scenes that each song played in, in the first pressing of the CD. It was an early CD-ROM-ish thing. And we were able to connect the song to the scene, which we were not able to do when we needed to do a repressing.

The first soundtrack was so successful that five more were produced over the life of the series.

Josh Schwartz: I can't believe that we made an entire Chrismukkah album.

Lori Feldman: At the end of *Mix 3*, we made a plaque for Josh, Stephanie, and Alex, saying that we had sold a million copies worldwide.

Which, as far as a TV soundtrack goes, I don't know that anyone had done that before.

Now Playing at the Bait Shop . . .

Season One's Rooney episode was such a success that it gave Schwartz and company the confidence to make live music—or, at least, an incredible simulation of live music—a regular part of the show. For Season Two, production built a new set for the Bait Shop, a local rock club where all the hottest indie bands of the day would appear.*

Josh Schwartz: We were excited about the Bait Shop. We wanted to create another shared space for everyone to hang out that wasn't at school. The show was very much identified with its music, and the first soundtrack had sold really well. And selfishly, I was like, *Oh, I get to build a candy shop and fill it with all my favorite, most delicious candy?*

The Bait Shop set was big and elaborate, designed to not only showcase the acts that were performing, but to allow various conversations and moments of drama between the main characters to happen at the same time.

Lisa Cochran: The Bait Shop had multiple levels. So you could have people upstairs on a graded upper level, and then down below there was the stage that backed up to the one wall. And it was round, to match a building down at the pier where we used to film exteriors.

Alexandra Patsavas: In college, I had booked a club and I felt like I was stepping back in time. But I realized that band time and TV time are not the same time. Early on, we picked up a band at five in the morning

---

* In a later season, the writers used Taylor Townsend as their mouthpiece for a meta joke about the improbability of so many big acts coming to Newport Beach.

for a shoot, and I realized we were going to have to adjust. But to book the Bait Shop, we went through who might be available in the two-week window that the episode was shooting in. Being on the Bait Shop set was so cool. They got it so right. It felt and it smelled like a real venue.

Typically, the bands would run through each song two or three times, lip-syncing to the prerecorded track.

Rachel Bilson (Summer Roberts): I remember always being really excited to meet the bands and see them, but also being like, *Gosh, this is probably boring for them. They just have to lip-sync and do this over and over again; they must be getting tired of it.*

Some acts seemed happier to be there than others.

Josh Schwartz: It depended on the artist. Modest Mouse, I remember being a bit more private and like, *What the hell are we doing here?* I tried to go say hi, and they weren't really into it. The Killers were super professional when they were on the show. We recorded it a couple of months before their first album launch. So they were just super hardworking and humble. Everybody was really professional, because it was early days for most of those bands. As excited as we were to have them on the show, it was important for them as well.

Michael Cassidy (Zach Stevens): My trailer was next to the Killers. And I remember distinctly, as a fucking white dweeb, walking into base camp one day and seeing all these dudes with long hair and tight jeans. I'm wearing a soccer jersey and basketball shorts to work that day. And I walk in and ask the third AD, "Is that a band?" And he's like, "*Absolutely* that's a band."

Josh Schwartz: With some bands, we hit it just right. The Killers appeared as that record was dropping and it was real kismet—"Mr. Bright-side" is being played on the show as it's exploding on the radio. It felt like we were exactly in the right place at the right time and everything was working. Sometimes, we got up our own ass a little bit about it. We had the Walkmen on, but we didn't want them to play [their single] "The Rat," because we thought that was too mainstream at that point. Only later to realize "The Rat" was popular with, like, fifteen hundred of us that lived in a small part of Los Angeles and New York at the time. We probably could've played "The Rat" and it would have been just fine.

Michael Cassidy: When Modest Mouse came through, it was the only time that I wrapped and went straight over to the set where they were filming. I was like, *Holy shit, there they are!* I was super-stoked to see them and hear their new song.

Adam Brody (Seth Cohen): Modest Mouse, I thought those guys were so cool. I always had my dog around, and I had my dog run up to them as a kind of bridge-builder. The lead singer, Isaac [Brock] petted him, and we bonded a little.

Lisa Cochran: It was always a concert that we were in the middle of. And a lot of us were upstairs in that balcony area, because none of us that worked on the show wanted to miss the bands. I thought it had a lot to do with the success of the show—having that kind of appeal to a young viewership.

Also, it is not a coincidence that the Bait Shop's initial manager shared a first name with the show's music supervisor.

Josh Schwartz: Alex loves to be compared to Olivia Wilde.

Alexandra Patsavas: I felt great about it. I still feel great.

Death Cab for Brody

No act came to symbolize the sound of *The O.C.* more than Death Cab for Cutie. Though only a handful of their songs appeared on the show, their status as Seth Cohen's favorite, most frequently name-checked band made the show and the group inextricably linked in the minds of many viewers. And the nakedly emotional quality of Death Cab's music sums up the sonic palette of the series better than that of any other artist featured.

Josh Schwartz: Brody loved Death Cab. That's what that whole group—the whole House of Seth—was listening to. The conversation around it worked its way into the show.

Adam Brody: They're not me. They have nothing to do with me. They're artists. But to be able to share something I like with the masses, that truly did speak to me and maybe wasn't as well-known, was really fun. I don't know, everyone wants to be a DJ.

Where many other acts featured in the early days of the show were just starting out, Death Cab had been around since 1997, had put out three albums prior to the debut of *The O.C.*, and had a hotly anticipated fourth one, *Transatlanticism*, due to drop in the fall of 2003. They were already doing very well within their particular lane.

Ben Gibbard: We were selling around 50,000 records. I think that's around what [2001's] *The Photo Album* had done at the time. At that point, [indie label] Sub Pop was joking that 50,000 was indie rock gold.

As the series was early in production, the band's management got a request for *The Photo Album*'s "A Movie Script Ending" to appear in an episode.

Ben Gibbard: We were told, "Hey, there's a show on Fox. It's a teen drama; they want to use 'A Movie Script Ending.'" The offer, I don't know how much money it was, but it was certainly more money than we'd ever seen. Indie rock was not going to be used in television or movies in the late nineties, early 2000s. It just didn't happen.

It was such a novelty that the band threw a watch party for the episode—
"The Escape," where the kids take their ill-fated trip to Tijuana—and
were startled to discover that not only was their song featured, but the
characters on the show were *talking about the band*.

Ben Gibbard: We were like, "What?!?!? Hold on." We weren't record-
ing it. There was no TiVo. So we couldn't back it up. So it's, "What just
happened? They said *what?*" Then it became fucking hilarious, but
we just figured that would be the end of it.

[*extremely fake Ron Howard voice*] That would not be the end of it.

Transatlanticism was released while *The O.C.* was on its brief Season
One baseball hiatus. It was greeted with rave reviews, but some of them
couldn't help noting the group's association with TV's newest It Show.
The *Orange County Register*, for instance, declared the album "a first-rate
work that, with any luck, will push the band beyond being a minor sensa-
tion and a footnote on *The O.C.*"

Ben Gibbard: There were a lot of attempts to dismiss our newfound
success as merely a function of *The O.C.* A lot of publications would
never miss an opportunity to try to connect us. That was annoying.
And it undermined all the work we put into the band beforehand. I
was worried. We participated, in the sense that we licensed our music
and we [later] agreed to go and be on the show.

Adam Brody: I can imagine that it was ultimately a thrill and financially rewarding for them, and afforded them opportunities. And at
the same time I'm sure they got sick of it—and to a certain degree, [I
did], too. In the sense of them being wedded to this show for so long,
and me being wedded to a band that, in my early twenties, was my
favorite band. It's nice, but it's not a permanent relationship.

After initially playing to small, homogenous audiences, Death Cab had already started broadening its fanbase prior to the release of *Transatlanticism*.

Ben Gibbard: It wasn't as if we were playing for all these hip kids in August of 2003 and then November 2003, we were playing to all the mall kids.

The mall kids did start to come, though, especially as Seth kept talking up the band on the show.

Stephanie Savage (executive producer): People would go to the Death Cab show, yelling, "I love Seth Cohen!" from the audience.

Josh Schwartz: I'm sure for some other bands, but for Death Cab especially, being known as, "*The O.C.* house band" was probably a little bit of a thing. I always felt for Death Cab. They were a successful, beloved band before the show. And there was a period of time where they were not written about without the words "Seth Cohen" or "*The O.C.*" in the same sentence. They were very gracious about it, because I'm sure they were like, *What the hell, man?*

Ben Gibbard: In a lot of cases, *The O.C.* was beating us to Europe. So we got over there [to tour] and we're like, "Why the fuck is everybody asking us about *The O.C.*?" We'd been a band for six years at this point, put out four albums and two EPs. And then I realized, *Oh yeah, because a lot of people see it as, "This American show made this band,"* because most people had heard of us on the show.

That said, there were certain financial perks to being so closely linked to Brody, Schwartz, and Alex Patsavas.

Ben Gibbard: Alex is probably responsible for me buying my first house. But I need to give ourselves credit, too. We had made the best record of our career. We were getting incredible reviews. The culture was starting to shift, due in some part to *The O.C.* But I think also *Garden State*, and it was this moment in the early aughts, where a lot of people who grew up on college rock and indie rock and R.E.M. and

Superchunk, Merge Records, Sub Pop, Matador, all that stuff, now they're in charge of shit. And it's "I want to get my favorite bands for money. Use them in the background." A large part of it is that it was a cultural shift for people who are now running shows and have some kind of sway in cultural circles, saying, "I want to use *my* music."

Death Cab played the Bait Shop late in Season Two, though one of the episode's jokes is that Seth misses the show because he's too wrapped up in other drama.

Ben Gibbard: There's a weird history of bands doing this. We thought that'd be hilarious, to have our name on lists of bands playing in the background of a movie or a TV show. Like, Andy Warhol and the Velvet Underground cool shit. This is slightly less cool, I think, but all the people on the show were really cool to us. And I met Liz Phair! She showed up to that taping because she knew somebody on the show.* That was huge for me, because I'm a huge Liz Phair fan, and we've gotten to know each other over the years since then.

Gibbard worried for a while that the popularity of the show would completely overshadow the band. After the Bait Shop appearance, he asked himself, "Did we just get totally used by Fox TV?" But the group is still putting out new music, and earlier this year set out on a world tour to celebrate the twentieth anniversary of *Transatlanticism*.

Ben Gibbard: There were moments when we were like, "Can we talk about something other than *The O.C.*?" But we've lasted way longer than the show—maybe to some people's chagrin. Now I look back on that time as a really crazy chapter in our band's history. It was certainly part of the band's growth and movement into pop culture, into more of a mainstream thing. But thankfully, it didn't come to entirely define us.

---

* Writer Mike Kelley is her Chicago high school pal.

The White Whales

Even after seeing what the show had done for Phantom Planet, Rooney, Death Cab, and more, not every band was excited about placing their music on a Fox high school drama.

Josh Schwartz: There were some bands that never said yes. Arcade Fire is the first one that comes to mind. Clap Your Hands Say Yeah, we began to refer to as "Clap Your Hands Say No." They did some interview where they went out of their way to say, "We'll never be on *The O.C.*"*

Alexandra Patsavas: Or we couldn't clear because of a publishing dispute. I remember "Dice" being a particularly difficult clearance. There's a lot of pieces to songs, and there's a lot of parties involved, and it wasn't so immediate back then. I was faxing out requests, and pieces of paper were coming back with a yes or a no. If it didn't add up to 100 percent of the rights, then [we couldn't use it].

Matt Ramsey: Before Season Three, Arctic Monkeys had just come out with a song, "Fake Tales of San Francisco." We wanted to put it in some big montage. And Arctic Monkeys was like, "No, we don't want to be one of these *O.C.* bands."

There were also groups that, like Death Cab, appeared on the show and then began to have second thoughts after the fact, like Rooney.

Allan Heinberg: I have met two of the four of them as fathers with kids. We've talked about how at that time, there was a little bit of resentment—suddenly, they become "*The O.C.* band," and they're re-

---

* In that case, Schwartz and Patsavas eventually got a victory of sorts, when Clap Your Hands Say Yeah agreed to let "The Skin of My Yellow Country Teeth" appear on Schwartz and Savage's 2019 Hulu miniseries *Looking for Alaska*, which was set in 2005.

sentful, because they want to be their own thing. So it was nice twenty years later to be able to talk about that moment, and have mutual love and respect. They were all in their twenties then. So I get it. But at the time, we were being, *Well, that's very ungrateful. We don't think of ourselves as a teen show. Why are we getting this backlash?* We were just trying to love them, and they were trying to distance themselves. But I get that you want to be cool rock 'n roll guys, and we're ostensibly a teen drama on Fox. Those two things don't live happily together. So it was a pleasure, all these years later, to look back and say, "Oh, we had this moment together."

Mischa Barton (Marissa Cooper): I definitely think it was one of the show's strengths. A lot of those songs were really iconic at the time. Music was such a huge part of my life, because I was so young. Those bands, some of them I knew, some of them I didn't. Looking back on it, it's kind of humorous, I ended up dating the guy from Rooney* and becoming friends with the guys from Modest Mouse. So it really did play a huge part in the show, and in my life in general.

"California," Here We Come

Phantom Planet became one of the first bands to experience the impact that being featured on *The O.C.* had on their career fortunes.

Alex Greenwald (Phantom Planet): The show, I think, had to be out for about six months before people really noticed that we were the band that sang the theme song. Then our shows got bigger, which was great. But even before that, we had gone on a world tour, and we started to notice that even at these really small shows, there were people in Japan who were there because of *The O.C.*, or sending us fan mail because of "California." We were like, *This is*

---

* Barton dated Rooney guitarist Taylor Locke in 2008.

insane. That's the coolest thing. Like, somebody in Japan and their grandma watched the show and loved the song. That felt like the biggest deal to me. All of a sudden, there are millions of people who have heard this song, whether they know it's us or not yet. That's the biggest thing we've ever done and maybe the biggest thing we'll ever do.

Beyond an increase in record sales, Greenwald and his bandmates began getting unexpected professional opportunities.

Alex Greenwald: There were a couple of crazy things we couldn't turn down. There was a corporate party in New York where, I don't love discussing money, but we were paid a huge sum, with airfare and hotels covered, for us to play seventy seconds of "California." I still don't know what the heck it was for.* And then because *The O.C.* took off in England, too, "California" got enough radio play for us to do *Top of the Pops.*†

Where Are We? What the Hell Is Going On?

If "California" is the song most linked with *The O.C.*, "Hide and Seek," played when Marissa shoots Trey, is a very close second—remarkable given that it only appeared in one episode, as opposed to being the theme music every week. It was a song Imogen Heap composed on a whim, to cheer herself up after a computer crash destroyed everything she had recorded for the previous few months.

---

* "I think this was for the Season Two Fox upfronts," says Stephanie Savage. "Josh and I are sitting in the audience, the emcee booming 'Last summer, a revolution happened!!' And we were like 'What revolution? OMG, there was a revolution?' And then Phantom Planet came out and did part of 'California,' and we were like, 'Holy shit, *we're* the revolution.'"

† A hugely popular and influential British music show that ran on the BBC from 1964 to 2006.

Imogen Heap (musical multi-hyphenate): I picked up this harmonizer that my friend had given me, because it belonged to Steve Winwood. I just recorded whatever came into my mind. It was the first setting I found, which was a four-note polyphony, that meant that if all the fingers went down, you only came out with the four notes, which it decided. Normally when you're improvising, it would be twenty minutes and maybe you'd find a bit in there you like. But this was really immediate, and it was a bit of an out-of-body experience in the fact that it was coming out so easily. In the middle section [of the finished version], there's a second voice that comes in, and I was playing it and thinking to myself, *Ooh, I must do that second voice.* But I thought I was being extremely self-indulgent and nobody would like it, and I didn't have any bass, rhythm, anything. I thought, *I'm just going to stick this one on, because I really like it. And if nobody else does, I don't care, because it's really good and I'm gonna put it out there.* But then there were some people who came into the studio and heard it and were like, "God, it's really good!"

Though *The O.C.* was playing in the U.K. at the time, it was not familiar to Heap.

Imogen Heap: I don't really watch TV, so no idea about anything. But you do a bit of research once somebody asks if you want to be in something. And then I was like, *Oh, that's quite good, actually.* So no, I didn't know about it, but lots of other people did.

While many songs featured on the show would have felt special even on their own, there was something alchemical in this particular combination of the song and the scene.

Imogen Heap: It's very special to me as a song, but if it was ever going to have an impact, it would have to be related to something visual. Nobody in their right mind would hear that for the first time out of context and give it the legs that it has, because not enough people would have sat down listening without any of their busy lives going on, if it wasn't for a TV show or a film. And that's the magic of getting a good sync: you sneak in there when no one's really noticing. But you would never commit to it if you were just looking around on the internet.

Josh Schwartz: The second we saw it in picture, it was like, *Oh my gosh, this is going to work so well.* It was really exciting.

At that stage of her career, Heap was acting as her own label, and had literally uploaded the song herself to the iTunes Store. Once it was featured on *The O.C.*, it exploded.

Imogen Heap: They put it on the front page of iTunes, which back then was massive, because there was only one front page, there was only one featured album, and they put my album there. I was like, *This is amazing. How did this ever happen?* This had never happened to me with the label before.

Heap did not share the regrets that some other *O.C.* artists felt, even temporarily.

Imogen Heap: Alex Patsavas really gave me confidence in making my first record. To have a thumbs-up from a major TV show and an amazing music supervisor, that was really encouraging. When they felt like it's good enough to put on in their TV show, I felt like, *Maybe I could mix this on my own; maybe I should just go for it.*

When You Get What You Want, but Not What You Need

Like Jeff Buckley's version of "Hallelujah," Coldplay's "Fix You" appeared on *The O.C.* soundtrack—accompanying Caleb's death late in Season Two—before the song would become a ubiquitous, if not utterly clichéd, soundtrack choice.

Josh Schwartz: We were invited to Capitol and told, "We're going to play you the new Coldplay record. Pick a song, and we'll hold it for you guys." We went in and we sat on the couch. They played us the whole album. "Fix You" came on. We looked at each other and we were like, "This is it. This is the song."

Alexandra Patsavas: It was Josh that identified "Fix You." I think they were hoping that we were going to pick an up-tempo song.

Josh Schwartz: I was like "This is a perfect song for Caleb to die to." It was not the lead single. It wasn't even the second single. I don't even know that they were going to release it as a single. And then after, it became a classic for them, but it certainly wasn't what they were leading with.

Staying Covered

In time, the show became known not just for introducing new songs, but offering fresh variations on older ones, with Patsavas taking special pleasure in commissioning cover versions of classic tunes—or, in some cases, of songs the show had used previously. (The final soundtrack album is filled with *The O.C.* covering itself, including Mates of State's melancholy riff on "California," from Season Four's Chrismukkah episode.)

Alexandra Patsavas: The songs that had the most discussion were definitely the bespoke covers.

An early cover was Nada Surf tackling "If You Leave," an Orchestral Manoeuvres in the Dark song famously used in the John Hughes–written *Pretty in Pink*, here deployed for Seth and Anna's farewell at the airport.

Josh Schwartz: I would say to Alex, "We want this to feel like an eighties John Hughes moment." But not do an eighties song itself, because that would not be the show, per se. "If You Leave" is obviously a John Hughes song and that's a great call, so we'd talk about who would be the band, and it's "How about somebody like Nada Surf?" With others, she would reach out to a handful of artists, and sometimes we'd get multiple submissions, different bands doing the cover, and then we'd have to pick one.

Alexandra Patsavas: How do we think about a spec song on a TV series rather than a movie, where you have time for a demo process? How do you have enough trust from the artist to know that it was going to be a great opportunity, to be able to say, "Can you do this on spec?"

British singer Jem's "Just a Ride" was featured early in Season One, and appeared on the first soundtrack album. For that year's finale, she was asked for her take on Paul McCartney's "Maybe I'm Amazed," to play while Ryan and Marissa are sharing what they think will be their final dance at the reception for Julie and Caleb's wedding. Jem is a huge Beatles fan—during a Zoom interview for this book, she gestured to a framed Abby Road album cover on the wall behind her—but had somehow never heard McCartney's most famous solo song before.

Jem (musical multi-hyphenate): They talked about what was going on in the scene, and that it was going to be very emotional. I was renting an apartment in Stamford Brook, and I sang it looking at the Tube going past. So I do vocals on my own at home, and then when we produced the rest of it, my producer went to his wall, and he got this rebab, a very traditional, ancient instrument. It really felt like there's magic in it. When I hear it today, it still feels super special, that song.

Jem was even invited to appear in that episode, as the wedding singer.

Jem: The cast were so lovely. Alan Dale used to be in a huge soap opera called *Neighbours*, so that was really funny for me seeing him, even though everyone [else is] so massively famous.

The Song Remains the Same

Alexandra Patsavas: I want to talk about how many times still people tell me how much the music mattered to them, how it opened their musical vocabulary to different music, that they knew how important it was. And that matters so much to them, to Josh, and to me.

Josh Schwartz: When people want to come talk about the show, almost always, one of the top two things—if not number one—is the music, and that they still listen to it. It's so gratifying and special. That's why music works. There's just a timelessness to music that is so evocative. It's like a time machine, and it can take you back.

Alexandra Patsavas: The music defined itself because it supported the story. It was the kids' music. It was the adults' music. I often get asked, "Can you do a modern *O.C.* playlist?" And I think I can't. At that time, there was this vast amount of music that was undiscovered in the zeitgeist—just huge, deep pockets of great music that we were able to use. And I don't know if I could come up with a current list that would have that much to pick from.

Josh Schwartz: It was just a unique confluence of events at a moment in time, when there was all this great music, and there weren't any other avenues for it to get discovered or heard. And we had the right team and the right show where it organically made sense to play. All these things came together, and for a couple of years, just became this really special vehicle to deliver music to people. And I will say—because Alex would never say this—that even when the show had its ups and downs creatively, the music always stayed good. And was probably the most consistent quality of the show.

CHAPTER 8

The Bizarro O.C.

SEASON THREE OF *The O.C.* was a calamity on almost every level, both in front of and behind the camera. It was a Murphy's Law year: anything that could go wrong, did. Network interference led to terrible storytelling choices, which led to even worse storytelling choices. The actors were so unhappy, the show's embarrassed creator literally started hiding from them.

Network Notes

There were many villains in the making of Season Three—along with a few surprising heroes—but the problems all began the previous season with a change in management. Late in Season Two, Gail Berman left Fox to take over Paramount Pictures. Schwartz and Savage were happy for her—"For someone from TV to move over to run a feature studio was a big deal," says Savage—even as they knew they had lost their best and most powerful ally at the network.

> **Peter Roth (president, Warner Bros. Television):** Gail was a champion of the show. And when she left, we lost our champion.
> Her successors were not nearly as supportive of the show. Nor did they believe in the show as much as Gail. We spiraled down after her leaving.

To replace Berman, Fox hired Peter Liguori, who had helped turn the previously obscure cable channel FX into a success with edgy, boundary-pushing dramas like *The Shield* and *Nip/Tuck*.

Melinda Clarke (Julie Cooper-Nichol): [*The O.C.*] wasn't his thing. Although with the success of *Desperate Housewives*, you would have thought that maybe they would have nurtured that a little bit more.

Josh Schwartz (creator/executive producer): Liguori was a nice, personable guy. It wasn't like he called and said, "I hate your show." Everybody comes in and rides what's working. *Prison Break* was working and *24* was working. They had football. At the beginning, we felt like we were a part of a culture at the network, and now that culture had very quickly morphed into a different kind of a culture, and had gotten very male and very action-heavy.

Even *O.C.* alums were feeling the change.

Amanda Righetti (Hailey Nichol): That was the year that Peter Liguori came in and just was like, *Fuck all this stuff. Get rid of it all.*

Craig Erwich (programming executive, Fox): I think Peter was neither here nor there about it at this point. It was a third season show. I don't think that's where his attentions were. I don't know that it was his cup of tea.

Stephanie Savage (executive producer): The quote that got back to me [from someone at the network] was, "This is the NASCAR network. We don't make shows about nerds that talk to plastic horses." I understand that from a business perspective—that was his job. But I felt very strongly about this. Part of my brain is my creative brain, but then my other part is my critical studies brain, which is like, "I know the history of Fox. You have adult animation with *The Simpsons*, irreverent family comedy with *Married with Children*, and *90*-fucking-*210*. We are that for you, and you are our network. You are not the NASCAR network. If you want to have NASCAR, that's fine, but that's not your DNA." I really felt like they were trying to make us into something that we weren't and that we didn't have to be. There were always the *Ally McBeals*. There was a world of lighter hours on Fox that people really enjoyed.

Josh Schwartz: The Season Three ratings for the premiere, I think were fine. On the main, the show was healthy, but the messaging from our new leadership at the network was that it was not broad enough. And it needed to get broader in order to remain on the air, which was very jarring to hear.

Stephanie Savage: "Promotable elements" was the term that got thrown around a lot in Season Three. Smoking pot wasn't enough; something had to be on fire because of it. Someone had to be slapping someone, going into a swimming pool—that's where we were.

Josh Schwartz: Peter Liguori felt like we needed to give him things that you could market. In his mind, "yogalates" is not going to be in a preview during *American Idol*.

Stephanie Savage: At the beginning, we were like, "We're going to build a Trojan horse. We're going to bring in these interesting, fun characters that you wouldn't normally see in a teen drama or nighttime soap. But we're going to give the network just enough of what they need that they leave us alone and let us do our thing, and life will be beautiful." And when that stopped working, they were like, "We want to kill all the soldiers that you've brought in here. And we only like the horse." There was a version of just saying no and letting the show be canceled, but I think we felt so much pressure to redeem ourselves, to keep the show going. You have two hundred people where that's their livelihood, and there's pressure on you to try and keep that going.

J. J. Philbin (writer/producer): Needing to have promotable big things in each episode took precedence over, "What do we want to watch and what's a good story?" And I think we had run out of things to do with our core crew, and didn't want to trouble any marriages anymore and things like that. So then you end up bringing in new people, and they weren't the right characters and it wasn't the right world and it wasn't what people came to the show for. As a young writer, it was certainly an education in . . . [*long pause*] what not to do.

Stephanie Savage: They were like, "If you don't give us any marketable moments, we're not going to market your show. And you know what will happen after that." So there was a really overt pressure; it wasn't unconscious or subtle. It was like, "You better give us some bangers that we can put in a 'this week on *The O.C.*' promo where something fucking crazy happens." Our job was to figure out what that was.

Josh Schwartz: Our show had a very loyal, fervent following that may have been bigger than the Nielsen ratings were measuring. But certainly we were not at the level of some of these bigger, broader juggernauts, nor was it the level of *Desperate Housewives*. I think that really drove the conversation, which was, "How do we try to turn you guys into *that*?"

Stephanie Savage: They had a sexier soap; they had a murder.

Josh Schwartz: And they had adult characters. Everybody was like, "You need more adult characters in the show." And that was what led to some of the stories in Season Three as well.

Stephanie Savage: We're trying to be optimistic: "Come on guys, we got to finish strong at the end of last season. We have the chance to rebuild! And get back to what people love about the show and tell new stories!" But we could feel that that energy, of riding the Trey wave to new heights, was being crushed by, "You guys need to be more like *Desperate Housewives*. You need to tell more adult stories. You need to introduce a mysterious femme fatale." Literally, that was the language. And this show is not a femme fatale kind of a show.

On the Move Again

The shift from Wednesdays to Thursdays had been rough enough, but at least the competition was a bit lighter at 8:00 p.m. when Season Three began: *Joey* was already running out the string on NBC, and *Alias* was in what would be its final year on ABC. Midway through the season—as the latest sign of apathy at best from new network management—Fox scheduler Preston Beckman moved the show to 9:00 p.m., where it would eventually have to do battle with two of the biggest hits of that era: *C.S.I.* and *Grey's Anatomy*.

Peter Roth: *Gevalt!* Why? I thought it was an eight o'clock show, not a nine o'clock show. The competition was absurdly difficult. Everything about the move, I thought was risky and a bit reckless.

Josh Schwartz: It wasn't a vote of confidence, and felt like they had to put something in the lion's den. Thursday, nine o'clock was just the most competitive time period. And moving us there at a moment where the show was not at its best creatively? It unfortunately exacerbated the challenges we were already facing.

Peter Roth: I'm a big fan of Preston, and I like him. I thought it was a terrible idea at the time. It proved to be a terrible move. It only hastened the demise of the show.

Stephanie Savage: It felt like a ticking clock at that point.

Yvette Urbina (programming executive, Fox): And Preston, honestly, was like "Because I said so, and I think you can do well here." That's generally Preston's response: *Because I'm right and I know things.* But I do think it was because he didn't care.

Preston Beckman (head of scheduling, Fox): Yeah, I can't remember why I did it. I don't know, to be honest.

Peter Roth: [*after hearing Beckman's answer*] Well, boy, if that doesn't add insult to injury.

Taylor Townsend for the Win

Before we revisit all the baffling story arcs and behind-the-scenes unpleasantness, let's pause to acknowledge that a handful of things worked very well that season. Chief among them were two additions to the ensemble, one wholly new and one mostly new. The former: Taylor Townsend, a type A student looking to wrest away Marissa's crown as queen of Harbor.

Stephanie Savage: We wanted to introduce a Tracy Flick character at school: someone who was a high achiever and not really a mean girl, but just a control freak. In Season One, we learned that Marissa's the social chair. And then as her life has become more tumultuous with her family problems, Ryan, and everything else, she's lost that thread of herself. She goes from the together, popular girl welcoming people on the mic at the fashion show, to somebody who was on the margins—and in Season Three, actually kicked out of school. And then Taylor comes in to create conflict for Summer, who's outraged that someone has filled the Marissa void.

Autumn Reeser was an actor in her mid-twenties who had been getting screen roles for a few years at this point, most notably as Marcia Brady in the 2002 TV movie *The Brady Bunch in the White House*,* albeit nothing nearly as prominent as *The O.C.* was even at this stage of its life. But she almost didn't go in for the audition.

Autumn Reeser (Taylor Townsend): I went back and looked through my scrapbooks from this period of time and read old interviews with

---

* She was not the only *O.C.* actor with a *Brady Bunch* past: Adam Brody had played Barry Williams (aka Greg Brady) in the 2000 TV movie *Growing Up Brady*.

myself, and apparently I was simultaneously up for a role as a dancer in a Disney movie. So I had to choose between the auditions.

Clearly, she made the right call.

Autumn Reeser: Sometimes you audition for roles, and they make sense to you on a different level. Like, "Oh, I know this person; I know who this is." And sometimes you audition for roles and you can never get inside their skin. I never end up booking those, because everybody can see I don't know what I'm doing. Whereas Taylor, I was like, "I know this person on a cellular level."

Taylor was meant to be a villain, conspiring with Harbor's new dean of discipline, Jack Hess (Eric Mabius), to get Marissa and Ryan expelled from school.* Reeser quickly proved too talented and versatile for such a limited role.

Josh Schwartz: The writers fell in love with her. Everybody was thinking she was really funny. It is definitely in the DNA of the show to take antagonistic characters, like Julie Cooper and Luke, and make them likable.

Lisa Cochran (unit production manager): Autumn was fantastic. Autumn was very, very funny. As a person, she has this personality that's very easy to be around. I'm not a director, but the recurring directors would tell you that she was easy to work with and easy to be directed.

J. J. Philbin: She brought so much energy, and she was also new. She hadn't totally checked out yet, and hadn't been through whatever the rest of the cast had been through at this point.

John Stephens (writer/producer): The first time we saw Autumn on-screen, it was like, *Oh, wow, where did she come from?* She had so

---

* Ryan managed to stay, with some help from Sandy.

much life, and she brought a different tone and flavor to the show. You're always trying to balance one character against another character. And she was not Summer. She was not Marissa. She was not Lindsay. She was her own specific thing. And she was someone who—both the character and the actress—you could put into any scene and they bring a scene to life. As an actress, she went for stuff, she was not afraid of going to the funny, and it was lovely. It was always fun to write for her.

Where the writers had once been barred from being too explicit about young female desire, they couldn't resist making Taylor into a very sex-positive character. While Seth and Summer are going through a sexual rough patch, for instance, Taylor tries schooling them with lessons from the *Kama Sutra* that she has clearly already put into practice for herself.

Stephanie Savage: It was a combo of J. J. and Leila being excited about those storylines, and also that may have been something where Liguori was more like, "Let's push it," versus Gail not wanting to have to testify in Congress again because of one of our storylines. Because Taylor was nerdy and matter-of-fact, I think that gave us a little bit of latitude as well. Because that was an unusual combination: that uptight type A girl who was also extremely sexual.

J. J. Philbin: I think the characters had aged enough that we could treat them somewhat like adults. And it made sense that Taylor had a wild sexual side that you wouldn't expect.

Autumn Reeser: One of my favorite things about Taylor that they wrote for her was this freedom of sexual expression. I've had so many young women come up and tell me how important Taylor was for them, in part because of that—because she had no shame about it. And there's so much cultural conditioning around that for young women. To have a girl who was nontraditional in her sexual choices and unapologetic about it, it was such a testament to the writers that they did that.

The Return of the Mini-Cooper

The season's other successful major addition was a revamped, more mature Kaitlin Cooper. Marissa's younger sister had appeared in a half dozen Season One episodes, but the writers packed her off to boarding school after that, to avoid constantly having to explain what she was up to in the increasing whirlwind of family drama around Julie and Marissa. Midway through Season Three, she returns and immediately begins causing trouble for Marissa and friends.

Stephanie Savage: We aged up Kaitlin, because it felt like Marissa had aged out of some of the activities—where it's not fun now if Marissa is drinking and driving and getting in trouble in that way. As with Kirsten at a certain point, you have to have an intervention and deal with some of these things. Kaitlin could be a pot-stirrer.

Shailene Woodley had continued working, but as was the case with the return of Trey in Season Two, the producers opted to hire someone new, eventually selecting Willa Holland.

Melinda Clarke: I think Shailene has discussed that she was a late bloomer. Even just being six months younger than Willa, she had not developed. And that's the way they wanted to go with the character. I guess she did audition for it, and Willa had a little bit more of that essence that they wanted.

Josh Schwartz: Shailene was young, and we wanted someone who could be the *Muppet Babies* version of the cast, like the next gen. She felt a bit too young. And Willa felt like Mischa. She had this great sardonic attitude and presence, and just felt like a really fun, new, potential antagonist.

Things turned out okay for Woodley, though—and for several other young actors considered for the part.

one-on-one. I can't remember verbatim what he said, but the tone of the conversation was, "Things are about to change. You're stepping into a world right now, and just be prepared. Know that when people are telling you things, you should listen. Don't let your head get clouded. Keep your head on your shoulders and your feet on the ground." It was smart and heartfelt and something that a kid needed to hear. There was definitely an air of tension. I think that that was maybe some of the purpose behind Peter Gallagher sitting me down. He was really adamant about like, "You're coming into a hot place, and things are crazy. It would be crazy regardless, but it's a little extra crazy here."

Peter Gallagher (Sandy Cohen): I wasn't really warning her that things are not great here. I was just trying to give her confidence to believe that she was enough. That she was valuable, and that the choices she made would have an impact on her future.

Willa Holland: I related a lot to Kaitlin. When I was a teenager, I didn't like admitting it, but now I can very much say that there's so many parallels between me and that character. Even just familial-wise, my upbringing, all that was very up and down—the rags-to-riches roller coaster was very similar. And there's a lot of things that I can relate to her in, like the angst and the rebellion and all of that.

In the penultimate episode of the season, Marissa visits Kaitlin and her roommate Hadley (played by a young Lucy Hale) at their boarding school, and gets Kaitlin out of trouble with a male classmate. This was the last remnant of yet another attempt to give Fox a spin-off or related series: *Pretty Things*, which Schwartz and Savage developed during Season Two, in between *Athens* and *Anthem*, a failed attempt to relocate *Athens* to the Dirty South.

Stephanie Savage: It was still that same quest of, "You guys refused to do the 'Summer moves to L.A. and becomes a fashion designer' spin-off. What you tried to do didn't work, twice—once for Gail, once for Liguori. Now, will you please spin off one of your actual characters and give us what we want?" *Pretty Things* was set at a boarding school in Santa Barbara, where Willa's character went.

Josh Schwartz: We already had attempted that, and we settled on this episode.

Stephanie Savage: As a consolation prize.

Josh Schwartz: Ghost Protocol

Schwartz turned twenty-nine early in production on Season Three—still very young by showrunner standards of the day, but no longer shockingly so. While growing older, he had also grown apart from the actors with whom he had once partied. But he had high hopes going into the new season. They did not last very long.

Josh Schwartz: A lot of the goodwill and drama that we built up at the end of Season Two just evaporated in that first episode of Season Three. I remember being in the editing room, watching that montage of them on the boat, and being like, *Where's the magic?* Everything felt very leaden. And I could feel in the performances, everybody was a little checked out.* I'm not putting this at the feet of the actors, by any means. But it didn't help. Sometimes if the story material isn't great or the scripts aren't great, you're hoping the charm of your cast can carry you, as it had in the past.

Some of the problems that followed may have been unavoidable, regardless of the directives from Fox, or the bad decisions Schwartz, Savage, and others would make regarding storylines and characters.

---

* Remember: just mentally add, "Well, except for Rachel and Melinda" after any and all statements like this.

Josh Schwartz: There's something inherent in teen dramas as you get into Season Three. The kids needing the adults in the same way starts to feel weird. The kids feel like adults. Some of [the actors] were well into their twenties at this point. It's harder to justify them needing Sandy's advice on something, or those two worlds interacting.

Adam Brody (Seth Cohen): If I had a criticism [with that season], it's not even the ridiculousness. I just think you need to take two or three times as long to get to where you're going. Then again, what do you fill the space with? You still need forty-five minutes of television every week.

Josh Schwartz: It was a lot of pressure, and I am someone who internalizes people's disappointment. I'm a real people pleaser. So when I knew I had a bunch of actors who were not happy with the quality of the scripts, that was hard for me. I felt bad about it. And I wish I had the ability to fix it, and I wish they loved it. But they didn't.

Ben McKenzie (Ryan Atwood): We all had various axes to grind, and Josh was trying to run a show and get through it all. And I'm sure the network was breathing down his neck over all sorts of stuff.

Very quickly, Schwartz decided the best way to avoid the actors' disappointment was to duck the cast altogether.

Josh Schwartz: I almost never went to set in Season Three, which is not something I'm proud of. It's not something I would do today. Becoming a parent very much informs how you act as a showrunner—not that actors or your crew are children, but you can't as a parent just not show up and expect your kid to thrive and grow and learn and feel loved. I delegated a lot of that to Bob or other people. It was my responsibility, and I should have taken it on more myself.

Stephanie Savage: I understood it, and in many respects I shared it. It wasn't fun to be there. Bob had more capacity to endure things that were uncomfortable.

Josh Schwartz: We took it much more personally. Bob wasn't on the pilot, so he hadn't had that initial bonding experience. He wasn't the same age as the actors and wasn't going out with them on the weekends, to feel the confusion of going from, *We're friends and we're doing this together to, Wait, the friends are rejecting the thing that we're making together? Are we even still friends anymore?*

The actors were not the only coworkers he was hiding from.

Josh Schwartz: There was a director upstairs in editing who I was having issues with, so I couldn't go upstairs. And I couldn't go into the writers' room because I wasn't seeing eye to eye with someone at the time. Bob found me sitting in the stairwell* with my hood on. He starts laughing and goes, "That is the portrait of a showrunner: Can't go to set, can't go to editing, can't go to the writers' room, just hiding in the stairwell with his hood on."

Stephanie Savage: There's also the feeling for the cast and the crew that if you're not on set, that you're not working on the show—you must be working on something else.

Josh Schwartz: By the time we got to Season Three, we were all burned out. We'd made so many episodes so quickly, and I think it wasn't a happy set for long stretches of it. Quite frankly, everybody was over it at that point. And I was one of those people who was over it at that point. It had been a great ride, but it had been a volatile ride.

Bob DeLaurentis (executive producer): It was like watching burnout in slow motion. On set, that's what you were seeing. Everything was just moving a little slower. Everybody was just a little less enthusiastic, less passionate, less engaged, more thinking about what other shows they could be on, or why the show wasn't doing better. It was just

---

* The same stairwell where they had filmed Ryan running to declare his love to Marissa on New Year's Eve in Season One.

the stuff that you would find fairly predictable in the environment we were in.

Josh Schwartz: Fundamentally, I felt like I was letting everybody down. We'd all bought into the promise of this thing, and I wasn't able to sustain it.

From Camp Gallagher to Unhappy Campers

Stephanie Savage: We went from a place of Season One, where we had the grips reading the scripts and coming in to work in the morning, laughing and quoting lines to each other, to the cast being very lackluster, starting to be a bit petulant with directors, having an attitude, reading a book during rehearsal instead of paying attention.

Melinda Clarke: We were very aware in Season Three of how disliked the scripts were, especially by the kids. Adam and Ben were like, *We're grown men and we're playing in high school still.* They didn't really ever talk to me personally about it, but that was the general understanding on set.

Peter Gallagher: I saw the seeds of our own demise in that [viewing party in Season One]. I think there were so many forces at work, opportunities for massive success coming at the cast. I'm sure it was challenging for the kids. And I don't think I ever really talked to them about it, because I was the old guy. They didn't really talk to me about all the cool stuff they were doing, I didn't get invited to all the cool stuff they were doing. I wouldn't go to the cool stuff, I was so happy to go home and hang out with my kids before they went to bed.

The older members of the ensemble, meanwhile, began to worry that they were being marginalized.

Bob DeLaurentis: There's a couple of times where we had conversations with the adult actors. And they were lobbying, or at least opening the discussion to the idea that we're missing a real opportunity not to have more family life, more adult presence in the show.

Kelly Rowan (Kirsten Cohen): I remember when they stopped [Kirsten] working and she started cooking. I was like, *Uh-oh*. I was holding the turkey up and suddenly I wasn't working at the Newport Group anymore. And I thought that was that character's whole identity. It was looped in with her father and everything.*

Peter Gallagher: I couldn't understand why we wouldn't continue to serve that world and that story. But then again, I am an actor. I am not a showrunner. And one thing I learned after that show was how little I know about the business [*laughs*].

The new actors did not arrive to the same sense of kinship that the original cast had experienced back in Season One.

Autumn Reeser: I was terrified. I was just trying to stay out of everyone's way. They were so famous and popular and cool. And had designers making things for them and were on the cover of every teen magazine. And the most expensive thing that I owned was a pair of $50 sweatpants. No joke. I felt so out of my league as far as the cultural world that I was entering into. I didn't feel unwelcome, but I didn't feel like part of a group, and I didn't expect to.

Rachel Bilson (Summer Roberts): The first year was really the year of the hangout. I can't remember Season Two, what was happening socially. But I don't think anyone was hanging out like that [in Season Three].

---

* One silver lining to being given fewer storylines was a lighter schedule. "There were a couple of times I was able to take trips for ten days," says Rowan. Such a long break in the midst of production would have been unimaginable in earlier seasons.

Autumn Reeser: We recently did a charity table read and everybody was talking about, "Those nights we used to go over to Peter's house for dinner and everybody was there." I was like, *I never got invited to Peter's house for dinner. I didn't even know that this was a thing that was happening.* Not that I needed to be. My point is that they'd had a whole two years of experience together before I ever came on. They had a completely different group dynamic.

Josh Schwartz: I mean this as a compliment, but actors are really unique, and they're like wild animals. Their whole thing is they want to roam and reinvent themselves. They're here for a little while, and then they go and they take on a new role and a new location. And when you're making a television show, you are the zoo, and you're putting these people in a cage. Those two things are fundamentally anathema. They don't line up the actor's need for reinvention and exploration and discovery and television's—network television, I would say at the time—need for status, repetition, reinforcing the fundamentals of the show. We tried to test that as much as we could. But network television, there are certain conventions to it: everybody at the end of the day had to revert back to who their characters were. That's why Sandy Cohen could not murder a home invader with a club! I think everybody was tired of being in a cage.

Preston Beckman: I think some of them wanted to move on a little bit. They became big stars in their minds.

Tate Donovan returned at the start of the season, first to play Jimmy angling to get a cut of Julie's inheritance, then to direct the eighth episode. Jimmy would leave town again in shame, while Donovan's directorial debut was nearly as messy.

Josh Schwartz: Tate's a relentlessly optimistic, upbeat guy. He was going to direct. I remember he had the sense of, "They're not going to do that to me. I'm one of them."

Behind the camera, Donovan had to deal with a much less collegial set than when he was a cast regular back in Season One. Early on, he filmed a scene with the four kids and was dismayed by the lack of enthusiasm and, from some, preparation.

Tate Donovan (Jimmy Cooper/director): Forget the script, they didn't read the scene! That doesn't happen in a vacuum. That doesn't happen because those four actors are lazy. That happens because the producer and the showrunner [needs to] come down and say, "Hey, get your shit together." I had heard that it was too painful for Josh to come down and see the actors not know his words. But so many times, an actor will read the scenes, like, "This is fucking bullshit, man. Why am I even saying this? It's so stupid." Josh found that painful. He always maintained a great relationship with all the actors. He was always friends with them. So he just decided, *Okay, I'm not going down there. I'm not [going to fight with them], I'm going to be friends and let the household management do all the [fighting].* [laughs]

The actors often felt like the ever-faster pace of production was hurting their work, and the end product.

Mischa Barton (Marissa Cooper): There was more [opportunity to think about the character] early on, when there was still time. By the third season, you were getting handed pages from episodes that weren't even written yet. So there was really nothing you could do when you were doubling up on episodes like that.

Josh Schwartz: In hindsight, had we had a big come-to-Jesus meeting and said, "Okay, you guys aren't happy, let's just air it all out and talk about it," they probably would have felt heard. They probably would have had some good ideas that would have enlightened us creatively. But you get very bogged down, because by the time a script gets to the cast, it's gone through the story breaking phase, where it's got to pass muster with the writers' room. It goes through the outline phase, where it's got to get past the studio and then the network; the script phase, where it's got to get past studio and network; the produce-ability phase, where it has to be something that can actually get made. And by the time it's gone through all of those iterations, that's when it gets to the cast. And so the idea that someone might be like, "I don't like the story," they are 100 percent valid to feel that way, and they may be entirely creatively justified. But you have so little time to adjust, and you've already gone through this whole process to get to this point of clearing all of these hurdles, that the idea of one more hurdle feels insurmountable. There's not enough time, and you're very defensive.

J. J. Philbin: I think we were all hiding our faces through that whole era, because we couldn't defend it. I remember being in tone meetings and being like, "I'm not exactly sure how you should play this, but maybe you'll get it . . ." And thinking, *Oh God, I hate myself right now.*

Peter Gallagher: I think we all felt like everybody was angry with us and disappointed in us and judging us harshly, and there were some other influences there that didn't really seem to understand or have affection for the kids. It was hard. I missed Josh.

Autumn Reeser: I was just trying to be respectful and do a good job. I think people were pretty unhappy. And I was in such a different place, where this was my big break. I was having a completely different experience. So there wasn't a lot that we could connect on. I remember at one point, everybody complaining in the hallway about the direction of the script. Peter was upset about something—some storyline that mostly the adults weren't happy with. And then the kids were joining in on that. I don't remember. It was just everybody really did not like the direction that the show was going in.

Mischa Barton: I remember a lot of actors complaining about the scripts.

Did she ever bring her own concerns about her material to the producers?

Mischa Barton: I said stuff to Stephanie and Josh and the showrunner. But that's the writers' room's responsibility, and I'm pretty sure it fell on deaf ears, to be honest.

Josh Schwartz: People were not getting along great. It was not a scandal. People weren't fighting, it wasn't hostile, the chemistry had just soured and we were no longer having fun making the show—myself included. And again, I should have sat everybody down, had individual conversations, and instead I just hid and tried to ride it out and get it over with.

Autumn Reeser: I didn't even know that you could complain about the direction the story was going! I was coming from this world where I'd been in an acting class with a bunch of young people trying to make it. And suddenly I was having "made it." So I was going back and forth between these two worlds, this world where everybody had everything that the other world was trying to get. It was a confusing period of time.

Peter Gallagher: I just noticed that there was a center missing—some source of affection and direction and appreciation. Success really will mess you up if you haven't had it before. You will stop asking questions and think you have all the answers and think, *Well, if I can do this, I can do that. I can do anything.*

Josh Schwartz: It was dark. When you're making a television show, you get very myopic. You can lose perspective, and every tenth of a ratings point can feel like a massive win or loss. Any episode that's received more or less positively feels much bigger than it is. And you lose the larger perspective of, *Hey, we're making something that people really enjoy watching, and we're bringing joy to a lot of people's lives.* I think that overall sense of appreciation—not for everybody, but certainly for myself and for some of the cast members—we all lost that a little bit. I remember going to the set of the first episode of that season, and nobody was into it. There was a real sense of exhaustion and ennui from day one, which I shared. I have to be honest, and I'm not saying this to shirk any responsibility, but I definitely was less creatively invested. The responsibility is still mine.

Ben McKenzie: The show had two generations of characters, and there was always a tension as to how much you were going to get out of the adult characters versus the kids. And I think an irony is that at some point the kids wanted less, the adults wanted more, and the show could not accommodate either of those desires.

The Guys Want Out

Adam Brody's and Ben McKenzie's discontent with *The O.C.*—and with the way their obligations to it were preventing them from taking other roles—had simmered for much of Season Two. In Season Three, it hit a boil.

Bob DeLaurentis: It was not at all surprising when [Adam] arrived at Season Three, I would say, generally unhappy most of the time.

Rachel Bilson: Because the show is such a success, certain people were in high demand. When you're on a show, you're committed for a lot of the years, and you can't do these other things. I think some of that frustration may have been a little too vocal.

Ben McKenzie: There were a lot of movies. Adam got deluged with offers. And I don't remember specific ones that got away for me, but I remember franchise movies and things where it's like, "There's interest, but they can't commit to you," and you're like, *All right, it is what it is.*

Josh Schwartz: You go from being the thing that's launching the actors into stardom, to being the thing that is prohibiting them from being able to do the kinds of things they want to do, or being bigger stars, at least in their perception.

Ben McKenzie: It wasn't as though I wasn't appreciative of the incredible opportunity. It was more a sense of restlessness, a sense that the thing that got you all this attention is the same thing that can be perceived as keeping you from taking advantage of it and doing all these other things that you want to do.

The producers tried to help the actors out with scheduling when they could, but it only sometimes worked out.

Josh Schwartz: Rachel got booked to do *Jumper*, that Doug Liman was directing. And it comes full circle, because Simon Kinberg, who haunted us during the filming of the pilot because of *Mr. & Mrs. Smith*, was reaching out because he was the writer-producer of *Jumper*. And Doug was directing and they wanted Adam.

Stephanie Savage: We couldn't release Adam to do it, because that was a bigger part.

Josh Schwartz: Ben was in an Al Pacino movie called *88 Minutes*, that we rejiggered the schedule to allow him to do.

Stephanie Savage: As we got later into the seasons, we realized we had to make some accommodations for them, because the level of unhappiness was extremely high.

Melinda Clarke: *Mad TV* wanted Adam and Ben to do a guest role as Seth and Ryan. They gave Adam a monologue, and it was very similar to the way Josh would write for Seth. And I guess the response from Adam was, *Oh my God, I'm doing a caricature of myself.* So the next time on set, he didn't want to continue to do what he had been doing.

Adam Brody: I think we started to get bored. So I would economize my reading of the scripts and my effort in a way, sorry to say. I was very okay, and going with the flow, and happy in my little actor bubble down there. I did a lot of reading and I was quite comfortable, and I liked everyone. I just did my thing and didn't worry about it.

Brody's disengagement became so palpable in his work that it led to one of the sillier plots in the run of the series: Seth becomes addicted to marijuana, which results in him missing his admissions interview for Brown University, and later burning down the Newport Group office with a carelessly discarded joint.

Josh Schwartz: Brody just changed his delivery, his investment in it. His style shifted to such a degree that we felt like we needed to account for it creatively. That's where "Kaitlin gets Seth hooked on pot" took root. We were like, "Well, how do we explain his lethargy on-screen? And at least if we can write that he's stoned, then we're not trying to write around it." It's the kind of storyline that we would have laughed at in Season One. And never would have done something that felt like it was a PSA or antidrug in any way, shape, or form.

Bob DeLaurentis: Adam was definitely more [worried about] the quality of his material going down. That was his specific objection. I remember at one point, in Season Four, he said to me in passing, "Does [Josh] think this is good?" But that was once. We'll give everybody a mulligan for having a really, really bad day.

Adam Brody: I was polite to everyone. I liked the directors, and the crew and I got on really well and I didn't keep people waiting. I would never scream or yell at anyone, or say anything fucking mean. But I think I very much let my distaste for the later episodes be known. I didn't mask that at all, and I'm sure I openly mocked it a bit. So I'm not proud of that.

Josh Schwartz: I remember Brody saying, "It's amazing. I get sent scripts all the time, for movies that I can turn down. I have to say yes to every single one of these scripts that come in." For an actor, that is frustrating.

Ben McKenzie: He was not shy about it. It was too bad, because I think that energy is an amorphous thing. It grows and seeps in, and it does feed on itself. And so everyone gets in the feisty, feisty mood. [It was] a challenge, and frustrating, and all those sorts of things. I think that at times each of us fell victim to that—except Rachel always had a good attitude. But it's impossible to determine causality. It just is this amorphous thing.

Autumn Reeser: I was disappointed. Because I thought he was a fantastic actor when I watched the show. And I think I was hoping to find more camaraderie there. But I have compassion for where he was at that time. I think the amount of pressure on those kids was extreme. Adam's a real artist and wanted the chance to stretch. And he was not feeling like he was getting that.

Stephanie Savage: When we started the show in Season One, it seems like the kids are juniors. In Season Two, they're also juniors. Season Three, they're seniors and I think all of them, but especially Ben and Adam, were freaking out that they had to stay in high school an extra year. I think we even had to adjust wardrobe, where they were like, "We're not wearing backpacks anymore, and no scenes of us sitting in desks."

Adam Brody: So you're a twenty-three-year-old tenth grader, yeah. [laughs] In looking at it again, what can I say? It's nice to look young. Not that we were fooling anyone, but it's nice to be youthful. And at the same time, a little infantilizing. The thing you want to do is be able to play a wise man with responsibility. And have a job and be an adult—you want to pretend to be an adult and not pretend to be a kid. But in hindsight, I had a baby face. I could have played a very baby-faced twenty-three-year-old, but I certainly didn't need to go be a lawyer or something.

Ben McKenzie: In my memory, and I could be wrong, I feel like Adam was much more strident about this stuff. But I'm sure there was some of that.

Adam Brody: I started to be creatively less interested. I blame myself for a lack of professionalism, and a disrespect to the work. In terms of engagement as a whole, I'll just say that they're different shows, Season One and [the later seasons]. Had the quality been the quality of Season One, I'm sure I would have been a lot more engaged. Not to say that I was just a fair-weather friend, and that that's okay. But I think the quality of it and my engagement went hand in hand. I think I could have been, and would now be, more respectful in that regard. But they really are so wildly different.

Brody could still be engaged at times, though, especially when he found the execution of the material interesting.

Norman Buckley (editor/director): Adam would come up to the editing room a lot. He was very, very skeptical of a lot of what I asked him to do in the first episode I directed. But then after he saw my episode, he never questioned me again. He was very cooperative, because he knew that I knew what I wanted, and knew that I was very clear about how I was going to put it together. We showed it to Adam and he was delighted. He was like, "Oh my God, I thought it was going to be a huge clusterfuck and it's great."

Peter Gallagher: I was not playing that many scenes with him by then. He was older, he was wiser, he was more famous—and, I'm sure, more in conflict about the future he envisioned. I could see maybe he was a little less patient, but not less good. When success happens, the molecules change. It doesn't make a person bad.

Rachel Bilson: Here is a thing about Brody: Even his half effort is still genius. Which is frustrating, cause you're like, "Dude, you can just phone it in and still be you," which is admirable in a way. [But] there were definitely times it was like, "Dude, sack it up." But it was a hard thing for me because on one side, it's my boyfriend, and the other side, it's my costar. So how do you balance that? Because you want to be supportive of the person you're with. But also I'm a firm believer in always being grateful, and gratitude comes first. And I think there were probably times where that went by the wayside. You grow up, you look back, and you can realize when you're young, you might behave in certain ways you wish you hadn't.

Adam Brody: Downstream of that, people really liked Seth and Summer together, which is great. So then break them up for a year, break them up for two years—really Ross and Rachel it. And instead, I felt like we were in this sitcom, where every episode we break up in the beginning over some misunderstanding. And then it'd be a comedic thing of me trying to get her back. And then I would, by the end, which was enjoyable. And like I said, I wasn't dying to do the melodrama, I was happy to do that light-stakes comedy. But I felt like in terms of stretching a dramatic storyline out to make people care—not just from the beginning of the episode to the end, but to make them really invested in the long haul—it sapped some of the power from potentially doing that.

Stephanie Savage: We still did hard copies of scripts then. So when the actors' new pages came out, they'd be delivered to their dressing rooms. Brody at a certain point said something like, *Oh, you can stop giving these to me. Because I am never going to read a script before I show up. I'll read the sides on the day, but you don't need to send me these blue pages anymore.* And we were like, "It might be a SAG rule that we have to send them to you." And he was like, "Whatever." And they would just pile up outside his door, symbolically.

Adam Brody: I'm not proud of this, but it became a bit of a game for me to see, *Can I find out what's going on story-wise by just my* *scenes?* And, again, is that professional? Not really. But I was on time! I was nice. And I knew my lines. I didn't keep anyone waiting. It's not a ringing endorsement for my conduct, but . . .

Norman Buckley: I reminded him on one episode I was directing in Season Three that he needed to be more invested—that I felt him going through the motions. I had a conversation with him where he was like, *Does it matter?* And I said, "Of course it matters. You have to play all of it. Just play it full out. I know you're better. You can read the phone book and make it great."

Josh Schwartz: I love Brody, I would work with Brody again in a heartbeat. And in the main, the character of Seth Cohen is obviously an enduring character. But he was so checked out in Season Three. Most actors, if they're unhappy with the material, if they don't like their costars—which is not the case here—when the camera is on, whether it's narcissism or vanity or professionalism, they're going to still deliver. And Brody had just locked into a new performance style, that was much lower energy, much less spark. He may not have felt that there was room for his brand of humor where the show was.

Ben McKenzie, meanwhile, didn't ease back on his performance in the same way Brody had, but everyone could sense that he was struggling with the job by this point.

Bob DeLaurentis: Ben's dilemma was not entirely dissimilar from Adam's. He wanted to be doing different work, work that he perceived to be of a higher quality. And in a different kind of show. We had gone out and had dinner one night near the start of Season Two. He was just up against that first wall of, *Wait a minute. This is my life for the next four years.* And the double whammy of, *I'm now going to be perceived as a teen star. And that's the only thing I'm going to ever get offered. My career is going up in flames. What do I do now? My future is gone.* And then at one point during the dinner, we had a couple of glasses of wine, and he confessed to me that what he really wanted to be was Sipowicz.

Sipowicz, for those too young to know or recall, was the main character on a popular nineties cop drama called *NYPD Blue*. He was a fat, bald, mustachioed, profane, bigoted middle-aged police detective played by Dennis Franz, a great character actor who, um, does not resemble Ben McKenzie.

Bob DeLaurentis: And I thought, *Wow, this charming, smart, good-looking kid, who's got the world by the short hairs, wants to be a character actor.*

Ben McKenzie: I was saying all kinds of weird shit like that [at that dinner]. I guess it's my nature, just pushing against the assumptions of, "You're the teen heartthrob. You love that and do that forever." Which [are] champagne problems. But I wanted to be taken seriously. The chip on my shoulder, it was pretty big.

Josh Schwartz: I was like, *I don't know how to deliver a Sipowicz experience with this character.*

Eventually, Schwartz found a way—sort of. In one Season Three episode, Ryan ends up at a strip club. A dancer wearing the fetish version of a police uniform introduces herself to him by saying, "Hi, I'm Sipowicz." An uncomfortable Ryan replies, "Hi, Sipowicz."

Bob DeLaurentis: Oh, my God! I did not write that.

Stephanie Savage: One hundred percent, it was a joke about that.

Josh Schwartz: He's a really smart guy. I don't know that he ever was fully on the ride in a way that wasn't without some level of complication for him as part of his journey. But I get it. You go in and read for a pilot. Next thing you know, you've signed a six-year contract and you're known as this character and your face is on magazines. It's great, but it's terrifying, and it's something to reckon with.

Ben McKenzie: At the time, you don't have any other work to show people. So there's an easy conflation to make that you're just the character—you're just a guy who only does the one thing, because you haven't done anything else yet. It's hard not to internalize that, and to get a little ornery about that. Adam certainly did as well. But then, life goes on, and you adjust, and you have new experiences.

The Bright Spots

There was still enthusiasm from the two newcomers to the ensemble, along with the continued good spirits of Melinda Clarke and Rachel Bilson—not coincidentally, two cast members who had grown up around the business and tended to view it as a job first and foremost.

Autumn Reeser: Going back over the show, Melinda's so funny, her character is so campy and glamorous and soapy and just delicious. She's so good at it. And beautiful, and appears to be having a great time, too. I always enjoy watching when you can tell an actor's enjoying themselves.

Melinda Clarke: I've always tried to be positive on set. That's the way my dad was on his show for forty years. I guess it just comes from, I'm grateful. I want to be there. I like the job and I want to make sure that they want to have me around. I once worked with somebody who rewrote every scene. I was like, "Oh, you've got to be careful about doing that. Eventually, they'll kill you off the show." It depends on what you want. If you don't want to be on a show, you can be hard to work with.

Willa Holland: I had never seen a writers' room before, and I had never seen the little writers' cafeteria. So I just lived in there and ate all the candy for thirty minutes. I remember being so excited, seeing behind the scenes, because I'd never really seen that too much before on that level.

Josh Schwartz: Rachel on the whole was always good-spirited, and didn't seem to have the same level of at least outwardly being disgruntled as the show wore on.

Rachel Bilson: I was a pretty go-with-the-flow kind of person. I don't like ruffling feathers. I just like things to be easy, so I try to be easy myself.

Autumn Reeser: Rachel always made me feel welcome, made me feel appreciated. She's just a little ray of sunshine. She's easygoing. I don't remember her complaining very much. I also think the amount of pressure on her was crazy. When we would shoot on location, we'd get paparazzi trying to photograph her and Adam. That was very scary. There's people in the bushes taking pictures of you, and it was expected to be part of their normal life, something they couldn't complain about. That was weird and unsafe and very unsettling.

Reeser's enthusiasm didn't wane over time, but she eventually came to understand the less eager mindset of her costars.

Autumn Reeser: I think everyone was exhausted. I didn't have that much to do and this was my dream coming true. It's a completely different experience. But Season Four, I was really tired coming out of it. I didn't have any creative juice left. And that was only after sixteen episodes of being a series regular. So I can't even imagine how exhausted they were after three seasons of twentysomething episodes each, and the amount of press they had to do and the amount of cultural pressure it was. I think it was a lot on all of them.

Still, it was hard not to feel frustrated that her dream job no longer seemed to be anyone else's.

Autumn Reeser: I went to the upfronts for Season Four. Which is, in all the acting schools around town, the ultimate goal: "You get to go to upfronts!" It means you've made it. So I finally get to go to upfronts, and none of the kids come. It's just me and, I think, Peter and Mindy. And I missed my best friend's wedding to go to this, because you're told it means you've made it. All of the bs that we believe, you're excited and your dreams are coming true and you think it's going to be one thing. And then it's something different.

Johnny Be Bad

Much of the cast's creative discontent centered around the season's biggest and most miscalculated storyline: Marissa is expelled from Harbor as fallout for shooting Trey, and enrolls at Newport Union, the public high school elsewhere in town. She soon befriends a trio of characters presented as funhouse mirror versions of Ryan, Seth, and Summer: respectively, aspiring pro surfer Johnny, Johnny's wisecracking best friend Chili, and Johnny's girlfriend Casey. The story was meant to be a reinvention for our heroine, and a chance for her to not be the damsel in distress for once. Instead, she would take on Ryan's role as the new kid from the other side of the tracks, who has to repeatedly save the unfortunate Johnny.

J. J. Philbin: We tried a few storylines that just weren't right for the show.

John Stephens: We made some decisions that I wish we could take back. [*laughs*]

Sara Morrison (Television Without Pity recapper): The whole public school storyline was both hilarious and annoying, because I went to public school. I remember [Newport Union] being full of horrible, poor criminals. And I was like, *I'm pretty sure my local school is in a less nice town than Newport Beach. Did any of the writers go to public school?* They spent a lot of that season picking on poor people.

Stephanie Savage: I'm not saying this would have been a good story, but coming out of the end of Season Two, we talked about how maybe we could start Season Three with Marissa in, like, a Sybil Brand prison. She could be in an orange jumpsuit and facing real consequences. Trey could really die; Sandy could be involved in a legal defense of her. There's some big juicy story here. But is "girls behind bars" really the show? No. Is Sandy in the courtroom helping to defend Marissa really the show? No.

Josh Schwartz: But at least that would have been a story where the adult world and the kid world met.

John Stephens: One of the things I learned from that was how easy it is to lose touch with what makes the show special. Part of the reason people watched the show was they were suddenly going to Orange County in Southern California, and they were on the beach, and there was sunshine, and it was this combination of aspirational and edgy at the same time. And all of a sudden it was like, *Oh, no, we're putting Marissa in this place.* And it wasn't even an accurate depiction of a Southern California public school. It's terrible! We weren't giving people what they actually were watching the show for.

Josh Schwartz: A lot of Season Two had felt like it suffered from, until Trey showed up, a lack of strong villains or conflict for the show. There were conversations around having strong antagonistic figures, which is what led to Taylor Townsend. It's what led to Dean Hess, and to Marissa going to public school. Seinfeld was the reference, like Bizarro Jerry and Bizarro Kramer and Bizarro George, but in public school, was something we were intrigued by. God, I can't even remember what the best hope was of what the Johnny archetype could be, but it was somebody similar to Ryan that Marissa could save, instead of Ryan saving Marissa.

Stephanie Savage: The idea of the Bizarro world, that made a lot of sense. But then the piece that didn't make sense is that the Ryan version of that character actually *is* Ryan. That's the same character. So the thing that could make it different is if now Marissa can show that she has learned and grown, and she has some more tools that she could actually help somebody else. That's the positive version. And then the more troubled, conflict-creating version is that she actually doesn't have those tools that she thinks she does, and she gets in over her head, trying to save somebody else, and needs to be saved again.

The producers didn't have to look very far to find an actor to play Chili, picking Adam Brody's former housemate Johnny Lewis.

Patrick Rush (casting director): We had him come back for Seth, and Josh Schwartz really loved that kid. I remember opening the door for McG's office, and there was a kid sitting down the hall with dark hair and really dark eyebrows that I didn't recognize. And it was him, and he had dyed his hair to look more like Peter Gallagher. And his eyebrows. He looked like Groucho Marx.*

The character of Johnny proved harder to cast, in part because Schwartz and Savage blew a chance to hire an actor who would go on to a very successful career.

Patrick Rush: I had seen Sebastian Stan audition from New York for some role, and they weren't testing him. And I sent it to Josh and Stephanie, like, "This kid's really good." And they flew him out to test, and still didn't hire him.

---

* In the years that followed, Johnny Lewis battled substance abuse and mental health problems, and was arrested multiple times. On September 26, 2012, he was found dead outside his home from a fall off the roof, shortly after he allegedly beat his eighty-one-year-old landlady to death. "I don't remember Johnny exhibiting any of those qualities when he was on the show," says Josh Schwartz. "I don't remember him being problematic when he was on the show. Knowing him through Brody in the years prior, he was the sweetest, most kind—just a really good person, and funny. It's shocking how it all ended up. It's just hard to even hold those two people in your head as the same person."

On a group chat, Schwartz and Savage confessed to no memory of Stan—
who would later appear on *Gossip Girl* before finding even greater celebrity
in the Marvel Cinematic Universe—auditioning in Season Three. Informed later that the specific role he read for was Johnny, Schwartz texted
"Oh my," while Savage responded, " 😬 wtf is wrong w us??" Instead, the
job went to Ryan Donowho—who probably would have been better off
also not landing this controversial part.

Josh Schwartz: We didn't remember seeing Sebastian Stan in person; I still don't think we saw him in person. We didn't even see Ryan
Donowho in person. We cast him off a tape, which is something we
rarely did back then. But we were late in the process. We couldn't
find anyone we liked for the part. We saw Ryan's tape and were like,
"That's the guy." He felt soulful and he felt troubled, and he felt like
this blue-collar kid. We didn't realize how much physically smaller he
was than his counterparts till we had started shooting, which was part
of the trick of it.

J. J. Philbin: [Newport Union was] the worst. And we knew it at the
time. It's that nightmare feeling of, you go down a road where, in theory, these things don't sound so bad. And then by the time you realize
it's a bad idea, you're so deep in that you can't extract yourself.

Josh Schwartz: The writers turned on Johnny pretty early. Nobody
really knew how to write him. I don't want to put this at all at the feet
of the actor. I've said some things in the past that've gotten to Ryan
Donowho in the press, that he has rightfully taken issue with. It's not his
fault. That character was ill-conceived, and an actor can be miscast
for a part. It doesn't mean they are a bad actor; it just means being
miscast for the part. Brody wanted to play Ryan. That would not have
worked. There's no knock on Brody's talent; he just wasn't Ryan. And
we cast someone who wasn't a Johnny, partially because we didn't
really know who Johnny was.

So who would have been the ideal actor to play Johnny?

Josh Schwartz: Well, clearly it was Sebastian Stan!*

Rachel Bilson: I feel bad, because Ryan Donowho is a lovely young actor and he did great. What else was he supposed to do? But I could not stand Johnny. Tiny Tim drives me insane every time. I'm like, "What the fuck?!" In our rewatch, we're at this point. Marissa, did she have feelings for him? I'm like, *What did I miss? When did Marissa have feelings for him? Like, where did that happen?* I never saw that happen. I saw Johnny being a little bitch. Sorry, speaking of the deceased, that way, I apologize. But I just . . . I was so angry. The whole storyline was so aggravating.

Josh Schwartz: I think part of the issue that the writers had with the Newport Union crew, and ultimately with Marissa's character and a lot of those storylines, was feeling like they were not fun. Everything was just ending up being very dark, very dramatic, very heavy. The storylines that always worked best for us, we were able to lace all of that with humor. Suddenly we had five Olivers in our show instead of just one.

Johnny, like Oliver before him, becomes fixated on Marissa, and his life is ruined as a result. Casey† breaks up with him, and his promising surfing career ends abruptly once he's hit by a car when he chases after Ryan to insists that he's not trying to steal his girlfriend.

Josh Schwartz: People were watching the show to watch our main cast. Very quickly, Johnny became what every storyline was about,

---

* Schwartz: "I said to Patrick Rush, 'This is the worst thing to come out of this book. I hate us.' He goes, 'You can just tell him not to put it in the book.' And I said, 'No, the shame must be publicly shared. We cannot hold this inside.'"

† Casey was played by Kayla Ewell, whose work Schwartz and Savage had admired in several episodes of *Freaks and Geeks*. But they never quite figured out what to do with her once Johnny fell for Marissa, and—unlike the rest of the Newport Union group—cut bait on the character after only three episodes.

and had more screen time than anybody else. And even an episode that conceptually I was excited about—Seth throws Ryan a bar mitzvah—somehow, that storyline ended up being to support a Johnny story. We were just bedeviling ourselves at every turn and challenging our audience.

Stephanie Savage: That's a lesson that we learned: People do not like when the focus of the story is the main character helping the guest characters. Guest characters are good antagonists. They create conflict. People do not like when everyone who they've been watching for three years and loved is here having conversations about, "How can we help Johnny?" They don't really care about Johnny. If Johnny's causing interesting problems between our characters, that's one thing. But just helping Johnny because he has lots of problems is not something that they wanted to watch.

When Marissa spurns his declarations of love, Johnny spirals emotionally and begins hanging out with Kaitlin Cooper, who thinks flirting with this guy will get under her sister's skin. Eventually, a drunken, embittered Johnny falls to his death off a cliff overlooking the Pacific. The whole Johnny arc was so cursed that even his death scene created postproduction difficulties.

Matt Ramsey (editor): My worst nightmare. Him falling off the cliff was a major problem. We had to go back and do some reshoots, like inserts of his shoe and his foot and stuff. The director couldn't get the camera where they wanted it, so he shot it on the other side of the line, and then we flopped the shot to make it work. It was all these problems.

Josh Schwartz: The final indignity for that storyline was when that episode aired, the music card came up and said, "This week's music brought to you by Rock Kills Kid," which was the name of the band that played somewhere in the episode. None of us had put that math together.

Willa Holland: A year or two after the show ended, I was in New Orleans filming a movie. I was walking down Bourbon Street, people were drunk, and I hear somebody screaming at the top of their lungs, "You killed Johnny!" They're coming at me full throttle. It was an intense, intense moment. And I remember having to coax her down. I'm like, "No, no, no, no. He's alive. That's not real. It didn't really happen. I'm not her."

Stephanie Savage: What's crazy is he falls off a cliff, and then *we keep telling Johnny stories*. There's stories about his cousin Sadie,* his mom. Even after he was dead, we have a whole episode of his funeral. It just went on and on and on.

About the only part of the Newport Union story that worked at all was Kevin Volchok, the bad boy who functioned as the Bizarro Luke to Johnny. The producers liked actor Cam Gigandet so much that they kept Volchok† around long after that story was over, even having Marissa date him for a while as part of a self-destructive streak post-Trey and post-Johnny.

Josh Schwartz: He was somebody who popped off the screen. In a year where it felt like marquee players were wanting off the marquee, he was somebody who felt like he had star quality, who women in the audience were responding to, as despicable a character as he could be at times. And the OG Luke-Trey archetype had worked for us in the past.

---

* Sadie was, like Alex in Season Two, a teenager already living an adult life, designing and selling her own jewelry. "McG's friend, Maya Brenner, actually designed Sadie's jewelry," says Savage. "Maya has become very successful since then—not because of designing Sadie's line." She was played by Nikki Reed, who had been on the producers' radar since her acclaimed debut performance in *Thirteen*, a film she cowrote as a teenager.

† Named after Adam Brody's agent.

The Ol' College Try

Though the actors weren't happy being in high school for another year, it gave the writers an opportunity to do some final coming-of-age plots before figuring out how to make the show work post-Harbor.

Josh Schwartz: We thought senior year would be a good organizing principle. We could build the season around college applications, who's going where, the future. That's good, rich, relatable, universal stuff.

While Ryan and Marissa each struggle with where to go—or whether they even want to go to college—Seth and Summer quickly settle on the idea of heading east together to Brown University. Seth, though, ruins his shot due to his ridiculous pot addiction.

Stephanie Savage: I actually think some of those storylines are good. When Seth didn't get into Brown and Summer did, and the emergence of Summer as not just not being superficial, but actually smart, I think is a really good one.

Leila Gerstein (writer/producer): The only thing that I know I contributed that year was asking, "Well, why can't Summer be smart?"

Josh Schwartz: There are definitely storylines that worked. But for whatever reason, we just kept doubling down on the things that weren't working.

Stephanie Savage: It really is like a bad relationship or like how you're trying to fix your relationship with your parents by dating people that remind you of them, but trying to have a different outcome. Doesn't work.

The Parent Trap III: Who the #$@! Is Matt Ramsey?

The Newport Union story arc was a fiasco. No one denies this. But there was at least a germ of a solid idea in reversing Marissa's usual role. There is, on the other hand, absolutely no explaining or justifying the sheer amount of time that Season Three devoted to Matt Ramsey, a cocky young executive who joins Sandy in running the Newport Group and does . . . something? It's really unclear what he is up to, or why—there's a contract to build a hospital, maybe?—or, most importantly, why the season is so dedicated to that character, played by actor Jeff Hephner.

> **Sara Morrison:** Oh God, I don't care about the Newport Group. Never cared about the Newport Group. No viewer of *The O.C.* is going to care about the Newport Group. Sandy's a lawyer. Why was he running the Newport Group? And Matt was weird and boring.

Schwartz and Savage put off this topic in multiple conversations for this book—even rescheduling several Season Three–related interviews for reasons that may or may not have been real—before finally running out of other things to discuss from that terrible year. At first, both respond to the "Matt Ramsey: why?" question with a shrug, only to be reminded that a shrug is not conducive to an oral history book.

> **Josh Schwartz:** Write, "Both stare at each other dumbfounded." I don't know. All I can tell you is we named him after our editor, Matt Ramsey.

> **Matt Ramsey:** It made me laugh at first, but then the guy is pretty douchey.

> **Josh Schwartz:** But God, if there's a storyline that I remember the least of from the show, it's got to be that one.

Stephanie Savage: The struggle of Matt Ramsey [the character] is that you wanted him to be a young hotshot, Tom Cruise kind of a guy who would be getting Sandy in trouble, doing dirty deals, getting Sandy to bribe people or bring prostitutes to the party, or test Sandy's limits in some way. Those stories could be fun stories. But then we never really let ourselves go there. So he was a nonstory every week. Nothing really ever happened.

John Stephens: Season One to a large degree was so successful because Josh and Stephanie knew what the show was. The stories they were telling on the Sandy side were the fatherhood of Seth, becoming a father to Ryan, being a husband, and those stories were told really well. And all of a sudden, we were telling the story about Sandy's moral slide. I don't think the show was built to tell that story.

Norman Buckley: I was directing these scenes, *I don't even know what I'm directing here, because nobody cares about this shit. What are they talking about?* When I did Melinda and Rachel's podcast, I went back to watch the episode, and I had totally forgotten about those scenes.

Marissa turns to Matt for advice on a few occasions, and even sleeps in his apartment one night, platonically, much to the disapproval of Sandy.

Stephanie Savage: If Matt Ramsey had crossed the line with Marissa in some way, at least it would have been a story. But a story where Marissa just hangs out with Matt Ramsey and nothing happens, that isn't a story. I can't quite explain it. I don't know why we didn't say, "If we're not doing the story where Matt Ramsey is a guy who's testing everyone's limits, then I don't know why we have this character in the show. And we should just not do Matt Ramsey stories." But we kept doing these watered-down, 60 percent interesting stories at best.

Josh Schwartz: It's the same reason why a lot of the Johnny stuff didn't work: we weren't fully committing to any of these things. The tone of the show was a tricky one. For the first two seasons, obviously it's not perfect, but we walk the line pretty well and knew what the show was ultimately. Season Three, we were trying to figure out what this new version of the show was going to be that could work for Fox, but it wasn't any of our natural creative instincts. I think we lost a sense of what the show was, because we were throwing it creatively in the opposite direction of any of our instincts. Left to our own devices, which is what Season Four was, maybe it skewed too much in the other direction.

Stephanie Savage: It's like being trapped in wanting to do something that was true to the show, but also wanting to do something that was big enough to get the ratings. The version of the show that we had made in Season One was not fit to survive as a Top 20 Fox show on Thursday night. Trying to get it to be that show but then also not wanting to go too far, or violate what we thought the show was, we didn't jump the shark; we just paddled around in the ocean trying not to drown.

Josh Schwartz: Season One, we were jumping the shark left and right.

The loss of Caleb, it turned out, had created a void on the adult side that couldn't be filled.

Josh Schwartz: With Caleb's death, it was a harder and harder story to serve in a way that felt like it was touching all the characters. Peter was always lobbying, "Put me in these sexy situations. That's what people want to see." And he wasn't wrong. But the Newport Group stories were not sexy situations. No one really knew how to write them. No one wanted to write them. And we assumed, correctly, that the audience didn't really want to watch them. That's not what you tuned into the show for.

At least one good thing came out of the Matt Ramsey storyline, even if Ben McKenzie didn't realize it at the time: Matt spends a few episodes flirting with a character played by Morena Baccarin, who would go on to marry McKenzie while they were working together on the comic book drama *Gotham*.

Ben McKenzie: She gives me grief to this day. It's her favorite story about me, that she was very polite, maybe even hitting on me, and I blew her off.

Femme Fatally Dull

Kirsten goes into rehab at the end of Season Two, and in Season Three, she falls under the sway of Charlotte, a con woman played by Jeri Ryan from *Star Trek: Voyager*. Like almost everything else about the season, it was a miss.

Josh Schwartz: The calls about needing to boost the ratings and broaden the adult appeal of the show led to Charlotte, who was named Charlotte because the big hope was that we would get Charlotte from *Sex and the City*—Kristin Davis. And that would be the kind of DNA to bring into the show to help broaden the audience.

Craig Erwich: Our head of research was like, "We need to broaden out the show." And then that started this very stupid conversation about, "Where's our Heather Locklear?"

Stephanie Savage: I have memories of being told that we needed to add "an adult femme fatale," and a pot-stirrer. And we were like, "We have a pot-stirrer. Her name is Julie Cooper." But I think the feeling from the network side was that Julie Cooper had become too soft and likable and well-rounded to fulfill what they wanted from this.

Craig Erwich: Julie, I think we'd run out of steam.

Stephanie Savage: Ironically, that story started to work a little bit better when Charlotte became friends with Julie Cooper, and you had those guys doing more mischievous things, versus this more hard con plot. I can't even really remember how that was going to work, but I think she wanted to somehow steal all of Kirsten's money. And she made Kirsten her pawn, only to find out that in our other story, Kirsten has lost all her money, and it wasn't going to work out.

Josh Schwartz: Was *that* the story? When you pitch it like that, I don't hate it!

Stephanie Savage: Lara Flynn Boyle came in to talk about playing Charlotte. She was really fun, and she was like, "I'd be interested if my storyline was sleeping with all the young guys." And that is what that version of that story should be on this show, versus someone trying to extort money from Kirsten, who doesn't have any money. Lara Flynn Boyle had a better idea than what we're being told to do by the network! Any story that didn't double back to the kids was always going to be a hard story for us to tell.

Craig Erwich: We basically put a gun to Josh's head and said, "You have to bring in Jeri Ryan." It was a stunt, which he really did not want to do.

The Charlotte story did lead to another silver lining, though. Julie discovers that Caleb died broke, and after she declines to rebuild her fortunes by helping Charlotte hustle the Newpsies, she has to move to a trailer park in a seedier part of town—a setting that frequently led to fun moments in a season that was desperate for them.

Josh Schwartz: Julie Cooper was a character who had proven that she was able to work in every world, and Melinda had chemistry with every actor that we put her in scenes with. It was just too delicious to turn down the idea of her back in her trailer park days, with Bob Seger and some booze.

Melinda Clarke: What's interesting is, have you ever seen Julie so happy as when Kaitlin's there and Marissa's there and they have this little scene together in the trailer? Her fear was, *What if I can't pay my bills? And what if I live in a trailer park?* Well, guess what? Julie discovered that she still has friends, she still has her family that love her, and she's never actually been happier. Doesn't mean she's not going to want for these things again. So I think it's so endearing to the audience. And then everybody accepts her.*

Prom Night

The Harbor kids' senior prom arrived at a moment late in the season when both of the two central couples were once again broken up. The writers decided to bring back Theresa and Anna (the latter of whom had already popped up during Seth and Summer's visit to Brown) to be Ryan and Seth's prom dates†—and as a Hail Mary pass from a more successful era for the show.

Josh Schwartz: We were just looking to find that old Season One magic wherever we could, like, *Okay, let's bring back two people that were part of that time when it was magical.* Samaire, when she came back to the show, she was not in a good place.

Samaire Armstrong (Anna Stern): I have to admit, I was going through my own stuff, so I was probably more self-consumed.

Josh Schwartz: It immediately felt like we were not recapturing magic, this is not working.

---

* Julie's time in the trailer park is over before the end of the season, though. She begins to date Summer's plastic surgeon father, Neil Roberts (Michael Nouri), and eventually she and her daughters move into Neil's mansion. When the relationship falls apart in Season Four, Dr. Roberts leaves town, but lets Julie keep living in his house.

† Marissa goes with Volchok, while Summer reluctantly accompanies the K-pop star cousin of Taylor Townsend's date. Taylor eventually takes both cousins home herself, later bragging, "It was hot and spicy, and let's just say I had my very own Korean barbecue."

Samaire Armstrong: It was so awkward. I felt again like the new kid. Everyone had been filming all season. They had their inside jokes. They were so lovely, but I did feel super out of place. I wish I could go back and do it all again. I would just soak up every moment of it and enjoy it. I guess that's so much of life, though.

As part of Theresa's return, we see that her son is now a little boy who looks much more like Ben McKenzie than Eric Balfour. So who is the father: Ryan or Eddie?

Josh Schwartz: Eddie.

Stephanie Savage: Eddie.

Navi Rawat: I always thought that it was Ryan's. And Theresa didn't want to tell him because she loved him as a friend, and because it was a decision that she ultimately made on her own. I think she did that in the spirit of their friendship, and in the spirit of loving him enough to set him free.

Goodbye, and Good Luck

There is still one major Season Three development that we will talk about at length in the next chapter. But before that catastrophe, the Cohens, the Coopers, the Atwoods, and the Robertses gather to celebrate their kids' graduations, and Sandy delivers this toast: "There's been tragedy and comedy and first loves and broken hearts and family members lost and found. It hasn't all been perfect, but we're all family here." It feels like the type of meta-commentary a character will offer in a series finale—or, at least in the season finale of a show with an uncertain future.

Josh Schwartz: I don't know if we thought that, but it was definitely written from a place of defensiveness. It was very much about both the characters and the making of the show.

Schwartz's own season-ending farewell to the cast and crew was much less poetic.

Josh Schwartz: In the video for the Season Three wrap party, I am featured hiding under my desk and just saying, "Is it over? Is it over?" And that aired at the wrap party, which I did not attend.

CHAPTER 9

The Death in the Family

ALL THE CREATIVE mistakes and backstage drama of Season Three converged in its final episode, "The Graduates," where Volchok, still fixated on Marissa—and angry with Ryan for screwing up a plan to steal a luxury car from one of Sandy and Kirsten's neighbors—runs Ryan's Jeep off the road, killing Marissa. It's a story with a lot of blame to go around behind the scenes, almost none of it falling at the feet of Mischa Barton herself.

Foreshocks

Barton was the initial face of *The O.C.*, but she never entirely seemed at home on the show in the way so many of her costars—not coincidentally, all of them older than her—had been.

Bob DeLaurentis (executive producer): The dominant image I have, Mischa is sitting in one of our fold-up chairs, reading a Penguin Classic. She was very much the youngest of the group. There's a huge, huge gap between seventeen and twenty-two, and as a result, I think clearly felt like the odd person out of the Core Four.

Josh Schwartz (creator/executive producer): A lot of fame came at her very quickly. And there's a lot of positive that comes with that. But even though the Internet was in its infancy then, it could still be a cruel place. Perez Hilton was hounding her, paparazzi, the critics weren't always kind to her.

Barton was also being asked to burn the candle at both ends in a way no one else on the show was.

Josh Schwartz: She was working all the time. If she wasn't working on the show, there were a lot of endorsement deals and appearances.

Mischa Barton (Marissa Cooper): There were years when I only had six days off in the whole year. It was tiring. It was a lot. And when you weren't filming, you were promoting the show and doing press and touring. There really wasn't any time off for me. It was exhausting. I don't think I realized how exhausting it was for a while, though.

Rachel Bilson (Summer Roberts): I think there was pressure from her mom wanting Mischa to be doing [a lot]. I think it was probably too much for this teenager to be doing as much as she had to do. And she did it gracefully.

Alan Dale (Caleb Nichol): I know all the stories and everything, but my experience of her was that she was delightful. I thought she worked really hard to fit in and do as well as she could.

Rachel Bilson: Nuala was always nice to me, but I think she definitely had that, *Make sure that Summer doesn't have more things to do or say than Marissa* vibe. And I do think it was, like, stage mom.

Josh Schwartz: When you are the breadwinner for your family, it's really complicated. As a family member, you have certain priorities for the person you are looking after, but when they're the manager and this is their client, it's a different set of priorities. And I think it can be very challenging to keep those priorities separated.

Patrick Norris (director): Look, it's hard being a mom of a teenager on a TV show. There's no doubt about it. There's a lot of boundaries that are pushed, and there's a lot of hours that are pushed. Sure, we can say the mom is a pain in the ass, but I've been on so many teen shows where I've seen this play out. Where the mom is the advocate for the teen that is working fourteen to sixteen hours a day, no life, and rushed back the next day to do the same. In that sense, I couldn't have anything negative to say. She was a protective mom.

Bob DeLaurentis: Her mother was concerned for Mischa's career—that she should be on the precipice, by Season Three, of starting to get some offers to be in the company of some other young female Hollywood actors. And they weren't coming.

Stephanie Savage (executive producer): As time went on, she had a lot of responsibilities outside the show, which I think contributed to her feelings of unhappiness. It would be that everyone would shoot on a Fraturday* and everyone would be so tired and spend the weekend sleeping and chilling out. And Mischa would have had to have flown to Ireland for the Irish Oscars, or gone to Harrods to open a boutique.

Lisa Cochran (unit production manager): Mischa wanted to leave. That's not a secret, I think.

Bob DeLaurentis: She was starting to, I think, be really, really distracted. I could see that all was not happy, that she was going through stuff, and that that their relationship was complicated. And guess what? Teenage girls and their mothers, it can be a bumpy road, especially when your mother is your manager and around all the time. And I think she was itching to get out and have a life.

Stephanie Savage: Mischa definitely had a level of unhappiness, which, again, if we had dealt with it directly, maybe we could have worked together.

Josh Schwartz: But she also wanted to go to college.

---

* A production day planned to begin relatively late on a Friday and end sometime after midnight on a Saturday.

Stephanie Savage: She was talking about going to NYU, not living in Los Angeles.

Bob DeLaurentis: When you're that age, you want to be out there having a normal life. You want to be at school. You want to do all of the things she couldn't do. I think that was really a terrible burden. I think that the wheels started to come off in Season Three. I know she was involved in a couple of relationships. I spent a lot of time with her mother talking about issues that she was going through.

Rachel Bilson: [By] Season Three, it was a lot of, "Oh, we're doing this again." It just seemed like maybe [she was] not as much into it. I don't want to speak [for her]; I think she's dealt with so much, and she's been pretty vocal about how awful this experience was for her. Come Season Three, I don't think she really wanted to be there. But I think there were a lot of people that maybe didn't want to be there.

Bob DeLaurentis: Even when you thought, *Well, she's not really passionate about this*, or, *She's not maybe as prepared as she could be*, she would always come in, hit the mark, say the lines, deliver the performance. I remember her as being in many ways the most reliable of the four kids—she had no problems with anything. She didn't ask for a line to be changed. She just came in and did her job like a professional. And I have very, very fond memories of her, because I think her life got incredibly overcomplicated from that point on.

Melinda Clarke (Julie Cooper-Nichol): Yes, there were days where you could feel negative energy. I can't even point to anything super-specific because everyone's so professional. I never saw anyone be unprofessional.

Josh Schwartz: I was not hyperaware of what was happening in her personal life. It wasn't impacting her work. I think she was just going through this process of growing up and being an actual teenager in a very public way. And on television in the public eye. There was paparazzi, and her relationships were being chronicled. I'm sure that was a really intense environment to be working in.

Stephanie Savage: Warners was very clear that they did not want us talking about that—that anything that fell into that zone of being a friend or being a parent-type of person was not our conversation to have. They were very clear that they didn't want us overstepping in any way. We're employers. These are employees. They have employee rights. They have to have their privacy respected. What they do after hours is none of our business unless it's impacting their work during the day.*

Norman Buckley (editor/director): She was never petulant. I feel like there's just a reputation over the years that's completely at odds with what my experience was. I really don't know where that comes from, because I found her to be a pleasure, in spite of the fact that she was under enormous amounts of pressure.

The producers have many decisions they wish they could have changed.

Bob DeLaurentis: If there was one thing that I would do differently if we went back to when we were casting The O.C., I would look to find an older actress. Because the other three had an ease and a facility with each other, and I don't think they ever had that with her. And it was hurtful. I think she felt it. I don't know how acutely she felt it, but she didn't mix and mingle a lot. She'd be sitting there with her book.

Stephanie Savage: There was one day when we were shooting, and it was a really nice vibe on set. Everyone was sitting around laughing, telling stories. Mischa was sitting in her chair out by the pool house by herself, with her back to us, reading a CAA script. And looking back

---

* This was at least a lesson learned for future Schwartz-Savage shows. "Later," says Savage, "when we did *Gossip Girl*, because I'd had this experience, I was like, *I'm not doing that. I'm crossing that line. Because however you think of us, we're still adults in these kids' lives, and they don't have that many of them. So I'm going to do what I need to do to be a good person and sleep at night.*"

on that moment, I'm like, *Why didn't I just walk over there and go,* "Hey, everyone's sitting over here having a nice time and chatting, and we'd love for you to join us"? Whether she said yes or no, that was up to her. But I remember just looking over with a very immature feeling of, *I guess she's too cool for us now to sit around and laugh,* versus a more mature feeling of, *Maybe she feels left out. Maybe she doesn't want to come over because she hasn't been invited.* Just not being able to see that from an adult perspective, and feeling more like my feelings were hurt that Mischa wasn't joining us, versus being a grown-up boss person who could be like, *I will go over and invite her to join us.* That's just a small moment, but that was definitely the vibe of it. Originally, we did a lot of things together, but as she got her different boyfriends, and was going to nightclubs with Paris and Nicole and being on Perez Hilton, she was more her own island. In retrospect, I think that was a very scary, dangerous island that she shouldn't have been on by herself. We had the ability to give her a little tugboat to go back and forth. And we didn't do that, and I regret that.

Josh Schwartz: There was a feeling from Fox and this new regime that the show needed to do bigger, crazier, more shocking things to stay relevant and boost the ratings. And it was also a feeling that maybe if we let Mischa off the show, it would be better for her in the long run, just as a human being.

Bob DeLaurentis: Mischa's passion for acting was diminishing, and in the realm of real life, of a young person, she wanted to have a life, not a career.

Stephanie Savage: When you're looking at agents, managers, publicists, momagers, boyfriends, studio executives, none of those people are really looking to be a moral mentor to a young person. I had that in me and I didn't activate it. Whether that was because I was afraid to activate it, because I didn't want to get in trouble, or I didn't want to get in over my head, or I was scared of what I emotionally would take on, or whether at times I would get my feelings hurt by how the cast was acting.

Craig Erwich (programming executive, Fox): I was very concerned. It seemed to be a fait accompli, just given the dynamics. Especially when you're dealing with young people, success is harder to manage than failure. The success of the show, with a lot of young people at the helm, just led to a lot of dynamics behind the scenes. I think Mischa may not have been in the healthiest situation. I know there was legitimate concern about that. But I think between whether it was her not wanting to be there, or them not wanting to write for her, you can't force the producers to keep somebody on a show that they didn't want.

Putting the Hit Out

However unhappy Barton may have been, Marissa might have survived if not for the shifting winds at Fox. After months of generic network pressure to generate "promotable" storylines, a more specific and definitive edict was delivered from on high.

Yvette Urbina (programming executive, Fox): Liguori, he's the one that wanted Marissa to die, so let's start there.

Stephanie Savage: The network was saying, "What you're doing isn't really working, and you guys need to do something big or this is the end." We had started joking about "faux-mos"—promos that they had cut that made it seem like things happened that did not happen, because they were so dissatisfied with the lack of incident on the show that they were making things up. Basically, they were like, "You have to kill someone, or equivalent," which, there really is no equivalent. And it had to be a main character. You couldn't bring another Johnny on the show and kill them. When they got to the promo, it was literally, "One of these people is going to die," and then you cut to the eight series regulars.

Yvette Urbina: No, I think it was specifically [Marissa].

Fox's orders coincided with the writing staff hitting a wall with Marissa as a character.

John Stephens (writer/producer): This comments so much upon the paucity of our imaginations, but we didn't know where to go with the story. The Marissa-Ryan relationship was so integral to the show, and we felt like we had gone through so many different permutations of it that we didn't know what the next step of it was. Putting them with other people always felt like they were waiting to get back together. So we thought at the very least, forcing Ryan to deal with the grief that would happen from that, we could understand how we could turn that into another season.

J. J. Philbin (writer/producer): Ryan and Marissa's relationship had this tragic feel to it. When we were actually taking time with them just being together as a couple, it was hard. I don't know, tragedy felt baked in, and you don't want her character to be a bummer.

Bob DeLaurentis: A big part of the problem the show had was that it was locked in to this relationship. The staff felt that we had written every iteration of this story that could be written. And there was no place left to go. And the discussion then turned to, "What do you do? Do you take Mischa out of the show? Because that is a huge deal. Or do we find a way to sideline Mischa?" The nature of the show was, we didn't really do stories that we didn't run through Ryan. If another character goes off, we didn't really follow that character.

Okay, but Why Not Kill Seth or Ryan?

If you've been reading everything thus far, you know Barton was not the only dissatisfied member of the cast, nor was she even the most vocal about it.

Rachel Bilson: I would say probably Mischa and Adam [wanted out the most]. Maybe Ben wanted to be done as much as they did. I don't know. But there was a lot of that going on.

No serious thought was ever given to killing off any of the others, though.

Josh Schwartz: We decided we would not kill Ryan, Seth, or Sandy. Because they were the core of the show. Though they would have gladly traded places.

Stephanie Savage: Not Peter, but Adam and Ben would have happily been killed.

Ben McKenzie (Ryan Atwood): Adam definitely said that, I'm sure. I don't remember my mindset at the time. So I don't know that I said it quite as strongly as Adam, but I certainly can understand.

Josh Schwartz: Quite frankly, creatively, the show is about these two. This was the calculation at the time, and in hindsight, it was a miscalculation. But the feeling was, we couldn't do the show without Seth and Ryan. Even when I've been approached about doing an updated version of the show—*that's* the show. It was those two guys in the Cohen family, and that was really the core of the show. But Marissa was an incredibly essential part of the show—more essential than we recognized at the time. We thought we could do this, it would be shocking, but it would reinvigorate the show creatively. Because it would so fundamentally shake up some of the dynamics of the show, which had probably started to grow stale at that point. And again, had I been smarter earlier, there was probably more life to have gotten out of the show by putting Marissa with Seth, or getting Luke and Marissa back together. There's a lot of dynamics we could have explored that I think would have allowed the show to keep reinventing itself, but still be itself. But we didn't do those things, and we were at a place where they really wanted something big and shocking, and it felt like the future of the show was up in the air. Were we going to even get renewed for Season Four if we didn't do something? So there were business reasons, and then there were creative reasons. We felt like Marissa was always a character who had a tragic strain to her. The end of the Tijuana episode and the end of Season Three echo each other. It wasn't outside of the realm of possibility that her character could die, as it was always on the table, even from the very beginning of the show. And where that would lead the show was something that was interesting creatively to explore. And it certainly felt—just very cynically—like we would be drumming up a lot of publicity for the show, in a year where we felt like we were becoming irrelevant.

Stephanie Savage: I think we didn't want to kill Summer or Julie, because they felt like reliable tonal anchors of the show. They were also characters with humor and light, we would need them to help with the aftermath. And Melinda and Rachel were both still very happy to be there.

Bob DeLaurentis: If you think about if it happened to Rachel or Adam, it would have been a totally different emotional experience and story for Ryan. And this is the knife you put in Ryan. We ask, "What hasn't Ryan gone through in the last three years?" The death of the love of his life would trigger a different rite of passage into adulthood.

J. J. Philbin: In a world where Marissa was still in the show, there would always be the feeling that they can't really be with anybody else. They can't really start over. They can't really do anything, because they're star-crossed lovers and will always be feeling that tension. I remember the argument being made that even if the character were to move across the world, you would still feel her there, and expect her to come back, and expect that the end of the series is Ryan and Marissa walking off into the sunset. There was a feeling of, *How do we break free from that?*

Stephanie Savage: And then the [Television Without Pity] message board not liking Marissa, I won't say it was the determining factor, but it definitely was a factor in feeling like, *Well, we could do this [kill her], and it would be okay.*

Sara Morrison (Television Without Pity recapper): On the forums [at the time], everybody loves Seth, everybody loves Julie, everybody loves Summer. People like Ryan. And then everyone hated Marissa. Just hated, hated, hated, hated, hated, hated, hated.

Daniel Blau Rogge (Television Without Pity recapper): Any rewatch or reevaluation of a show that came from a time before the present is going to require a tough look at our treatment of women overall. I'm sure my recaps of *The O.C.* were at least 37 percent, "Marissa, well she's really skinny, isn't she!"

Bob DeLaurentis: I was out of town. I got on a pay phone, and I called Josh, and I said, "I think we finally have to deal with this as a reality. Do we want to take this step?" I had come up with, I don't want to say what it was, but it was a version of sidelining her that kept her in the Ryan world. It was a bad idea. As you say in the writers' room, "Here's the bad pitch version." And Josh thought about it for about a second and a half, and he said, "No, if we're going to do it, we should just do it." I said, "Josh, it's your show," but I agreed with him 150 percent, and he knew that. I think it was the right thing to do.

Breaking the News

Savage had generally gotten along well with Barton, but she and Schwartz were afraid to even discuss the idea with their star before committing to it.

Stephanie Savage: Again, instead of talking to her about it as adults, we were like, "Well, we think that would work out great for her." And then just made this decision.

Josh Schwartz: And then made it Bob's problem to deliver the news. Because again, I was too chickenshit to have those conversations. Bob had the first conversation and tried to lay it out for Mischa and her mom. And their response was not excitement and gratitude and relief. They were angry—and rightfully so.

Bob DeLaurentis: I had a good relationship with Mischa, and when we decided that Mischa wasn't going to continue on the show, I called Nuala, and we had an hour-long conversation that wasn't fun for either of us.

Mischa Barton: It was a little bit of a bummer. But it was sort of headed in the direction that it was becoming inevitable, I guess. The character was just doing too much. And I think they ran out of places for her to go. It was not the best thing in the world, [but] there wasn't much you could do at that point. It was whether she could sail off into the sunset, or die. At that point, I guess it's better to have the more dramatic ending.

Stephanie Savage: We were driving home from Manhattan Beach, and somehow we ended up in some part of South Central that I'd never been in before. This was before phones had GPS, and we were lost.

Josh Schwartz: It was a perfect metaphor. And I was tasked with calling the rest of the cast to inform them that we were going to be losing a cast member at the end of the season, and that that cast member was Mischa. I feel like Brody was like, "*Really? Couldn't be me?*—whether he fully articulated that or not. Some of the actors were very upset to hear the news, obviously. I think Peter thought it was going to be him. So there was a moment where he was greatly relieved it wasn't him. And then obviously, he was sad about the Mischa piece.

Peter Gallagher (Sandy Cohen): That was a confusing time. I felt sad for her, just to be cast out like that. I didn't know all the ins and outs of all the stuff that was going on, because why would anybody tell me anything?

Ben McKenzie: I do remember her being upset before. And yeah, I guess that sounds right that she was probably also upset [to be killed off]. It's a "damned if you do, damned if you don't" thing. She was younger, so she was dealing with this whole mess of feelings that we were all dealing with to some degree, but hers were probably even more acute. So I don't blame her. But it did become this situation that I think something had to give. So Josh, Bob, and Stephanie did what they had to do.

Was everyone right in assuming Barton wanted to leave?

Mischa Barton: I really don't want to get into it at length. But there was a lot going on with the producers. I ultimately don't get to make any decisions. That's a fact. I had to do whatever my contract said I had to do. But I think that it was decided it was the best thing for the show in general.

The Crash

The writers had been forced to abandon plans for Marissa to be involved in a car accident at the end of the first batch of Season One episodes. Three years later, they went back to the idea.

Josh Schwartz: We had originally talked about a storyline where the car went into the water, and Ryan was trying desperately to open it, like a Chappaquiddick thing where Ryan is free of the car, and he's trying to save Marissa as the car is filling up with water, and eventually has to let her go. And that was so horrific. And, frankly, quite hard to produce.

Stephanie Savage: Also, *One Tree Hill* was having a car drive off of a bridge into water?*

---

* This does, in fact, happen in the *One Tree Hill* Season Three finale, which aired a few weeks before "The Graduates."

Josh Schwartz: It's the old *Skin** thing again.

Stephanie Savage: And Peter Roth said, "Come on, Stephanie, they need this."

The atmosphere in the days leading up to the car crash scene was complicated for all involved.

Mischa Barton: It was starting to get emotional for everyone. But we're all professional. So we had some really nice last scenes together, like when we're all hanging out in the pool. There were some good moments to be had because of it.

Bob DeLaurentis: It's a terrible way to work. It's one thing to have to leave a show. But to be working there, knowing you've been asked to leave, it's pretty bad. In the conversation I had with Nuala, she kept circling back to, "How can you guys do this? She's one of the Core Four."

Ben McKenzie: I remember it being awkward. I think everyone had feelings that they weren't able to articulate at the time, or certainly didn't want to share with each other. But it was also sad to mark the end of this run of her character.

Josh Schwartz: [After Bob told them], they made it clear that they actually didn't want to talk to me from that point on, either. When we shot the final episode, Mischa's dad came—and we were not really seeing him over the course of the show—and I was told that I was not to come to set. Which, again, had I been less of a coward, I could have dealt with. But I just was like, *That's my excuse. I will hide.*

Lisa Cochran: Shooting that final episode was incredibly emotional

---

* We *think* this is the last *Skin* reference in the book, but we can't promise. Everything is a blur, other than that his FATHER is THE DISTRICT ATTORNEY!

for everybody. We all had been on pins and needles, and then as we're out back shooting the car wreck, it became real for me, and I think some of the crew as well.

Melinda Clarke: She's unhappy on the show, but does she want to be killed off? I remember her being very sad that last week. We were having some moments where I could tell she was sad that she was leaving the show.

Ben McKenzie: She was pretty closed off at that point so I'm not sure [how she was doing]. I'm sure she was upset, but I don't really know.

Mischa Barton: The crew was quite upset. It was pretty emotional at that point, because we'd formed such close bonds. I just really wanted to do the character justice at the end of it. I don't think that had been depicted that much on television for teenagers: she literally dies and she's covered in blood and he pulls her out of a wrecked car. It's just heavy material. And once I saw that the crew was getting upset, it became quite an intense shoot.

Bob DeLaurentis: In Mischa's way, she did a good job. I don't think she phoned it in.

The aftermath of the crash is a triple callback, with Ryan carrying Marissa out of the car as we cut to footage of him similarly carrying her out of the alley in Tijuana, while Imogen Heap's cover of "Hallelujah" is meant to invoke both the Season One finale and the shooting of Trey. Ryan offers to go for help, but Marissa—whether aware of how badly she's hurt, or just afraid to be left alone—begs Ryan to stay with her, until the life leaves her eyes.

Matt Ramsey (editor): One of my favorite memories of working on the show is when Stephanie came up to my edit room, and I said, "I've got to show you this daily of Marissa. It's of her last breath." Mischa was *so* good in the moment. I built the whole cut around this one moment. I watched that with Stephanie, and she was crying. People talk about the Imogen Heap song and him lifting her. But to me, it's that moment right before.

"Oh My God, What Have We Done?"

While some members of the creative team at the time thought the story was a worthwhile gamble, it's hard to find anyone willing to argue in favor of it now.

Adam Brody: I felt then, and still do, that you could put her on ice in an economic way. I remember on *90210*, characters going to rehab for a while, or people would disappear for a year but not *disappear* disappear. I'm sure she was a little unhappy. I'm sure she was a little bored. I'm sure she was sick of X, Y, and Z. And at the same time, I highly doubt she wanted to be publicly, dramatically killed and quasi-fired. Even though I'm sure she enjoyed some newfound freedoms, I don't think she wanted it, or wanted it that way. And she was very young. I'm sure it didn't feel good.

Kelly Rowan (Kirsten Cohen): I thought it was the biggest mistake they were going to make. That whole foursome, the chemistry with those four actors, screwing with that, I thought was a big mistake. I don't know the specifics of why that decision was made. I was almost killed by a semi.* There was this whole thing going on, where we don't know which cast member we're going to kill. We were all worried about our mortgage payments at that point; "Oh, are we unemployed and looking for a job?" But then when we found out that it was Mischa, it was sad to lose that character.

Norman Buckley: I was very against the idea of killing her off at the end of Season Three. That was a big mistake. I was very vocal about

---

* Kirsten got into a car accident when her drinking problem grew out of control in Season Two.

that. As far as I was concerned, she was the face of the show. And even though there were many other elements of the show that were equally as important, she really was part of the initial structural paradigm of it.

Stephanie Savage: The first time I watched it, I watched it with Josh and Matt Ramsey, and I was just bawling. I was like, *What have we done?* Not just that it was sad that Marissa died, but that we made a terrible, terrible mistake.

Savage's tears about this episode were not isolated to 2006; by the time she has finished delivering this answer, she is again crying heavily.

Josh Schwartz: J. J. and Mike Schur came to my house to watch the episode, because they had been on a trip and hadn't seen it. Mike Schur was like, "Really good episode of television." And J. J. was sobbing hysterically, I'm sure having the exact same feelings that [Stephanie] had. And I'm feeling like, *We've saved the show. This is going to be epic. No one's going to see this coming.*

Well, not exactly.

Josh Schwartz: And then Mischa did an interview where she revealed that she got killed, right before the show.

"It's true. My character dies," Barton told *Access Hollywood* in a heavily promoted interview earlier that week. "I think the show is moving in a new direction. You know, they needed a big season finale at the end of this year, and we've had three great years. And my character has been through so much, and there's really nothing more left for her to do. So I hope this fulfills everything that the fans want and everything that the people wanted for our characters."

Josh Schwartz: I don't think it was intentional. Maybe it was, but it certainly drew a lot of eyeballs to the show that night. And the night that it aired, the message boards were lighting up with all of these people [upset]. All I had in my head was the criticism of the Marissa character and people feeling like we were in redundant storylines, and hitting the same level of melodrama, and that the story had run out of gas, and the writers didn't know how to write for the character. It had only been this inevitable march to Marissa's demise, because of the creative exhaustion with the character. And then all of these voices on the Internet and early Tumblr exploded, like a primordial howl from the early Internet into the night sky. Of grief, disbelief, anger, *way* louder than any voices had ever been complaining about the direction of the character. I very quickly realized, *Oh my God, what have we done? I think we made a terrible mistake.*

Stephanie Savage: Television Without Pity—the eight people that were controlling 90 percent of the discourse about the show—had one opinion. And even they were like, "Wait, I'm not sure that's really what I asked for. Like, why am I not happy about this?"

Daniel Blau Rogge: I think there's an extent to which the boards would judge the character—"Marissa is entitled!" "Marissa is annoying!" "Marissa is too skinny!"—but that the rhetoric would at times spill over to more of a judgment of Mischa Barton herself. The show killing her off led to a backlash when viewers were like, "THAT IS NOT WHAT WE MEANT."

Sara Morrison: People get joy out of picking apart or talking about or making fun of some things on your show. I guess that's true for the recaps, too. It doesn't necessarily mean that they know more about how to write a TV show than you. I think a lot of the sentiment was that it's really fun to pile on something and be a part of a group effort. I think even if you don't like the character, it's that you don't want to see her so much. It's not that you want her to die.

Morrison is horrified to be reminded that her headline for the finale recap was "A Twig, Snapped."

Sara Morrison: Oh, no. Oh, that's terrible. I would not have [written that now]. Oh, that's really mean.

Stephanie Savage: But then there were all these other people that were not on the Internet in the same way, that were less articulate, that were less snarky, that didn't have the tone of that Television Without Pity board. They were just beside themselves with grief, they did fan art of angels carrying Marissa to Heaven, or a thousand tears on the ground—religious iconography, like Virgin of Guadalupe–level Marissa worship. And I felt, *Oh, I guess there was a whole other audience that was connecting to this character in a different way, that was not voicing their experience and opinion in the same way as these other people were.*

Sara Morrison: Tell them I'm sorry!

Yvette Urbina: This isn't a Dick Wolf show where you can plug and play characters. Killing her just made you go, *I don't want the show to go on anymore.* When you're thinking about [killing] a character at the center of your show, then you just said to the audience, "Sorry, but we don't really care."

Mischa Barton: I remember after Marissa died, people being pretty hysterical and coming up to me in airports, crying about it. I thought that was shocking, because it's TV, you know?

John Stephens: Every now and then, people will learn I was on the show, and usually the first thing out of their mouths is, "Why did you kill Marissa?" Once, my wife and I were on our honeymoon, on a safari in Botswana, and we're sitting around the campfire in the Kalahari Desert, and this woman's there with their teenage daughter and they find out I was on *The O.C.* I'm here under this glorious African sky. And this girl said, "Why did you kill Marissa?!?!" I'm like, *Really?!*

J. J. Philbin: Now that I've had a little bit more experience, I realize that killing off a character is a violent and unsettling thing for the audience.

Josh Schwartz: I think we could have pulled our punches and come back in Season Four and she's not dead. You give everyone the summer to think it's happened. If we killed Trey at the end of Season Two, we could've done that. She survives the thing with Volchok and ultimately says, "I need to leave," and gets on Seth's boat. That said, Season Four, the show did have a creative rebirth as a result of that.

But was it worth it?

Kelly Rowan: My daughter says to me, "Mom, why did they kill Mischa's character?" I don't know. I really don't. From the show's perspective, messing with that foursome, it never recovered.

CHAPTER 10

The Silly Swan Song

THE FOURTH AND final season of *The O.C.* was easily its lowest-rated. It is also, if you are a fan of the show's more comedic side, maybe the best after Season One. In the wake of the disastrous third season and the regrettable death of Marissa, the creative team decided to just have fun again, resulting in a year full of amusing material that few people noticed at the time.

The season began with Josh Schwartz in a hopeful mode, even after Fox only ordered sixteen episodes, an unusual total suggesting the network's patience might be running out.

Josh Schwartz (creator/executive producer): Our secret thought was, *If the show is good enough, maybe they'll want to extend it, or we'll have a ratings resurgence when the show's back creatively.* Because the end of Season Three, as much as we may regret it now, was successful from a ratings perspective, and did make the show feel more relevant than it had in a while. So I think our hope was if we could build off of that, and the show felt rejuvenated creatively, the ratings might follow and we could potentially extend our lives.

The show did feel rejuvenated, but it didn't matter.

Josh Schwartz: Unfortunately, it's like when the popular girl leaves the party—everybody else wants to leave the party, too. And Marissa was the popular girl.

I'm in a Steel Cage of Emotion!

Rather than resume right where we left off and show Marissa's funeral and the immediate aftermath, the season premiere begins several months later. Summer is a freshman at Brown, Seth is waiting to go to RISD for spring semester, and Ryan has moved out of the pool house and is living in a storage closet at the bar where he's now working. But everyone is still grieving the loss of Marissa, particularly Ryan and Julie.

> **Melinda Clarke (Julie Cooper-Nichol):** I was living that heartbreak for those first three [episodes], which to me felt like three months. The summer after we wrapped, maybe I had too much to drink, but I remember just bursting into tears about how sad it was that Marissa died—but in real life.

Some fans, as well as members of the cast, were surprised to not get a funeral scene for such a beloved character.

> **Josh Schwartz:** We felt like it would be such overwhelming grief. A, what story are you telling, other than everybody is just so sad and heartbroken over this? Ryan going to Mexico for Volchok is not something he would have been thinking about necessarily in the immediate aftermath of the funeral. And B, we knew we needed the characters to be able to get to a place where they were able to integrate this tragedy in their lives and move forward. Some time and distance was going to be needed to achieve that—in three episodes. We only had sixteen episodes; we didn't want to stew in the misery, but hopefully still memorialize the character in a way that felt respectful for her and for the audience.

> **Yvette Urbina (programming executive, Fox):** They wanted to be done, just move on. They wanted to be in fun times.

The show works through the grieving process within that opening trio of episodes, including Julie encouraging Ryan to go to Mexico to find and murder Volchok,* and Ryan taking up cage fighting for the self-flagellating opportunity to get beaten up by his opponents.

Josh Schwartz: I remember Brody, when he heard about the cage fighting, was like, "I fucking love this." As bad as he had been on the show, he was like, "This is what I'm talking about." And Ben embraced it.

Ben McKenzie (Ryan Atwood): I thought it was completely ridiculous—and also awesome. It's one of those moments where you're like, *At least it'll be fun, you can throw yourself into it.* Gave me a reason to exercise, although I don't think I had much advance notice. Like, *Oh, I guess I'm a cage fighter now.*

Josh Schwartz: It was definitely pushing the envelope, but at least it felt like it was pushing the envelope in the way that the show used to be able to commit itself—like, *Let's just go right off the shark to begin with.*

Stephanie Savage (executive producer): Ryan hates himself. So he has taken himself away from the people who love him, the world where he's safe, where he has a future. He's punishing himself. The first version we talked about was Ryan goes to bars and instead of taking drugs or getting drunk, he's going to pick fights in bars. But that's a hard story to tell. Is it unlikable? Does he now become a bully, because he's picking fights for no reason, just because he wants to get beat up? There was a conversation about if we could codify this in some way, as Bob would say, it has to be very clear that someone is choosing to do this for a reason. And so we put a cage around those fights.

Josh Schwartz: I had seen [pro wrestler] Sgt. Slaughter fight Kamala in a cage match at Madison Square Garden. So this is a story that has always been near and dear to my heart.

* Instead, the arc ends with Volchok returning to the States to throw himself on the mercy of the courts, with some help from Sandy.

The Humor Strikes Back

Stephanie Savage took over the writers' room for the season, and decided it was time for a significant change of tone from the angst and tragedy that had typified the previous year.

Stephanie Savage: I felt like for the morale of the room and the morale of the show, we just needed to embrace that it doesn't matter now. This thing we've been trying to do is not working. So let's just be true to ourselves. Go back to the roots of why we love this show. It was a teen comedy, or a teen drama that had comedy in it. The things that Josh imbued in the voice originally, the characters that, like Seth, were unexpected in a show like this, let's embrace more of that ingredient. And fuck "This is the NASCAR network" and "We don't make shows about nerds who talk to plastic horses," because you do. And they're going to talk to a lot weirder things than plastic horses this year.

Melinda Clarke: The writers did some really wacky stuff in Season Four, where we were all having a lot of fun.

J. J. Philbin (writer/producer): I think we were all feeling really depressed by not just the reaction to Season Three, which was not positive, but also, the storylines we'd been writing were so bleak. Stephanie said, "Everyone in this room is really funny and has stories to share. Let's write things that bring us joy. If a storyline is making you happy, then let's go towards that." I remember being really relieved that that was the directive. If Season Four was too silly, it was a reaction to writing a really dark season that felt heavy and was hard to execute.

Leila Gerstein (writer/producer): We had the greatest time breaking Season Four. We would speak in French accents. I'm sure it's bonkers storytelling, and I bet it's too broad. But we amused ourselves to no end. We thought it was hilarious.

J. J. Philbin: We had the giggles and we were just enjoying ourselves. As we were breaking the stories, it kept seeming ridiculous. But they actually worked for the story.

John Stephens (writer/producer): We were in that point where I don't think the show had a lot of life left in it from the idea box. I think the network executives [implied that] this was the last season, so we could go out and do what we wanted. If we had been a massive hit at that point, then we wouldn't have been able to.

That year's Chrismukkah episode took a different approach from seasons past, putting Ryan and Taylor Townsend in a scenario straight out of *It's a Wonderful Life*, where they get to see what life for everybody would have been like if Ryan had never moved in with the Cohens. This includes Sandy being a ruthless politician now married to Julie, while Kirsten has finally gotten back with Jimmy. Marissa, meanwhile, died even earlier in this reality, because Ryan wasn't there to save her when she overdosed in Tijuana.*

Stephanie Savage: Ryan in Season Four is carrying around this weight that he's killed Marissa. And if we could take that away from him, and replace it with the idea that he actually gave her extra years, it would relieve him of that. When I was at Flower Films, we did *Donnie Darko*, and I liked that idea of playing with time, playing with what-if, having a do-over, and what that would look like.

Knowing what went down at the end of Season Three, Tate Donovan was puzzled that *this* was the episode he'd been asked back for.

Tate Donovan (Jimmy Cooper/director): I remember not really knowing what's going on. I just showed up. And I was like, *They brought me back for this, and they didn't bring me back for any funeral for my daughter?*

---

* In a blink-and-you'll-miss-it joke, we find out that one character is *much* better off in this time line: the comic book shop has a poster advertising an in-person appearance by rising surfing star Johnny.

While the season was much more fun than the previous one, it was also such a big deviation from the original formula as to leave some members of the cast and crew confused about how they had gotten to this weird place.

Norman Buckley (editor/director): Autumn was a wonderful addition. Willa Holland was a wonderful addition. Chris Pratt was a wonderful addition. There were some really great people that were added. But there were all kinds of storylines that I completely forgot about until I went back and was watching the show just to catch up for Rachel and Melinda's podcast. And the reason why I forgot is because it didn't resonate.

Peter Gallagher (Sandy Cohen): It felt like the show kept looking for somewhere else to land, or somewhere else to be.

Adam Brody (Seth Cohen): The fourth season, I'll be honest, I was checked out. And in my defense, besides just selfish reasons—*I've done this enough*, and except for financial reasons, you want to move on—if you watch the [series] pilot and the last episode [of the fourth season], they're different shows. Just truly, truly different shows.

Norman Buckley: The pilot was the template for the show. It was much more successful when it hewed to that, and when it was deviating from that, it was not as good. It was the balance of the love, the pathos, and the comedy that made the show work. When it just became a screwball comedy, basically, there was no *there* there. There was an undergirding of a certain reality that the show lost.

How About Pratt?

Because Ryan, Seth, and Taylor were all out of school at the moment for various reasons, production built an outdoor mall set where the characters could hang out, Seth could work at the comic store, and an emotionally healthier Ryan could work at a Mexican restaurant.

Stephanie Savage: We knew we bought ourselves at least a year of figuring out before, if we had had the opportunity to do a fifth season, what college would have been for everyone. But college is a show killer, man. It's really, really tough. That was another thing—if Marissa dies, then maybe everyone doesn't have to go to college next year.

But when the season began, Summer was still three thousand miles away from the group, which meant Rachel Bilson was going to need somebody with whom to play scenes. The writers came up with a character known as "Che"—an environmental activist who would raise Summer's political consciousness.

Stephanie Savage: We had to have Brown stories for her at first. Which meant partnering her with someone—and no offense to any of our guest actors from previous seasons—who we knew was going to be really fucking funny and lively and make you want to fast forward *to* those scenes, not fast forward *through* them. Because those stories where Summer is becoming an environmental activist, without someone as funny and engaging as Chris Pratt was, are potentially not great stories.

Patrick Rush had once cast Pratt as Emily VanCamp's older brother Bright on *Everwood*, and knew how funny he could be.

Patrick Rush (casting director): I just loved him. He was just a good kid. Everything he did in the first *Guardians of the Galaxy*, where people fell in love with him—he *was* that goofball.

Josh Schwartz: Pratt is so irrefutable. Everybody had to raise their game around him, because there's no denying him.

Stephanie Savage: Because he'd been a series regular on *Everwood* (which shot in Utah), he came at our cast like, "Oh my God, you guys, what the fuck is wrong with you? You shoot in L.A., you have great

VIP perks everywhere you go, you're on a fun show. What's wrong?" Which I think did have some impact.

Patrick Norris (director): I met this guy, Chris Pratt, and I thought, *Man, this guy's a movie star.* Because we rarely had that. And him and Adam did a lot of great stuff together.

Rachel Bilson (Summer Roberts): Fucking love Pratt. He's super-funny. I had a blast. Nothing but amazing, positive things to say. I had so much fun with him and he was just hilarious. To this day, one of his jokes is my favorite all-time joke, where he's like, "Okay, you name this movie: 'Welcome to Jurassic Park.'" And the way he delivered it! And then he wound up doing the *Jurassic Park* franchise! Who knew?

After a few episodes, Che* makes Summer the fall guy for a protest at the campus animal lab, resulting in her being suspended from school for the rest of the year. By that point, the writers were so in love with Pratt's performance that they kept finding excuses for him to visit Newport, including an absurd episode where Che takes Seth into the woods to figure out what his spirit animal is. (It's an otter, because of course it is.)

Autumn Reeser (Taylor Townsend): He was a ball of energy. He was a breath of fresh air. He was full of joy.

Stephanie Savage: We did not want this to be a Johnny or Matt Ramsey situation, where we were writing a very middle-of-the-road character. We wrote something that was really bold and crazy.

Though Seth is concerned at first that Summer is spending so much time with another guy, Che never falls for her in the way that, say, Zach did in Season Two.

* Later in the season, we discover that Che is actually a child of WASP privilege cosplaying as a revolutionary, and that "Che" is short for "Winchester."

John Stephens: We thought it would be more interesting to present him as a romantic rival in the traditional sense of how a teen drama would work, but then quickly defuse that and say, "Oh, no, he's actually going to stick around and become a part of their lives in a very different way." That would be surprising for the actors, more interesting for people to watch, and also a bit truer to the way things usually work out in real life. And then when he kept appearing to Summer as the spirit guide in that episode, that felt ridiculous, so we should do it.

Leila Gerstein: I'm really into otters, so I know that I picked the otter, because I wanted to see an otter. But I don't remember actually meeting the otter. I wrote that and was like, *This is never going to air. This is insane.* And then I think it aired as completely as written.

Pratt's work as Che inspired J. J. Philbin's husband to hire him on *Parks and Recreation*, putting him on the launchpad to stardom.

Michael Schur (executive producer, *Parks and Recreation* and *The Good Place*): I loved him that season, and *The O.C.* writers loved him, and J. J. always came home raving about funny things he did. That character became a real room favorite. When we were casting *Parks and Rec* and I was telling her about the character of Andy, he was the first name she suggested, and when she did, I got really excited. Then the real kismet was, I emailed [casting director] Allison Jones and told her the idea, and she said, "Oh yeah, he's already coming in to read."*

---

* Schur (whom you might remember as Dwight's creepy cousin Mose on *The Office*) also has a brief, extremely stiff cameo in this season as a representative for GEORGE, an activist organization that recruits Summer. "I was not, in my professional opinion, 'good,'" he says, recalling that he was extremely anxious just about remembering his lines, "which is, like, stage one of a multistage process known as 'acting well.' Rachel was very kind and patient. Because she is a professional actor, who knew what she was doing."

Taylor and Ryan: The Reese's of Ships

Marissa was gone, Ryan was moving past his grief, and Autumn Reeser had, like Willa Holland, been promoted to the main cast for Season Four. If you understood the arithmetic of series television, you knew that this would inevitably add up to Ryan dating Taylor Townsend, who was back in Newport after a short-lived marriage to a French author.

Josh Schwartz: [Marissa's death] did allow us to go all in on Ryan and Taylor in Season Four. Which for some people was the most successful pairing on the show. And for others, they hated it, because Marissa and Ryan were endgame.

Autumn Reeser: I'm pretty sure every article about the show that year talked about that controversy. Weren't there shirts made that were "Team Marissa" or "Team Taylor-Ryan"?

Stephanie Savage: If there is a continuum of Marissa and Theresa and Lindsay, then Taylor's on that continuum. She's just a little further down on the crazy side. But she and Ryan did have things in common and could connect. We wanted to make sure that we could build Taylor in a way where she felt like a real, grounded character, that would be able to meet someone's emotional needs in a relationship and not just be funny.

J. J. Philbin: She had this energy which, through no fault of the [rest of the] cast, we needed. After Ryan's relationship with Marissa, which had been just so tragic in so many ways, we really liked putting him with someone who lifted him and lightened him. Did we go a little too kooky with Taylor? Probably. But again, we had been in this very dark Season Three, and we were like, *Oh my gosh, Taylor and Ryan can have fun.* And we were happy for him. So we maybe went a little crazy.

Ben McKenzie: That was fun. Autumn Reeser was lovely and had a very sunny disposition. So the whole thing felt lighter. I know people have very strong feelings on that. You either liked Season Four, or you hated it. But I have to say, just from the doing of it, the doing of it was more fun, and honestly more fitting with I think what the show really was. Like, it didn't need to be trying for such weight all the time. I certainly appreciated being able to tell a joke or two.

In the season's sixth episode, "The Summer Bummer," Ryan is forced to confront his attraction to Taylor when he begins to have fantasies of her as an eighties-style music video vixen. Autumn Reeser did not require much convincing when asked if she wanted to do it.

Autumn Reeser: I'm pretty sure it was the double-elbow "Yes!" I like any opportunity to chew some scenery. I certainly don't get enough opportunities now to have that level of ridiculousness and fantasy and loved that episode. I shot that episode on my birthday. And I was like, *Happy birthday to me!*

Stephanie Savage: I think Autumn loved doing that because it was so out of character for Taylor. And she got to show off her moves, got to have a smoke machine on set, and I thought it was funny.

Even with spotlight moments like that, it was hard for Reeser to shake the feeling that she didn't quite fit in.

Autumn Reeser: I felt this pressure to be on the same playing field. And I just wasn't. I was asked on a red carpet, "Now that you're a series regular, what are you going to do with all your money?" I was like, "I'm going to pay my electric bill." Like, I don't have Jimmy Choos. It's completely different worlds. I remember the photoshoot for the posters and stuff for Season Four, they, I was so excited. This is the first I'm doing anything like this. And they were like, "Bring anything you want to wear, but we'll have things there, too." And I'm thinking, *Oh, great, they're going to have some beautiful gowns; it's going to be really fabulous.* And Rachel comes with this custom-made Zac Posen dress. Perfection. I come with nothing, because I don't have anything to bring in. I'm expecting dresses. And there were, like, three shirts there. So I hate everything I'm wearing in all of the photoshoot for Season Four, and this is another example of how I always felt out of step. I'm like, *What am I missing here? Who's setting the rules and why am I not getting the rule book?*

But there were lovely moments, too.

Autumn Reeser: Ben wrote me a really nice thank-you note when the show ended, thanking me for the lightness and the fun—which, of course, I think had a lot to do with the scripts as well.

I Think, Therefore . . . *Je Pense*?!?!

No episode sums up the absurd, fuck-it aesthetic of Season Four better than "The French Connection," written by J. J. Philbin and directed by John Stephens. In one story, Taylor's ex-husband Henri-Michel* arranges for their favorite French philosophical talk show *Je Pense* to record an episode in Newport Beach, as part of his campaign to win her back. In another, Seth is in the midst of an immature tiff with Summer where he has proposed marriage to her more or less out of spite, while she has agreed only because she stubbornly wants him to back down first. So he travels north to get permission from Summer's father, who has taken a job at Seattle Grace, aka the hospital from *Grey's Anatomy*.† The entire episode is

---

* Henri-Michel (played by Henri Lubatti) initially comes to Newport to promote his novel *A Season for Peaches*, which Taylor recognizes as a roman à clef inspired by their torrid love life. As Ryan begins to fear that he's not sexually adventurous enough for her, she tries to convince him that Henri-Michel exaggerated and outright invented parts of it, insisting, "Even if I was that limber, you know I would never do that in the Chunnel."

† In a parody of the show that had been kicking *The O.C.*'s ass in the ratings, Dr. Roberts monologues about a patient who got impaled after dressing his horse up as a unicorn for his daughter's birthday. "Things went terribly awry," he tells Seth, "but it taught us all about the value of family."

hilarious, both for the actual content and for the sense that it was made on a dare.

J. J. Philbin: The *Je Pense* talk show is totally absurd. But I remember thinking, *Well, we're* kind of *serving a story purpose?*

Stephanie Savage: They were excited about writing it. I wasn't worried about us getting canceled anymore. I felt like we committed a sin against the universe by killing a beloved character. *Je Pense* all the way!

But how did the network that once demanded promotable moments and character deaths allow something this goofy and arcane to air?

Stephanie Savage: I honestly think at that point, they weren't paying attention. They were like, *We gave these guys sixteen episodes. They're going off the air. We don't have anything else to put in their time slot. We're not going to cancel them before then, so just let them do what they're going to do.*

Yvette Urbina: Notes? Of course we had no notes. I just thought, *That's so Josh. No, I don't have notes.*

Late-Arriving Guests

Having brought Ryan's mother and brother to Newport Beach, the writers decided we should finally meet his father, Frank Atwood. Played by former *Hercules: The Legendary Journeys* star Kevin Sorbo, this Frank is not the abusive monster from Ryan's childhood, but a mild-mannered recovering alcoholic who wears nice suits and is just looking to make amends with his son.

Stephanie Savage: The idea, again, that this is the more fun version of the show, is that you set up the expectation that Ryan's dad is going to be a really scary dude, and then he actually has used his time in prison wisely and come out the other side. He's not Trey. It was something different, and somebody who could potentially be folded into our world in a larger way, like become a Julie Cooper love interest.

Frank also gets involved in one final Julie love triangle, as she's torn between her attraction to him and her fondness for Gordon Bullit, a colorful Texas oil tycoon who becomes a father figure to Kaitlin. Played by character actor Gary Grubbs, "The Bullit" quickly became a favorite of the writers, and the remaining viewers.

Josh Schwartz: Little did we know the charismatic adult who was going to steal Season Four was going to be—BANG—Bullit.

Luke's slack-jawed younger brothers, Brad (Wayne Dalglish) and Eric (Corey Price), became part of an unofficial next generation show-within-the-show focusing on Kaitlin's escapades at the Harbor School.

Stephanie Savage: It was one of the few things that Liguori actually liked about the show. When he watched one of the first episodes of the season, he had a comment, like, "It's really funny when those two guys walk down the driveway with that girl."

To continue appeasing Fox's desire for stunt casting, the producers brought in singer Chris Brown to do an arc as Kaitlin's new love interest, Will, a nerdy kid in the Harbor marching band.

Leila Gerstein: The Chris Brown thing, we still make fun of it. Like, "We have Chris Brown coming to the show. Let's do something really surprising and make him a total dork. That'll work!" I think it was also an unmitigated disaster, because it wasn't funny.

Josh Schwartz: We still wanted to be relevant, and we liked the opportunity for some guest casting that could potentially pop. And Chris was pitched to us as someone who was this bright, young, super-talented dude in music who was looking to start acting. We were open to that, and we were trying to figure out a Kaitlin romantic story. We obviously cast him completely against type, which we thought would be a bold, creative choice. We did the Season Four version of not letting the Walkmen play "The Rat"—of not playing to his strengths at all. Don't let him sing. Don't really let him dance. Have him play a nerd in the marching band.

Leila Gerstein: My memory is he did it without complaint. I can't believe he did. He should have complained and been like, "I can't do this." But he just did it. Obviously, we didn't know then what [he would do later].

Patrick Norris: He was playing soccer with my daughter Genevieve in a parking lot at the beach. I couldn't believe his path after he left *The O.C.* But he seemed like a nice person at the time, really connecting with people. And it was cool to have that excitement over this rapper in there.

The End of *The O.C.* as They Know It, and They Feel Fine

The sixteen-episode order was a pretty clear indication that the show was on borrowed time. Official word came down from on high a third of the way into producing the season.

Josh Schwartz: We may have been deluding ourselves that we could keep this thing alive, and reality crashed in after the Season Four ratings were down. I think we were editing "The Summer Bummer," when Liguori called and said, "Look, I'm really sorry I have to make this call, but we're not going to be picking up more episodes."

Instead of casting a pall over the remaining months of production, the news seemed to improve the mood among the cast.

Autumn Reeser: It felt lighter, like maybe there was a sense of relief. People knew it was coming to an end, and they would finally get their chance to do the movies they wanted to do, or just take a break.

Willa Holland (Kaitlin Cooper): I think everybody just wanted to have, if it was the last season, then a good season. So everyone was in the best of spirits that they could have been in, trying to make the best out of the situation that we were in. I think people were happy to be working, happy to be together, and happy to try to maybe not have as much negativity surrounding us at the time.

Josh Schwartz: Certainly, for some of the cast who were hoping they would be the ones who were killed off, they took the news well.

Adam Brody: It wasn't crushing disappointment. I felt like, *I've done this a lot already. We really have told a lot of this story, lived in these characters for a while.*

Josh Schwartz: I think everybody was enjoying the show. The idea that this will be the final season, while it's disappointing, it's always nice to know what your ending is. And at least we're ending the show at a place where everyone is engaged again. So it did not feel like a bummer. It felt like we accepted our fate.

Adam Brody: I also think everyone was sick of each other by the last season. It was that exciting, warm bubble, and then it wasn't the same. Mischa hadn't been there for a minute now, and there's a bunch of new people, and we like them, but it's not the same thing. I feel bad for the crew, who are like, *I just fucking wanted a steady job.* I sympathize. I really do.

Beyond the crew being out of work—at least, until many of them were hired the following season to work on Schwartz's NBC spy comedy *Chuck*—there was one other big disappointment: the show would end with only ninety-six episodes, rather than the hundred that had long been a marker of a successful run in network television.

Stephanie Savage: We all felt like in success, maybe we could get a hundred episodes, which for me personally, I was deeply invested in. For readers that don't know, in the old days, the idea is your show could now be syndicated.* People would buy you congratulations ads in the trades. You would get a big party; you'd have a sheet cake that said "100 Episodes" on it. I really, really wanted that for myself, but also for everybody else working on the show. With all the ups and downs and the roller coasters and the tears and the triumphs, at least if we got our cake, we did our jobs right and we delivered a syndicate-able show with a hundred episodes that crossed the finish line. So to not get that was a huge bummer.

Yvette Urbina: It's just such a failure on the company's part to not see it through to [one hundred].

Stephanie Savage: When we started the show, Fox was a really fun place to be around, and there were lots of young people. It was Paris and Nicole, and the *That '70s Show* kids, and Wilmer Valderrama was dating Lindsay Lohan, and our whole crew knew the other kids. There was a vibe. And then there was a vibe shift. In Season Four, there was the TCA party in L.A., and it was at a venue with a bar, and they weren't letting people in who were under twenty-one. Willa and Chris Brown literally couldn't come to the party—not even with a wristband that said, "Don't buy this person alcohol," or whatever. The network had changed so much in four years that they were creating events that excluded cast members.

---

* i.e., selling reruns of the show to local broadcast stations or cable networks. It could be done with fewer episodes—the original *Star Trek* became a syndication phenomenon with only seventy-nine—but one hundred was the traditional benchmark.

The Short Goodbye

The early call from Liguori also gave the creative team enough warning to begin plotting out the series' endgame. They decided, for instance, that there would be an earthquake where an injured Ryan would be rescued by Seth, and that the quake would damage the McMansion so thoroughly that Sandy and Kirsten would decide to move back to their former home in Berkeley.

Stephanie Savage: I wanted to do one where Seth had to save Ryan, and figuring out what possibly could be that scenario. I also felt really, really upset that we had to tear the sets down, so I decided to incorporate that into the story so that the rest of the world could be upset too, seeing the Cohen house destroyed.

Another part of the closing stretch involved Kirsten—who had spent most of the season running a dating service with Julie (which inevitably morphed into a male escort service while Kirsten wasn't looking)—discovering that she was pregnant again.

Stephanie Savage: We had a lot of conversations over time about how crazy the math of our show was. Melinda's child was a toddler when the show started and Melinda was playing the mother of a sixteen-year-old. And Kelly was not married and didn't have kids yet. On our show, a woman's fertility was between sixteen and twenty-two. Mathematically, there's no way Kirsten even could have gone to college and still be Seth's mother. So the idea that people have babies when they're thirty-eight, which is what was happening to our cast members, felt like that would be a fun story to tell.

Kelly Rowan (Kirsten Cohen): It was a storyline that they decided to do. It just felt like they were trying to tie everything up into a bow. And I don't know if we needed to tie everything up in a bow.

Beyond the Cohens leaving Newport en masse (Ryan belatedly enrolls at Berkeley, Seth finally makes it to RISD), there were other threads to be resolved—and a fitting farewell for the show's central pairing.

Stephanie Savage: If you asked in the pilot, I'm not sure I would have said that the core relationship was Seth and Ryan. I might have said Ryan and Sandy, or Ryan and Marissa, but especially as Seth just grew into himself as a full character, that relationship really grounded the show and was something that we wrote to every week.

Allan Heinberg (writer/producer): I appreciated that we could portray the homoerotic nature of the boys' relationships. Maybe "bromantic" is a better word, because it was never sexualized. But Josh and Stephanie never shied away from the love. We were always very clear that The O.C. was a love story between these two boys.

Josh Schwartz: The show was, at the end of the day, Ryan and Seth at the core. And that's why the end of the series is them hugging in the driveway. That final moment was very poignant.

That hug, along with a brief sequence of Ryan walking through the empty McMansion and flashing back on his arrival there, concludes the present-day narrative of The O.C. It's followed by a montage showing what happens to the characters after, including Summer protesting a nuclear plant (and Seth proudly clipping out newspaper coverage of the protest); Ryan matriculating at Berkeley while Sandy now teaches law there; Julie graduating from college (cheered on by Kaitlin, Frank, and the Bullit, all of whom have seemingly teamed up to help Julie raise the son she had with Frank); and Seth and Summer getting married in the backyard of Sandy and Kirsten's old-new house.

Josh Schwartz: We felt like we needed to make good on devastating Ryan and Marissa fans with something a little bit more authoritative about the fate of Seth and Summer.

The timing was less than ideal for Rachel Bilson and Adam Brody, though.

Rachel Bilson: We had broken up [in real life], and it's the end of the show—so many things coming to an end at the same time. It was really bizarre. When you're that age, you think you're going to be with that person forever. And I remember feeling like, *I don't want to wear something that I would ever wear for my own wedding. That feels weird, because we just broke up.* I was like, "Give me a dress I would never want to wear." So they did!

In the series' final moments, we see an adult Ryan Atwood leaving a construction site, a roll of blueprints in his hands. He has emerged from all the trauma of his younger years to become a successful architect. As he approaches his Range Rover, he spots a kid sitting forlornly by a pay phone, looking very much like Ryan himself in the moments before Sandy Cohen picked him up and drove him to a new life. Ryan hesitates, considers the implications of what he's about to do, then calls out, "Hey, kid. Need any help?"

Josh Schwartz: Is that kid his kid? Is it just the cycle starting over again? We really wanted to leave it in that ambiguous note and cast someone who obviously felt like that could be a young Ryan—metaphorically or literally.

While some people were relieved to be moving on, many others were deep in their feelings about having to say goodbye to a life-changing experience.

Kelly Rowan: I felt the wrap-up of the show was a bit rushed. But yeah, it was sad, and it was particularly sad that they were taking down the sets as we were going.

Rachel Bilson: I remember one of the last days, just feeling sad and being close to Adam, sitting on his lap and going through all the emotions. It was a big chapter of life closing. And surreal to be filming the wedding, but we still had fun filming it. I stuck my tongue out at him, and we laughed and we had fun still together. We were able to still be good.

Josh Schwartz: The girls were all disasters. Rachel and Melinda and Stephanie, I don't know who cried harder. That's true of the series wrap on any show I've ever done with Stephanie—she will cry as hard or harder than any of the cast members. Willa was really sad. She loved being there. Autumn was really emotional.

Autumn Reeser: You get clapped out. This is so arbitrary and something nobody else remembers, but in my spontaneous thank-you speech to everybody, I said the word "fuck" twice. And then went home and was like, *Oh, my gosh, why did I do that?* I don't know why this is what I remember from it. It's another example of me somehow being awkward or not saying what I meant to say or judging myself.

Josh Schwartz: Peter and Kelly wrapped together. Unclear if they both wanted to get the last word in, it was like a *Bridesmaids*, "And then . . . and then . . ." thing. And right before Peter wrapped, he leaned over the monitor, looked at me and said, "One day, we'll talk about everything that happened." It was unclear to me if that was a threat at the moment or if he was reaching out. But then he reached out shortly thereafter, and everything is good.

Not every goodbye was tearful.

Josh Schwartz: Adam wrapped with the infamous send-off: "It's been lucrative . . . for some of us." I don't think he meant any malice. I think he just didn't know what to say in the moment.

Rachel Bilson: I called him out on the podcast on that, and I think he apologized for it. He felt really bad about it, looking back. But I remember him saying that. I think at the time I didn't know what "lucrative" meant, and I was like, *What did he just say? What does that mean?* And I told him, "You're an asshole."

Brody does not remember this, but he also does not dispute it.

Adam Brody: I can take it two ways. Part of me thinks, *Wow, surely I was kidding.* I might have been a brat about the work and immature—and I was, 100 percent—but I was nice to people. I was nice to everyone around me. By virtue of not respecting the work enough, am I disrespecting people and people who've created it? For sure. But to anyone I'm talking to, I was nice. I don't have total recall, but I stand by that as my nature. And I believe her that I said that, but clearly it was a joke. I don't remember 100 percent the context, but it certainly sounds like a fucking asshole. I still don't think I was. But cocky. Cocky about the work for sure.

Rachel Bilson: It was his sense of humor. Like I said, before I knew Brody in the beginning, his sense of humor could come off dickish at times.

Stephanie Savage: I feel like Adam was going to a more emotional place, and then he stopped himself. He made a joke and was like, *I can't do this.* And Ben just tipped over the edge.

Josh Schwartz: Ben was really fucking emotional. He was the last shot of the show. And I think he was surprised because he had been ready to be done with the show. The show changed his life, and whether he thought it was for better or for worse at that moment, I think it was really significant. He was the last shot. It was a pickup shot against the blue sky of the set that was supposed to be exterior Berkeley campus. But we just had to shoot it out of the Cohen backyard, with him in his Berkeley sweatshirt with the backpack on. And when we wrapped, he got really emotional.

Stephanie Savage: He teared up.

Josh Schwartz: It was nice to see that it meant something to him. It meant something to all of us, in ways that I think we are still grappling with and understanding.

Ben McKenzie: I filmed the last scene. I remember speaking to the crew. And I said the truth, which was, "Before the show, I'd been in L.A. a year and I didn't have any friends. And now I feel like I have hundreds. And if we run into each other at any point in the future, I hope we can grab a beer or a coffee and reminisce." And that actually did happen on a number of occasions. So it was nice, a nice feeling.

Josh Schwartz: We felt a tremendous amount of sadness that the show was ending, that we probably are still processing to this day, but didn't allow ourselves to process in that moment. It was head-spinning in so many ways. I personally felt like I had failed, that the show ending was a failure, and I just wanted to keep moving forward and not allow myself to get mired and drown in the pity that it was over. So how emotional that last day was, and how emotional the series wrap party was, caught me by surprise. We made a video set to Coconut Records' "West Coast," that played over this montage of everyone in the cast and crew saying goodbye. And I think that's when it really hit me that not only was it over, but it had been a really meaningful experience for a lot of people and was a positive experience in the end.

CHAPTER 11

The Distance

Every New Beginning Comes from Some Other Beginning's End

IN EARLY 2007, while series finale scenes were being filmed at Sandy and Kirsten's once and future house in Berkeley—but in reality in Pasadena—fans of the show gathered in the street outside to take pictures and get autographs from the cast before *The O.C.* said goodbye for good. Josh Schwartz wandered over to talk with some of them.

Josh Schwartz (creator/executive producer): Someone said, "*The O.C.* can't end! What you going to do next?" I said, "Oh, working on a show called *Gossip Girl*, based on the books." And every kid out there screamed, "WE LOVE THOSE BOOKS!"

This would be one of two series that Schwartz and/or Savage worked on the following season.

Josh Schwartz: I remember very distinctly the last day of shooting *The O.C.*, because that was also the day that Patrick Rush showed me Zachary Levi's audition tape for *Chuck*.

Since *The O.C.* ended, Schwartz and Savage's Fake Empire Productions has produced more than a dozen new series and miniseries, often working with members of *The O.C.* cast and/or crew along the way. The past sixteen years have taken the show's actors in a variety of directions. Adam Brody and Ben McKenzie have both done time in DC Comics adaptations, for instance—Brody in the Shazam films, McKenzie as James Gordon on *Gotham* (where he continued to work with *O.C.* writer John Stephens)—but McKenzie also recently coauthored a book about the dangers of cryptocurrency. Like *The O.C.* itself, the show's afterlife contains multitudes.

Gail Berman (president, Fox): It created an incredible partnership in Stephanie and Josh, people I've worked with since then. Stephanie leaves McG and joins Josh, and they form a company that has been remarkably successful.

The Cast Looks Back, Not in Anger

Adam Brody (Seth Cohen): It was such a wonderful time of life. We were so young and hopeful and idealistic, and it was all so exciting and uncomplicated. It was a big lovefest. In the beginning, at the very least, everyone got along so well, and it was just so joyful.

Peter Gallagher (Sandy Cohen): It was a great three and a half years, regardless of how things may have meandered or whatever. It's one of those rare, rare, rare, rare moments where the story you're telling has a place in the world that you live in. And when that happens, there's just nothing like it. And I'm really glad that *The O.C.* introduced me to all those guys, from Josh to all the people who made the show, because it was really fun. And I love seeing the delight on people's faces when they see Sandy Cohen. My daughter said, "Dad, you have a pretty good reputation. It's all pretty much because of Sandy Cohen, though." I'll take that.

Autumn Reeser (Taylor Townsend): You're working so much and you don't have time to process what it is that's happening until afterwards. When I look back, it was an experience that changed my life. There was a lot of joy. I really feel like I got to bring a lot of myself into the role, which doesn't always happen. I have a lot of gratitude for that, for the amount that I was allowed to stretch, for the writers' trust in me, and for the amount of comedy I got to do on a teen drama. It was really fun. Most of the time. It was really fun.

Rachel Bilson (Summer Roberts): It hits me now. Rewatching the show and doing the podcast and watching these episodes and seeing me young and seeing where I was then and seeing where I am now, I get super emotional a lot of the time.

Peter Gallagher: My daughter was just in Ireland and her cabdriver, for whatever reason, had to stop off at home. And while they were in there, the daughter was crazy about *The O.C.* and said, "Could you do *yogalates*?" And my daughter called: "Dad. Can you do *yogalates*? And what about this?" My refrain to the people who remember Sandy and that show, I just say "Sandy Cohen loves you."

Rachel Bilson: I think Summer will always be OG number one. I feel for Brody, too. Probably Seth is still number one for him.

Adam Brody: I was doing what I wanted to do on it at the time, and I'm very thankful and appreciative that it connected with people—that the character has a place in pop culture history, I think.

Autumn Reeser: The thing that means the most to me is when I hear from a girl who resonates with Taylor, who watches the show when she's a teen or early twenties, in that period of trying to figure out who she is, and she recognizes something of herself in Taylor, and receives permission to be who she is. Even if who she is doesn't fit into the mainstream. There was a lot of the power of Taylor in all of her quirky too-much-ness.

Kelly Rowan (Kirsten Cohen): I still have my Captain Oats T-shirt.

Peter Gallagher: My daughter was working on Broadway in *Jagged Little Pill*. And across the street, Ben McKenzie showed up in his play. So she sent him a cake that said, "Welcome to Forty-Fourth Street, bitch."

Changing Reality

Depending on your perspective, *The O.C.* either deserves enormous credit or enormous blame for inadvertently inspiring one of the dominant strains of reality TV over the last couple of decades. This started with the debut of MTV's *Laguna Beach: The Real Orange County* in between the first and second *O.C.* seasons.

Gary Auerbach (cocreator, *Laguna Beach*): [Fellow *Laguna Beach* producers] Liz Gateley and Tony DeSanto were talking about how Liz grew up down there. She brought it up in a meeting that it would be cool to do something similar to *The O.C.*—"What can we do in that space?" I said, "What if we approached it like we would approach a one-hour drama, like *The O.C.* already is?"

Stephanie Savage (executive producer): Those kids were compelling. They were good characters, and the realness that they were offering, we were in a different business. So it felt like, *Is that a better business? Should we have done that show instead of this show?* I had a queasy feeling.

Willa Holland (Kaitlin Cooper): The way that *Laguna Beach* and all those shows came out after it, I don't know if it was 100 percent modeled exactly after us. But the fact that they specifically picked that part of [California] to start with, I don't think it was a coincidence. There was a bit of a fascination going on at the time with that area and teenagers in that age range because of that. The zeitgeist narrowed in there. At the time, you felt like you were a part of something big. But looking back on it, I don't think we knew how big.

Stephanie Savage: We ended up befriending some of those kids. They would come and read for us, and we'd run into them when we were out places. Everyone was always very nice. But it was a weird feeling at first, and not a good feeling. It didn't feel like, *Oh, flattery, that's so cool.* It was like, *Sharks in the water!*

Yvette Urbina (programming executive, Fox): I ended up hiring the DP from [*Laguna Beach* spin-off] *The Hills*. The show I was doing had to have that look, and the lighting, but I needed it to feel unscripted. And he said they had modeled it after what we had done [on *The O.C.*]. It was really full circle and wild.

Gail Berman: And then, of course, Andy Cohen goes off to create his version of *The O.C.*, which is *Housewives*. And that's its own story.

The first episode of *The Real Housewives of Orange County* debuted on Bravo on March 21, 2006, late in *The O.C.* Season Three.

Lauren Zalaznick (president, Bravo): *The O.C.*, at the time, had a fairly significant impact on how we conceptualized not only the tone of the show, but the possible appeal of the show for our audience on Bravo at the time. There were two layers to that show: a soapy, easy to take, didn't have to think about it twice, lean-back, plotty drama; and a social critique and relationship critique. A layer that if you wanted to turn your brain on or if you read media in a certain way, there's something there for whatever percentage you want to call of a viewing audience—is it 5 percent? 10? 20?—who are getting it, similar to today's *The Bachelor*. We know that that has two kinds of audiences. And we recognized it in *The O.C.* It also functioned as a model for what Bravo [became].

As with *The O.C.* and then *Laguna Beach*, there was just something in the zeitgeist about Orange County that the TV business couldn't get enough of.

Lauren Zalaznick: The locale was really coming into view. And the two last attributes of that show, that informed our name, *Real Housewives of Orange County*, were that it was a very earnest show, but there was a certain distance, maybe irony, to it. And it was a little bit sexy.

Melinda Clarke (Julie Cooper-Nichol): When you look at the *House-wives* now, Julie is subtle compared to that.

Gail Berman: At first I was very angry. I don't know why. Maybe it was because I hadn't thought of it? But I was also like, *Well, I guess we inspired something here.* It never really crossed our minds, to be perfectly honest. We were doing much more provocative [reality] concepts.

Though Schwartz and Savage have had long runs with scripted soap operas like *Gossip Girl* and their *Dynasty* reboot, it's hard not to feel like the reality TV space has taken up most of the pop culture real estate that traditional prime-time soaps used to dominate.

Stephanie Savage: When I'm getting my nails done, or in a world of women chatting about things where I don't know them, and they're not in my peer group, those *Real Housewives* shows, *Selling Sunset*, those shows get talked about a lot in a way that when I was growing up, women would talk about *General Hospital* or *Dallas* or *Dynasty*.

Daniel Blau Rogge (Television Without Pity recapper): My current job as a network executive really makes me analyze why shows like this worked, and how they influenced and informed everything from *The Hills* in the aughts to something like *Siesta Key* today.

"Mmmm, Whatcha Say?"

On April 14, 2007, *Saturday Night Live* aired a Lonely Island short film called "Dear Sister," where seemingly innocuous conversations between a group of people (played by Bill Hader, Andy Samberg, Shia LaBeouf, Kristen Wiig, Fred Armisen, and Jason Sudeikis) keep being interrupted by them randomly shooting one another. Each gunshot is followed by the familiar "Mmmm, whatcha say?" portion of Imogen Heap's "Hide and Seek" from the Season Two finale of *The O.C.*, and usually with one of the actors looking in disbelief over their shoulder, in the same manner Trey gawked at Marissa at the end of that episode. It was an unlikely homage, perhaps impenetrable to anyone who did not get the reference.

Josh Schwartz: My friend Andrew Singer, who works for Lorne Michaels, sent it to me, and I was so confused. I was like, "Did I miss this from two years ago?" He was like, "No, this is on tonight." We had met Andy a couple of times, and [the Lonely Island] got their start doing something called The 'Bu, which was a web series parody of The O.C.* So the show was very much on their minds. And anytime we ever met Andy, he was super nice and complimentary about the show and everything.

Imogen Heap (musical multi-hyphenate): They didn't ask permission. So it was totally unexpected. There was all this fuss about this song and I was like, *Where's this coming from?* And then afterwards they got permission. But [retroactively]. And from that, the memes.

Back to the McMansion?

You may have noticed that in recent years, the easiest way to get on television is to have already been on television. Revivals and reboots are viewed as an efficient method of getting attention in a world where more than five hundred scripted TV shows air each year. Unsurprisingly, Schwartz and Savage have been asked many times to consider a return to Newport Beach.

Josh Schwartz: We get approached about that maybe once a year. There was a very serious overture that was made about two years

---

* In a 2007 *Entertainment Weekly* oral history of "Dear Sister," the Lonely Island's Akiva Schaffer explained, "We knew that most people wouldn't know *The O.C.* reference, so we weren't like, 'This is only for *O.C.* fans.' We figured it was funny on its own to some degree."

ago. There was a conversation that I had with Ben and Adam about it, which is further than it had ever gone before. Returning to the show doesn't work without those two guys. Ben said he would direct it, but wasn't necessarily interested in moving back from New York and acting in it. I said, "I'll tell you what: You get Brody to say yes, you can direct it." I made it his problem, and they had a nice conversation about it. But ultimately, I didn't have much of an idea. I just said, "It opens with Seth and Ryan, and they've both gotten vasectomies as the opening scene." It would be a way to explore middle age.

Stephanie Savage: The version where a new family moves into the Cohen house doesn't feel like that's really recapturing the spirit of what people loved about this show.

But would the actors want to come back if this ever actually happens?

Rachel Bilson: Fuck no. [*dramatic pause*] I'm just kidding! I would do anything any day with Josh and Stephanie. I will also say that for the rest of my life.

Adam Brody: Not really. Unless there was a radical idea, and that's not what anyone wants. I just think we're in such a different place as a society. I love escapism, and it's not that I think everything needs to be self-hating flagellation. But post-Trump, something would need to be done and said, and I don't think anyone's really interested in what that would be. I understand reboots are all the rage and I understand money is nice, but in everyone's heart that you're talking to, do they really want to know or have a deep desire to explore what everyone is doing now and graft it onto 2023? I doubt it. It's such a time capsule. And I'm all for the nostalgia pieces. I don't even hate reboots at all. I hate that most of them suck—most of them are spitting on the graves of the original but—but in theory, I have no problem with it. I don't know. It'd be pretty hard to recapture the magic of that first season. That said, we're all older and wiser, so who knows? Maybe that should be worth something.

Forever Young

While working on Season Two, Allan Heinberg gave Schwartz some issues of *Runaways*, an exciting new Marvel comic whose devil-may-care pacing felt very much of a piece with *O.C.* Season One. Years later, Schwartz and Savage adapted *Runaways* for Hulu, and tried not to make those same *O.C.* mistakes.

Josh Schwartz: The *Runaways* comic was accused of moving too fast, and blowing through a lot of stories. I was especially hesitant to move through that story too quickly, and, in fact, kept them from running away till the end of Season One. Even though the show is called *Runaways*! And that was a direct result of *The O.C.* experience.

As they've moved into streaming, though, with its shorter seasons and its shorter runs, Schwartz and Savage have realized that the reckless abandon of *O.C.* Season One works just fine when you've got ten episodes to fill instead of twenty-seven.

Josh Schwartz: There was all these rules that had been ingrained to us in network television, that were not going to be relevant to streaming anymore.

They've applied the many lessons learned on *The O.C.* to all the shows they've made since then.

Josh Schwartz: On *The O.C.*, we didn't pair different members of the Core Four together. And on *Gossip Girl*, we saw the value in taking characters that people were invested in and just going, "Oh, now Dan can date Blair, and there's opportunity for moving those people around."

Stephanie Savage: Now we know that no one's ever going to love anyone as much as they love the pilot characters. Don't kid yourself. So really lavish love and attention on those characters, and use them as much as possible for your storytelling versus bringing in new characters. And we learned from the Oliver story about not telling stories where the audience knows something that the characters don't about an interloper. We had a couple of versions of that kind of a character on *Gossip Girl*, but we treated it very differently, so that the audience was engaged in the pursuit of that truth along with our main characters.

It's hard for them to escape the feeling that, on some level, they are still making *The O.C.*

Josh Schwartz: We did *Looking for Alaska*, and we set it in 2005, which is the year the book was published, and two of the characters are briefly caught watching *The O.C.* on a laptop. *City on Fire*, we transposed the time period of the book from the 1970s to 2003. The blackout of '77 is the culmination of the book. There was a blackout in 2003, and we wanted to tell a story about post-9/11 New York. But we keep returning to this period of the aughts. Most people remember their high school age with the vividness of yesterday. And I think for us, *The O.C.* is like our high school days. And we remember every single band, every single news story, everything that was happening with a higher intensity—things are more colorful and just more imbued. So we keep finding ourselves returning to telling stories in this time period, which is obviously informed by our experience making the show then.

Stephanie Savage: Yeah. Not when we were in high school, but when we first made a high school show.

Josh Schwartz: And now we have young actors to ask us to gather around and tell them what the aughts were like.

What Is a Legacy?

For the series finale, production returned to the real McMansion in Malibu for the first time since very early in Season One. The house was later destroyed in the Woolsey fire that ran through Los Angeles and Ventura counties in November 2018.

Adam Brody: There's something symbolic there, obviously, with it no longer existing.

For the people who worked on *The O.C.*, memories of the show have proved more durable.

McG (executive producer): You can't hold on to magic forever, and it belongs to the world and it's reflective of a point in time, and societal standards change. And what was perfect at the moment couldn't possibly sustain. No shooting star can last forever. It's a moment in time. You enjoy it for what it is. It's magical. And you're thankful that it happened, and it's destined to burn out.

Melinda Clarke: There's popular TV shows. But then there's popular shows in the industry, and popular shows with a demographic. And it was all of those things for a short time.

Autumn Reeser: They built a whole industry around it. When I was going back through these scrapbooks, there was a fragrance called *The O.C.* What on earth did that smell like?

Craig Erwich (programming executive, Fox): I really think it's one of the best shows of the last twenty years. The show not just put its finger on what was going on, what people say, but it created its own weather in terms of popular culture. Like Chrismukkah.

Stephanie Savage: We still hear stories of people being like, "I found my Seth Cohen because I realized nerds were cool," and that kind of geek chic. I honestly think it affected people's marriages, who married who, who hooked up in college. There's definitely some happiness in the world that can be traced back to that archetype.

Kelly Rowan: I got letters. One person had said that they were in a difficult situation at home, and watching the show and watching the family relationship gave her courage to actually leave her situation. You don't realize how much of an effect you can have on people's lives. Television is a powerful tool both ways. So when you are able to affect somebody in a good way, that feels good.

Peter Gallagher: You know what the cool thing is for me? I believe that that show is every bit as powerful as I suspected it was when I first read that script, because I still get contacted by people around the world. For ages, when Twitter started and stuff, people would have a final exam or something they'd be nervous about, and they'd want some help, and I'd give them the bagels or the schmear—the fatherhood stuff. And the show itself, it just keeps being rediscovered, and it makes me feel really good inside that after all these years, it's still out there, still moving people and delighting people, and they still respond to the kids and the parents. They still dig Sandy and Kirsten. So it was nice to see, after that suspicion when I read that script, that it might really have a place. That there are a lot of parents out there that are busy, and fathers are out there that are busy trying to make a living, and don't have the time to be around and be available and talk to the kids and it's a deficit, and that I'm not the only one who has felt that.

Samaire Armstrong (Anna Stern): My son, who's now nine, he goes, "Just so you know, *The O.C.* is a pretty big deal." I was like, "Yeah, I know that." And he goes, "Well, it's on streaming. People are watching it."

Alan Dale (Caleb Nichol): My youngest is now twenty, whose friends have just recently watched *The O.C.* I find it really was influential and so, so very, very L.A. I don't know that it can survive much longer because it might start to date, but it so far has very well.

Rachel Bilson and Melinda Clarke's podcast, *Welcome to The O.C., Bitches*, as well as the interviews for this book, have given many members of the cast and crew an excuse to rewatch the show for the first time in years.

Kelly Rowan: I did the podcast, so I've watched a couple of episodes, and I popped my head in when my daughter was watching. And I'm shocked that it still holds. Even all the stuff with Luke on the beach fighting Ryan, and then finding out that the reason why Luke is so messed up is because of his father and the secret relationship. All those things, people could go, *Oh, okay, I can relate to that.* So even though there was all this, these crazy events happening, underneath, there was still something real going on.

Rachel Bilson: A lot of it holds up. There's certain things you could never get away with now. Certain jokes, there's definitely tone-deaf things, and all of that stuff would need to be reworked. But as a whole, I'd say it holds up.

Adam Brody: Creatively, the sadness of the first few episodes really got to me. And of course that's coupled with my own nostalgia and the bittersweet nature of looking back in your yearbook, at yourself as a young man and all the people you knew much younger. We were all at different points in our lives, but we were all starting such a significant journey for all of us together. And it was pretty emotional to watch it.

Peter Roth (president, Warner Bros. Television): I think the most important legacy is the audience's appetite for a series like this. Not simply a teen angst–filled drama, but a story of outsiders, a story of loneliness, a story of characters that were desperate to fit in, that didn't and eventually weren't able to. And I think that story is so universal in its appeal, especially to young audiences

Susan Rovner (programming executive, Warner Bros. Television): At the end of the day, all the right things ended up happening. Even though there were so many obstacles, and so many things like losing McG right before production starts. It ended up being a story where so many things could have gone wrong that ended up where everything that happened was right, which I think is fascinating.

John Stephens (writer/producer): I think the show especially has a legacy in the shows and the characters that came out of it. Seth Cohen as a character, as someone who is obsessed with comic books and certain elements of pop culture, I think that has just proliferated. You see that character that sees every Marvel movie that's out there. I also feel like the complexity of storytelling, and the adult-y version of a lot of the show, really had an influence on a lot of the teen dramas that came after it, whether it's what Josh and Stephanie did with *Gossip Girl*, or other shows like *Riverdale*. I feel like *The O.C.* continues to live on through those shows.

Stephanie Savage: I think the legacy in terms of the industry, is the idea of having a really voice-y, really potentially comedic aspect to a nighttime soap. Self-awareness, meta characters that wouldn't normally be in a show like that, first opened the door for other shows. Marc Cherry has said to Josh that he wouldn't have been able to do *Desperate Housewives* if *The O.C.* didn't exist.

Allan Heinberg (writer/producer): All of my favorite TV, it's always about a new voice that you've never heard before, speaking to you in a way that you've never been spoken to, but touches you very deeply. Amy Sherman-Palladino with the first season of *Gilmore Girls*. Shonda Rhimes with *Grey's Anatomy** was that. David E. Kelley with *Picket Fences*, Steven Bochco with *Hill Street Blues*, Zwick and Herskovitz with all of their shows, Winnie Holzman with *My So-Called Life*. And Josh had that voice. Josh had a voice that was unique and entirely his, and was charming and smart as fuck and insightful and sneakily emotional.

McG: "Pop" is such a dirty word. And I think *The O.C.* is the consummate example of smart pop. The show is unapologetically cool. It's as

---

* Heinberg wound up writing for *Grey's Anatomy* after leaving *The O.C.* He was unaware that Summer's dad later worked at Seattle Grace until he was interviewed for this book.

fucking cool as anything I can think of. And it was pop. It was a teen soap. And the ability to create that is the greatest trick Josh Schwartz could have up his sleeve.

The popularity of both the show and Luke's catchphrase even led the people of the actual Orange County to make peace with the "the."

McG: At first, they loved to hate it and then they acquiesced to simply loving it. Now, Josh Schwartz has completely and utterly changed the vernacular. And dare I say, anything associated with Orange County has the orange "O" and the orange "C" that are specifically of the show. It's been effectively adopted by the County of Orange. So yeah, it's just fun to have that level of social influence prior to the days of social influencers.

Chris Carmack (Luke Ward): I think for about ten years, I heard from people from Orange County: "It's not the O.C., it's O.C." The cultural legacy of the show is that there's now a "the" in front of "O.C."

Craig Erwich: To this day, people say, "Welcome to the O.C., bitch." It's like quoting a line from *The Godfather*, or Butch and Sundance. Rachel Bilson going "Ew," you still remember that. There's not that many pilots you can remember those things from.

Josh Schwartz: That the show has a legacy [at all] is unbelievably gratifying. Because as we've discussed, when it ended, I felt like we had failed. My mom kept scrapbooks, including ones about the end of the show, and "Fast success—even faster failure" was the headline. Everybody seems to have a different takeaway of what the show meant to them or why they remember it. Some people say, "I moved to California right when the show came out" or "I moved away from California right when the show came out, but it reminded me of home where I was in my dorm." Or, "I was in love with this character or that character." "The music." "I always dreamt of going to California." For me, I would think it's about the family and the wish fulfillment. Not everybody is born with the family that they want. But this gave you the opportunity to dream about being able to find the family that you really deserve.

Acknowledgments

Nineteen years ago, I wrote my first book, with the extremely 2004 title *Stop Being a Hater and Learn to Love the O.C.* The publisher was eager to get something on the shelves tied to TV's newest It Show, as quickly as possible, so the whole thing was completed in the span of about three weeks. My editor was concerned about violating copyright if I got too specific in describing literally anything that had happened on the series. Yet somehow, I managed to fill up 150-odd pages by doing things like listing every song featured in Season One, or recommending graphic novels that Seth Cohen fans might be inclined to read. Calling it "a book" is perhaps wildly overstating things.

So when Josh Schwartz and Stephanie Savage reached out to ask if I'd like to author an oral history in time for the show's twentieth anniversary, it felt like an opportunity to do it right this time. This required more time, more effort, and many more actual details about the show itself—which in turn required a *lot* more help than I had the first time around.

Welcome to the O.C. could not have been finished on time, never mind as well, without the thorough, tireless, brilliant aid of my researcher, Oriana Schwindt. Oriana shared the interviewing load with me, often asking questions that would have never occurred to me, leading to some of the best quotes in the whole thing. (You can thank her for Chris Carmack's shack and chili dog stories, for instance.) She also served as exhaustive transcriber, reliable sounding board, and invaluable assembler of quotes into roughly the order the story needed. She was, and is, an incredible collaborator, who also never objected to me texting her random *O.C.* screencaps at all hours of the day and night.*

---

* A favorite of these: an awkward (and inscrutable from a 2023 perspective) bit of product integration where Lindsay tells Ryan, "No, but I a9.com'd him last night."

It also would not have been possible without the love and support of my incredible wife Marian and our even more incredible kids, Julia and Ben. This book was completed amidst the most trying twelve-month period of my entire life, which featured enough drama to fill an entire bonus season of *The O.C.*, along with a medical mystery straight out of fellow mid-2000s Fox drama *House*. Without my family around me, I'm not sure how I would have stayed sane, let alone found the energy or focus to write about Johnny and Chili.

Thank you to my fantastic editor at Mariner, Molly Gendell, whose notes were always on point, and who helped me cut down a draft that was approaching the length of *Infinite Jest* into the more manageable version you've just read.

Thank you to Maria Fontoura, Noah Shachtman, Sean Woods, David Fear, Marlow Stern, Andy Greene, Angie Martoccio, Alison Weinflash, Rob Sheffield, and the rest of my colleagues at *Rolling Stone*, past and present, for allowing me the freedom to do this in between reviews and features, and/or for bouncing off ideas.

Thank you to the many friends who helped point me in the right direction whenever I had some obscure question about pop culture in the mid-aughts, or needed reminding of some long-ago *O.C.*-adjacent conversation I only half remembered: among many others, Joe Adalian, Kate Aurthur, Patrick Cotnoir, Brian Cronin, Dan Fienberg, Lesley Goldberg, Eric Goldman, Linda Holmes, Cynthia Littleton, Jason Lynch, Joanna Robinson, Sarah Rodman, and Mike Schneider.

Thank you to Nishima Gupta for enabling all the conversations with Josh and Stephanie that formed the spine of the book, and to all the publicists, managers, agents, and assistants who helped facilitate interviews with the cast. Thank you to Melinda Clarke and Rachel Bilson, whose podcast served as an excellent resource throughout the process. (Melinda was also the person I turned to whenever I couldn't find the contact info for someone who had worked on the show; she inevitably had emails and/or phone numbers for them all.) And, obviously, thank you to everyone from *The O.C.* who was willing to make time, even under complicated circumstances, to revisit this memorable chapter in their lives.

And of course, thank you to whoever created yogalates.